MW01030181

ELITE WARRIORS
300 Years of America's Best Fighting Troops

by

Lance Q. Zedric and Michael F. Dilley

Pathfinder Publishing

Ventura, California

ELITE WARRIORS

Published by:
Pathfinder Publishing of California
458 Dorothy Avenue
Ventura, CA 93003
(805) 642-9278
FAX: (805) 650-3656

Library of Congress Cataloging-in-Publication Data

Zedric, Lance Q., 1961-
    Elite Warriors : 300 years of America's best fighting troops / by Lance Q. Zedric and Michael F. Dilley.
        p.   cm.
    Includes bibliographical references and index.
    ISBN 0-934793-60-3 (hardcover)
    1. United States — Armed Forces — Commando troops — History.
I. Dilley, Michael F., 1943- . II. Title.
U262.Z43 1996
356'.1673'0973 — dc20   96-5910
                                                                          CIP

ACKNOWLEDGMENTS

We would like to express our deepest thanks and appreciation to the following people. Without their help in providing source material, guidance, and photographs this project would have never got off the ground (in many ways this is as much their book as it is ours):

Gary and Mike Linderer, publishers of *Behind The Lines* magazine; Brad Melton of *Arizona Highways* magazine; the staffs of *Infantry* and *The Retired Officer* magazines; Patricia Tugwell, Reference Department, Pentagon Library; Beverly McMaster and Richard Baronne, Donovan Technical Library, Infantry School, Fort Benning, Georgia; Karla Norman, Research Department, U.S. Army Command and General Staff College, Fort Leavenworth, Kansas; and all the fine people on the staffs of the Crofton Branch of the Anne Arundel County (Maryland) Public Library and the Parlin Ingersoll Library, Canton, Illinois; Rich Boylan, National Archives, Suitland, Maryland and Sharon Culley, Still Picture Branch, National Archives, College Park, Maryland; Jack Green, Naval Historical Center Photo Branch, Washington; Delores Oplinger, U.S. Army Signal Corps Museum, Fort Gordon, Georgia; Terry Van Meter, Museums Division, Fort Riley, Kansas, and Tony Wolusky, United States Air Force Academy.

Special recognition to Dr. John Partin and Lt. Col. Bill Darley, U.S. Special Operations Command, MacDill Air Force Base, Florida; Dr. Richard Stewart and Roxanne Merritt, Command Historian's Office, U.S. Army Special Operations Command, Fort Bragg, North Carolina; Lt. Commander Jim Fallin and Petty Officer Mike Hayden, Navy Special Warfare Command PAO, Coronado, California; Maj. Debbie Malle, Air Force Special Operations Forces PAO, Hurlbert Field, Florida; Lt. Brad Lewis, Navy PAO, New York; Sgt. Kyle Olson, Marine Corps PAO, Washington; Dan Dunmire for taking the time to offer his views on John Singleton Mosby; Holly Pellowski for her help researching the Alamo Scouts, and fellow military history writers John B. Dwyer, George F. Cholewczynski, and George A. Bray III for providing valuable insights and suggestions.

We would also like to convey our deepest gratitude to Eugene Wheeler and to the entire staff at Pathfinder Publishing for their confidence and dedication to this project, and to our family, friends, and co-workers for their encouragement and support.

Thanks everyone.

The Authors

Lastly, thanks to my best friend, my wife Sue, not only for her help, but for her patience and understanding with my "hobby."

Michael F. Dilley

FOREWORD

Wars are ultimately won by footslogging infantrymen, slugging it out in the fields and trenches and grinding ahead to seize and hold critical parcels of real estate. Seldon do news cameras seek out the tired and grimy faces like those of "Willie and Joe," Bill Mauldin's unforgettable caricatures of the dog-face soldier of World War II.

Conversely, small, elite units of volunteers engaging in dazzling feats of derring-do are often in the headlines, despite the fact that they seldom, win major battles, let alone the war. More often they flame up meteor-like, exciting the public, and then disappearing as historical footnotes.

Why the public fascination with "warrior elites?" Simply stated, greater and immediate drama exists in their efforts. More is required of such elite units in a compressed period of time than is the case with their more conventional counterparts. Their operations are high-risk/high-gain, pitting small, elite forces against numerically larger, more powerful forces—a situation where the combat-multiplying factor of complete surprise is a **sine qua non** and where the chances of annihilation in event of failure are infinitely greater.

These "warrior elites" can play a pivotal role in influencing how the battle begins and on what terms, even though the main event still must be left to the heavyweights.

Unfortunately, some envy and tension exists between the more conventional and the unconventional elements of our armed forces. One faces the dreary tedium of continuing danger under miserably adverse conditions and gains scant public attention while the other appears briefly in a starring role and exits the bloody stage under thundering applause.

However, the truth is that both roles are essential and both players need each other.

In this context, Messrs Zedric and Dilley have accomplished an admirable and highly useful feat with their survey history of 52 "warrior elite" units from America's military past...men from whom, on occasion, the impossible was asked, and who sometimes achieved it, men to whom the nation owes its profound gratitude for their sacrificial efforts. In the backdrop, however, lurk the fatigue-lined faces and haunted eyes of "Willie and Joe."

Samuel Vaughan Wilson
Lieutenant General, US Army-Retired

(**Note:** General Wilson served in the Office of Strategic Services and subsequently in Merrill's Marauders in Intelligence and Reconnaissance during World War II. Additional assignments during his 37-year military career include command of a Special Forces Group; Deputy Assistant to the Secretary of Defense for Special Operations; US Defense Attache to the Soviet Union; Deputy to the Director Central Intelligence; Director, Defense Intelligence Agency. He is a former Honorary Colonel of the US Army 75th Ranger Regiment and is the recipient of the fifth Arthur S. "Bull" Simons award for exceptional contributions to US Special Operations.)

CONTENTS

DEDICATION

This book is Dedicated to The Rangers, Scouts, and Special Operators of the United States, past and present.

PREFACE

I'd like...to have two armies: one for display, with lovely guns, tanks, little soldiers, fanfares, staffs, distinguished and doddering generals, and dear little regimental officers who would be deeply concerned over their general's bowel movements or their colonel's piles: an army that would be shown for a modest fee on every fairground in the country. The other would be the real one; composed entirely of young enthusiasts in camouflage battledress, who would not be put on display but from whom impossible efforts would be demanded and to whom all sorts of tricks would be taught. That's the army in which I should like to fight.

Jean Larteguy , *The Centurions*

This book is a 300-year survey history of the elite warriors of the U.S. military forces. Our intention was not to write a detailed history of such forces. Others have done that, usually taking one unit, battle, or war at a time. Rather, we preferred to paint with a broad brush and take an all-services, all-wars approach. It is our hope that this book will serve as a useful reference tool to historians, former and active duty military personnel, and provide the general reader with an entertaining and informative account of the origins and operations of some of America's elite forces.

When we initially discussed this project, our first step was to arrive at our definition of "elite warriors." In this work we have defined them as a special purpose, special mission organization that:

- Conducts missions atypical of units in its branch of service.
- Is formed to conduct a particular mission.
- Receives special training for a mission.
- Uses specialized or prototype equipment or standard equipment in non-standard roles.
- Performs scouting, ranging, raiding, or reconnaissance missions.

10

- Conducts or trains indigenous people in guerrilla-type or unconventional warfare operations.
- Results from separate recruiting efforts, either in-service or off-the-street.

The reader will find that many of the units discussed in this book meet more than one of the criteria. Some of them are fairly obvious choices and would be on just about anyone's list, while others might stretch the definition somewhat. For example, the authors believe that parachute units, such as the 82nd and 101st Airborne Divisions, Pathfinders, and others, along with the submarine service and the crews of the *Enola Gay* and *Bock's Car* should be included. But due to the strictures of publishing and the sheer number of such units it would be impractical to include them all. Instead, we tried to include a variety of units which not only met the criteria, but were also exceedingly colorful, audacious, or highly unconventional.

Others that are not included are: Ethan Allen and his "Green Mountain Boys;" the Mexican Spy Companies of the Mexican War; the early air or tank corps; the Intelligence and Reconnaissance platoons of most Army regiments during World War II; the so-called "smart weapons" units of the modern period; and other *ad hoc* units such as Patton's "Household Cavalry." All of these and several others easily fit the definition we have established.

Essentially, two things make a unit "elite" or "special:" its mission and its people. All of the units in this "elite" category, however, are part of larger conventional organizations and supported their missions. As a rule these units did not act on their own. Rather, they played an integrated, sometimes isolated, but not exclusive, role in executing that larger mission. We discovered that many of the units were *ad hoc*, that is, they were created, trained, and employed for a specific purpose. When that specific purpose or mission was completed, and the unit was no longer needed, it was hastily disbanded.

Some units executed their specific missions so well that they were given larger conventional missions that were often beyond their capabilities. This misuse often resulted in disaster. Some commanders had no idea of how to use the elite units or what their particular capabilities were. Others properly employed these units *specifically for* those capabilities and achieved outstanding success.

When many of the *ad hoc* units were disbanded, such as at the end of World War II, it left a void in the military. Much of the experience gained was lost when the veterans were mustered out of the military or sent back to conventional units. This meant that later, when the need arose for similar units, such as in the Korean War, the units had to be reorganized, and new personnel trained and equipped. The lapse in continuity required time for the new units to "ramp up," that is, spend valuable time training before they could be used effectively in action. Some lessons, it seems, need to be learned again and again.

The U.S. military has never had a shortage of volunteers to fill the ranks of elite units. Whenever the call has gone out, there have always been more who stepped forward than were needed. Regardless of the risk, or the overwhelming odds against success, someone believed the mission could be accomplished. Usually, the volunteers were strong-willed individuals who required equally strong-willed leaders. The leaders pushed them to the limits of their endurance but kept them focused on their mission. They provided them with the latest weaponry and equipment, and trained them with the newest but sometimes unconventional methods.

Our analysis shows that America, either in colonial or republic form, has called for special military units throughout every major conflict, except, perhaps, World War I. The earliest units discussed are English units that fought in America before there was a United States, and the most current are those involved in the latest military venture in Bosnia. Wherever the U.S. military goes its "elite warriors" are usually the first to arrive and often the last to leave. Their missions are normally cloaked in secrecy and protected by operations security, since forewarning gives an enemy time to prepare. Some even change their name or designation to confuse the enemy or make it appear that they no longer exist. When they succeed in battle, we don't always hear about it. Unfortunately, we hear more about their failings, but when they do succeed, it's because they dare. To paraphrase David Stirling, when they dare, they win.

PART I

PRE-REVOLUTIONARY WAR

INTRODUCTION

In the first century of the European colonization of America several bloody clashes occurred between the native Indians and the colonists. As a result, some of the colonies raised forces of local citizens, gave them rudimentary military training, and designated them to be a protective force against further Indian attacks. The local force units were called various names, but the one most often used was "militia." These militia units differed from the consolidated militia organizations that existed in England, a military system dating back to the 12th century, in that each colony raised its own units and were subject to local government control.

Soon, militia units mounted punitive expeditions against Indian settlements. These attacks differed in style from the raids by Indians on colonial areas. The Indians usually favored ambushes and hit-and-run raids, while the militia generally employed the conventional linear battlefield tactics of the period. Each side adopted tactics suited to the capabilities and limitations of its weapons, whether the lance, bow, or musket.

Walled forts were built to defend outlying houses, cabins, and small villages from Indian attacks. Parties of soldiers, sometimes mounted, patrolled, or "ranged" between the outposts. Thus, the term "ranger" came into popular, military use. Soon, however, the term included more that just patrolling.

The early ranger units were small, usually about company size or smaller. In those days, a company was of indeterminate strength, containing approximately from 50 to 150 men. This number refers to rangers actually present for duty and does not include the "contingent men" or any other term used to describe numbers added for "billets not occupied," one of the customs of the period in the British Army. This practice, which allowed more money to be authorized and paid by Parliament or other paying authority to the unit commander, was a convenient way for unscrupulous commanders to line their own pockets. These ranger companies had combined missions of gathering information about their area of operations and conducting raids. Some, like the Georgia Rangers, were even assigned peacekeeping or law enforcement missions. While some of these ranger units operated on their own, most operated in support of a higher headquarters. Many ranger units employed Indians in their ranks, and at least one black ranger served with Major Robert Rogers. The Indians taught the colonists their ways of fighting and the lore of the woods. Other units combined classic military tactics with woodcraft and better use of cover.

Rangers usually supplied their own weapons and horses when needed. Most did not wear the typical bright red or blue usually associated with the military uniforms of the period, but generally dressed alike and wore clothes appropriate to operating in the woods. Virtually all early rangers were colonists or provincials as opposed to regular soldiers.

It was not until near the end of this early period, during the French and Indian War, that there is evidence of any special training for the ranger units. During that war, two of the units, those led by Rogers and Colonel Henri Bouquet, had training for the individual rangers, irrespective of their previous experience.

Research material briefly mentions other ranger units during this period. These include: the Massachusetts Rangers that had seven companies during the years 1703-1704 and companies during King George's War; the Carolina Rangers (referring to North Carolina) during the war with the Cherokee Indians following the French and Indian War; and three companies of the South Carolina Rangers. Rangers are also mentioned as operating in New York (during 1702, 1721, and 1747) and New Jersey, where the companies were called the Frontier Guard, between 1756-1760. The New Jersey Rangers started with one company in 1756, led by a Captain Gardiner. He is mentioned in 1758 as the commander of two ranger companies from New Jersey and in 1760 as commanding a company of 120 rangers at Oswego, New York. Captain Hezekiah Dunn also raised a company of New Jersey Rangers in September 1757. As was true with most ranger organizations, members furnished their own weapons. Dunn's rangers fought a band of 50 Indians near Westfall, New York on 13 June 1758. During this battle, the rangers dropped their packs and quietly approached the camp. When the rangers were in position, they ambushed the surprised Indians. At the siege of Louisburg, Major George Scott commanded an *ad hoc* unit composed of light infantry troops and rangers but the command was disbanded after the siege. Little else is known of these units and of some of the ranger organizations discussed, especially Moulton's Rangers.

The battalion of the Royal American Regiment raised by Colonel Bouquet is included because of the training it received. Many of Bouquets training techniques had their basis in Rogers' concepts. After the French and Indian War, it became standard practice for British regiments to have a light infantry company. These units are included here since they form part of the mosaic of the special operations forces history, although more for their training than for their actual operations. It is interesting to note that more than 200 years before the Ranger School, BUD/S, or the Special Forces Qualification Course were designed, military men realized the value of training.

Most of the men who led early ranger units had very strong personalities which often put them at odds with commanders of the regular forces that they were supporting. However, it was necessary for the ranger organizations to have strong leaders who could control the many individualists.

Here, then, are brief histories of some of America's earliest "Elite Warriors."

WILLET'S & CHURCH'S RANGERS

$\mathbf{T}$he ranger units of Captain Thomas Willet and Captain Benjamin Church mark the beginning of the history of elite or special operations forces in America. The first ranger units appeared during the period of King Philip's War. Metacomet (or King Philip, as the colonists called him) was the chief of the Wampanoag Indians in the Rhode Island colony. His battles with the colonial authorities began in 1664 when his brother, then chief of the Wampanoags, died after being released from colonial custody. Metacomet resisted colonial attempts to annex the tribal land, but war broke out over accusations and counter-accusations concerning the murder of a baptized Indian. In 1670, Captain Thomas Willet, a militia leader in Rhode Island, formed a ranger unit to scout the Wampanoags and determine if they were, as suspected, preparing to mount war against the New England colonists. Later that year members of Willet's Rangers reported on the movement of Metacomet's armed warriors in the vicinity of Bristol, Rhode Island.

King Philip's War lasted from June 1675 to August 1676, although the United Colonies of Rhode Island, Plymouth, Connecticut, Massachusetts, New Hampshire, and Maine did not "officially" declare war until 9 September 1675. In the many battles, the Indians inflicted thousands of casualties, prompting a militia officer, Captain Benjamin Church of Massachusetts, to criticize the way the Plymouth authorities were conducting the war. In time, the Plymouth Council told Church to correct the problems and to capture Metacomet.

Church formed a composite unit of hand-picked frontiersmen and friendly Indians called Church's Rangers. Church employed Indians' most effective tactics, ambush and lightning raid, against them with great success. The Rangers scouted prior to their ambushes and learned two key pieces of intelligence. First, the Wampanoags did not employ sentries around their camp, and second, they did not like to move or fight at night.

Church learned several tactical lessons from Indians he recruited. The Indians noticed that, when on the move, the

English "always kept in a heap together," making the choice of targets easy. Church also learned that if the Indians discovered a company of English soldiers in the woods, they could be certain that no other troops were in the vicinity. The English, unlike the Indians, never divided and scattered their troops. Church used this information to devise new tactics to confuse the Indians.

In several of the early engagements where his rangers and militia units combined forces, Church became angry at the conventional tactics employed by the army troops. Following one poor showing at Mile's Bridge, Church wrote, "The Lord have Mercy on us, if such a handful of Indians shall thus dare such an army!" For the duration of King Philip's War, Church criticized "formal European battle tactics," and urged any who would listen, to learn from his Indian scouts, from his rangers, and from his own observations.

On an operation in Rhode Island, with a force of militia commanded by Thomas Matthew Fuller, Church was amazed when their attempted ambush of Wampanoags in the Pocasset Swamp was spoiled because several of the militia gave away their positions by lighting tobacco at night. Church, his rangers, and about 20 volunteers from Fuller's force pursued the fleeing Indians. A running battle fought over the next six hours was inconclusive and Church's force withdrew under heavy fire.

In December 1675, Church's Rangers scouted for the army of Josiah Winslow in an attack on the previously peaceful Naragansett Indians near Kingston, Rhode Island. Winslow marched his men through a driving snowstorm on the 18th and attacked the next day. In the battle that followed Church was shot three times, wounded in the hip and thigh. He tried to persuade Winslow not to burn the Indian houses after the battle, arguing that the English would need them for shelter from the storm, but Winslow didn't listen. This act only hardened the Naragansetts and drove them into an alliance with the Wampanoags and the Nipmucks.

In the months after the "Great Swamp Fight" in the snow, the Indians defeated the colonists in many battles. In early summer of 1676, the tide turned and the colonial troops pursued Metacomet relentlessly, employing a strategy of attrition.

Church, through personal diplomacy, finally convinced several smaller Indian groups to stop fighting. In July, the Naragansetts were soundly beaten in two decisive battles in Rhode Island. At about the same time, the Abenakis, Sokokis, and Pennacooks all signed a peace treaty, ending the fighting in Maine.

Church's Rangers fought Metacomet's warriors twice in July, defeating them at Middleborough and Manpossett on July 11, and at Taunton the following week. After the latter battle Church recruited several of the defeated Wampanoags to help him run Metacomet to ground. On July 31 and August 1, Church's Rangers captured several members of Metacomet's family.

Several days later, a deserter guided the rangers to Metacomet's camp. The rangers surrounded the camp without being detected and attacked savagely. When the short, swift battle was over, Metacomet and most of his warriors were killed.

In 1689, long after the end of King Philip's War, the Plymouth authorities arranged for Church to continue scouting the various Indian tribes in the New England area. Following the death of Metacomet, the Indians' movements and actions were severely restricted. For at least the next 15 years, Church continued to select, train, and lead companies of rangers. These units conducted raiding operations against Indian tribes that violated any of the restrictions requiring them to stay in their own villages and leave the colonists alone. During the operations against the Saco Indians in 1696, Church chose Captain John Gorham as his second in command. Gorham would later raise a ranger company of his own.

Indians were not the only target of Church's Rangers. He also considered the French, especially those in Port Royal and Quebec, proper military targets and launched several raids against their settlements. Unfortunately, his smaller force was no match for the "superior forces entrenched on their own ground." But not all the attacks against larger French settlements failed. In 1704, Church's company of rangers raided the French at Les Mines and burned the settlement to the ground.

Although he started mostly with wild Indian fighters and frontiersmen, Church insisted on military order, appearance, and discipline. Throughout his command he succeeded in turning his company of rangers into a taut military force. Church's Rangers relied on surprise and ambush along with intelligence collected beforehand. Their coordinated teamwork and precision marksmanship set the standard for America's special operations units for centuries to come.

VIRGINIA RANGERS

The New England area was not the only part of Colonial America to experience problems with native Indians. Farther south, in Virginia, almost constant warfare existed from the beginning of the colonial period in 1607. Unlike authorities in the north, Virginia's governors refused to raise military units or authorize militia units to fight the Indians. In the 1670s, William Berkeley was the Governor of Virginia. Berkeley liked the idea of having a series of walled forts with mounted patrols ranging between them. He thought they were sufficient to meet the needs of the colonists and signed a proclamation saying so. Not all colonists agreed.

In April 1679, following the end of Berkeley's second term as governor, the colonial legislature authorized a force of militia units and rangers to be raised. The rangers were to scout and report on Indian activity.

These rangers operated, on and off, for more than 100 years in the Virginia colony, serving local militia and the few regular English units with information about the local Indians, as well as fighting in several wars. Many young, adventurous Virginians joined the rangers. In fact, for some it was steady work.

In 1682, the colonial legislature provided a pay system for the rangers. It stipulated that the rangers were not to stand guard at a particular place but were "expected to maintain regular patrols for intelligence of Indian movements." These rangers were also required to provide their own weapons and horses. In June 1684, Captain George Cooper, who was to raise a ranger company to support the fort at Rappahannock, reported difficulty in raising the required 30 men. The legislature then authorized him to recruit in nearby counties. By 1691, mounted companies of rangers were raised. Each "company" consisted of a lieutenant, 11 rangers, and two Indians, and was stationed at the heads of principal rivers in the colony. The following year, Maryland built three forts on its frontier and the Provincial Council arranged for the formation of a "body" of rangers. While half of them patrolled the area between the various forts, the other half rested. Each week, these rangers switched duties. In 1716, several companies of rangers from the settlement of Germannia, were sent into the Valley of Virginia on scouting and exploring expeditions.

As late as 1755, during the French and Indian War, the Virginia colonial assembly authorized the recruitment of five or more companies of rangers. In July 1755, five of these companies, along with one ranger company from Maryland and one from North Carolina, accompanied General Braddock on his ill-fated campaign against Fort Duquesne. At the site where Braddock was killed, the ambushing French and Indians fired from protected positions in the trees, moving out among the British only to take scalps. The regular British units were caught in the open, and did not know how to react. But the rangers knew and moved into the woods to fight back. At one point a British detachment fired on rangers maneuvering in the trees and killed almost half of them, forcing the rest to withdraw.

As a result of the casualties, Virginia called for more ranger companies to be formed, but these were never fully manned. For some time, the rangers were not paid and morale and efficiency of these units suffered. The mission of the ranger companies raised at this time was to protect the colonial frontier, specifically to ward off Indian raids, under French sponsorship, into the Valley of Virginia. Captain John Ashby commanded one of these companies, raised near Winchester in Frederick County. Daniel Morgan, who later led his own rangers during the Revolutionary War, served in Ashby's company. Some ranger companies even used dogs to help them track the enemy. In October 1756, Colonel George Washington disbanded ranger companies because he thought they had mediocre leaders. Ashby's was one of the companies disbanded.

However, several months later, more ranger companies were organized to replace the disbanded ones. These companies served throughout most of the French and Indian War, becoming better as time passed. By 1763, during Pontiac's Rebellion, over 1,000 Virginia Rangers were on regular duty, compared with a much smaller number of rangers in Pennsylvania. The war damage in each area shows that Virginia suffered little, while Pennsylvania had "its whole western region ravaged by Indians."

In 1774, Dunmore's War broke out. Dunmore, the governor of Virginia, granted titles for land on both sides of the Ohio River that, according to a 1768 treaty, belonged to the Shawnee and other Indian tribes. Following some initial incidents in which both Indians and settlers were killed, Dunmore raised a force of 1,500 men and headed toward a rendezvous with a similar sized force raised by Anthony Lewis. Pennsylvania, opposed to Dunmore (he accused Pennsylvania of being in a conspiracy with the Indians to stop him), raised a "Corps of Rangers" that numbered about 100 men. Dunmore had several ranger companies as part of his force, while others were raised but ordered to stay behind to range the frontier. The War lasted from 10 June to 26 October. Only one major, but inconclusive battle was fought, in which Lewis lost over 200 men.

During the Revolutionary War, Daniel Morgan raised several different commands of rangers. Numerous other companies were also raised and fought against "superior numbers of Indians in the woods." One of the most prominent ranger commanders during this period was Captain Samuel Brady, who raised a company in 1777. Pennsylvania, which had learned a lesson from its experience during Pontiac's Rebellion and Dunmore's War, raised several companies of rangers early in the Revolutionary War, and maintained them on active duty throughout the war.

Following the ratification of the Constitution in 1787, the Federal government discouraged state and territorial ranger forces from conducting offensive raids along their frontiers against the Indians. This meant that the rangers had to stop any pursuit at their border. Finally, in 1789, the Federal government ordered Virginia to disband all of its rangers. The following year, many of the state rangers were re-formed and placed on the Federal payroll.

MOULTON'S RANGERS

Queen Anne's War, the second war between England and France for control of North America, ended in 1713, but local antagonism continued among the colonists. In 1721, Captain Jeremia Moulton, described as an experienced Indian fighter, raised a force of rangers to conduct raids against the Norridgewock mission village Indians in Maine, and to report on the French influence among the Indians there. The English colonists had increasingly viewed French Jesuit missionaries and fur trappers with suspicion because they lived peacefully with the Indians. Many of the English believed that the French were trying to influence the Indians to fight the English.

Moulton raised several companies of rangers to operate under his command. He chose three other captains to lead companies, Bourne, Bane, and John (or Johnson) Harmon. All were experienced Indian fighters, but Harmon had the reputation of being the most savage. The Indians of eastern Maine knew of Harmon's reputation and, between 1722 and 1724 throughout New England, referred to his company as "Harmon's dreaded ranger band."

In one operation, in the vicinity of the Kennebec River, Harmon and his rangers found a party of 20 sleeping Indians. Harmon directed his men to follow him quietly up to the sleeping band, to take careful aim, and, at his direction, to shoot. The first volley killed the entire group.

During August 1724, Captain Moulton led a combined ranger force of about 150 to another part of the Kennebec River, this time targeting a French Jesuit named Father Sebastian Rasle. Rasle lived with the Indians. The New England authorities feared his influence over them, believing that he incited the Indians "to kill, burn, and destroy." Although it is probably true that Rasle promoted hatred of the British among the Indians in his village, he was concerned about losing some of his power of persuasion over them. Moulton's Rangers traveled up the Kennebec to a point near the village and split into two elements, the second led by Harmon. This division of the ranger party suggests that perhaps Moulton may have scouted the village ahead of time and knew the strength of the Indians.

At about three o'clock in the afternoon of 12 August, Harmon took half of the rangers and began to destroy the village cornfields. Moulton led the other half in an attack on the village. Moulton sent detachments to the north and south of the village and led the remainder in from the east. This pinned the Indians against the river, situated on the west side of the village. The rangers achieved complete surprise and a quick, violent victory. Moulton found several well-known Indian leaders among the dead, and the body of Rasle as well. The rangers spent the night in the village and departed the following morning, burning the village behind them.

GEORGIA RANGERS

When the colony of Georgia was established in 1732, its charter, which was typical of the time, specified that the local militia bore the burden for defending the citizens and territory. Although the Governor of South Carolina was the commander of the Georgia militia until 1738, this did not stop James Ogelthorpe of Georgia, from organizing and conducting the drill of the early Georgia militia units.

Georgia's full-time military force, initially established in 1734, included a small force of rangers that, as in other colonies that used them, conducted scouting and ranging operations between garrisons to detect and, if possible, counter the threat raised by the French, Spanish, and Indians. Since garrisons were built on the edge of what was then the frontier, the rangers patrolled on horseback.

One of the first, formed in May 1734, was a unit called Mackay's Rangers or Mackay's Independent Company of Rangers, led by Captain Patrick Mackay. These rangers did not wear "uniforms" but wore practical clothing suited to the mission and area of operations. This included buckskin trousers, leather leggings (or "leggins," as they were called, adapted from similar garb worn by Indians), shoes, coats, and broad-brimmed hats.

Their weapons were usually long-barreled muskets with the usual accoutrements of cartridge box, powder flask, and some rangers even carried cutlasses. This company was initially posted to the Tallapoosa River area and eventually established Fort Okfuskee, in that area. In 1736, Mackay's Rangers were divided. Part of the company patrolled the frontier while the rest moved to the Atlantic coast. Those on the coast were integrated with scout boat units, specifically organized to patrol the "frontier" along the east coast of the colony.

In 1739, a troop known as English Rangers was raised but did not remain together as a specific organization. Instead, it was split into smaller forces and stationed at various places within Georgia, depending on the local need. In 1743 Captain James MacPherson commanded a troop of 19 rangers of this company. The English Rangers provided their own clothes, weapons, and horses. Civilian clothing, not a uniform, was worn, consisting usually of deerskin or wool trousers, leggings, shoes, checkered shirts, waistcoats and jackets, and cocked hats. The rangers carried "Brown Bess" muskets, only recently available in Georgia, with shortened barrels, a pistol, and a hatchet.

At about the same time, near the settlement of Darien on the Altamaha River, members of a highland Scot area formed a troop of so-called Highland Rangers. This unit generally patrolled in the area where it was raised. The following year, a Highland Independent Company of Foot was formed in the same area and it is likely that the rangers were the basis for this unit. The Highland Rangers wore clothing more closely associated with traditional highland dress. While kilts were not worn, clothing included buckskin trousers, leggings, shoes, tartan waistcoats and jackets, blue bonnets, and, on occasion, tartan shoulder plaids. They, too, carried shortened "Brown Bess" muskets and pistols, but also had dirks, broadswords, bayonets, and even shields.

Many of these ranging units employed warriors from the various Creek tribes as scouts to supplement their size. These Indian scouts supplied information on the movement and hostile intentions of local Indian bands.

From October 1739 until June 1747, Georgia fought in two wars. The first, the War of Jenkins' Ear between England and

Spain, started when an overzealous Spanish Caribbean coast guard cut off the ear of an English sea captain named Jenkins. This happened in 1732, but Jenkins did not report it to Parliament until seven years later. In 1740, the War of Jenkins' Ear merged into a continuation of the War of Austrian Succession, in which England sided with Austria against Prussia, Spain, France, Bavaria, and Saxony. The colonies called this King George's War. Eventually, the Treaty of Aix-la-Chapelle settled the war in 1748.

Ranger organizations in Georgia fought in four major engagements during this period. In 1739, Oglethorpe led a raid into Florida with a composite organization consisting of Georgia's ranger units, other militia troops, and a band from South Carolina called Rangers or Southern Scouts. The raid failed when Spanish reinforcements from Cuba forced the colonists to retreat and the Highland Rangers suffered heavy losses. This is the only known mention of military action by the South Carolina Rangers or Southern Scouts. Other engagements involving the Georgia Rangers included the attempted invasion along Georgia's coast by the Spanish commander of St. Augustine in 1742, which culminated in a Spanish defeat at the Battle of Bloody Marsh. In 1743, Ogelthorpe, accompanied by the Highland Rangers, again attacked St. Augustine. The attack failed to draw out the wary Spanish, and the English force returned to Georgia.

The strength of Georgia Rangers during this period peaked in 1746, with 15 officers and 122 men. In June 1747, despite several efforts by Governor Oglethorpe and others in the colonial government, King George II ordered these units disbanded. He believed they were too expensive to maintain and unnecessary since the war was almost over.

1756

In 1754, Georgia became a royal colony; that is, the trustees returned the charter to the king, having been thwarted by "[a]n unforgiving frontier and too many impractical ideas." Soon after, on January 24, 1755, the colonial assembly passed the militia act of 1755. This established, as did similar acts in many of the other colonies, that all men in the colony aged 16 to 60 were required to serve. Militia captains were appointed and authorized to form companies to "suppress pirates, sea rovers, Indians, and fugitive slaves." Two regiments were authorized in 1758 and a third in 1759. The first ranger organization that was specifically authorized was a troop of 6 officers and 70 men, formed in September 1756.

As the French and Indian War intensified, the governor looked for a way to support his rangers. He petitioned the commander-in-chief of English military forces in North America to accept his rangers as regulars. In addition, the assembly asked the governor to authorize and raise two additional ranger troops. Eventually, on 18 May 1759, the First Troop of Rangers became part of the regular British military force, followed on 1 January 1760, by the Second Troop of Rangers.

In 1760, Governor Henry Ellis, for many years the champion of his ranger units, ordered rangers from coastal forts to those inland to assist in the Cherokee-Creek crisis. Friendly Indians were once again added to the strength of rangers to bolster the size of patrols. These patrols "dealt with suspected spies, runaway slaves, deserters, cattle and horse traders en route to the Spanish garrison at St. Augustine, and whites squatting on Indian land." They often served as ceremonial troops, taking part in the announcement of the accession to the throne of King George III in February 1761, in the declaration of war against Spain in May 1762, in the king's birthday celebration (June 4) in 1763, and in marking the end of the French and Indian War in September 1763. On occasion, they escorted and provided protection for the governor. This was perhaps the first use of special operations troops in a personal security role.

By 1763, rangers reached a strength of 14 officers and cadets and 140 men. Each troop was authorized five officers: a captain, first, second, and third lieutenants; and a quartermaster. These troops of now full-time rangers performed the same duties as had similar units up to this time, ranging among the various frontier garrisons of the colony. In 1761, they were located at Fort Halifax, Fort Augusta, Fort Argyle, and Fort Barrington. Within a year rangers also garrisoned Fort George and later Fort Frederica.

Following the end of the French and Indian War, the two troops of rangers, supplemented by detachments of the 60th

Regiment of Foot (Royal American), constituted the full-time military force in Georgia. The rangers continued to take part in ceremonies. During one such ceremony, Governor James Wright, was accompanied by a force of about 50 rangers, some from each troop, on a "parade" of about 140 miles. Those of First Troop were led by Second Lieutenant Moses N. Rivers, and Second Troop by Third Lieutenant Mungo Graham. Increasingly, the rangers enforced the law along the frontier. For example, in November 1765, Lieutenant Robert Baillie of First Troop searched the vicinity of the Canoochee River for a "Nest of Villains."

STAMP ACT CONTROVERSEY

However, both the North American colonies and the Georgia Rangers were headed for a crisis that would change both forever. In March 1765, the British Parliament passed the Stamp Act. This was an effort to raise money to pay for the costs of defending the colonies. The act's sweeping coverage required stamp duties on a wide range of items, including "legal papers, commercial papers, liquor licenses, land instruments, indentures, cards, dice, pamphlets, newspapers, advertisements, almanacs, academic degrees, and appointments to office." There was widespread opposition to the imposition and enforcement of the Stamp Act, principally from the colonists who had organized themselves under the name Sons of Liberty.

In many of the colonies, the Sons of Liberty prevented the arrival or use of the stamped papers, or the appointed stamp collectors from performing their jobs. Georgia was the only colony to distribute and use the stamps. A force of rangers assisted in this process.

On 2 January 1766, Governor Wright heard that 200 Liberty Boys intended to seize and destroy the colony's stamped papers, then stored at Fort Halifax. He ordered the Ranger Troop commanders (Captain James E. Powell of the First and Captain John Milledge of the Second) to assemble as many of their rangers as possible at a guardhouse. In a short time, 54 rangers had gathered. Wright and the rangers later dispersed a crowd gathered to prevent the distribution of the stamps. Then Wright and the rangers marched to Fort Halifax, loaded the stamps, and removed them to the guardhouse they had used for their initial assembly.

For the next several weeks a force of rangers guarded the stamps and patrolled the city of Savannah. On January 3, rangers escorted the stamp collector to the Governor where his oath of office was administered. The stamp collector sold stamps for two weeks and then left town. On January 30, just ahead of an angry crowd, Wright ordered the rangers to move the stamped papers to Fort George, located on an island. The rangers established a guard force. Three days later, Wright and a force of rangers and sailors dispersed a gathering of the Sons of Liberty who had demanded that the Governor release the stamps to them.

Protests died down and peace, of a sort, was restored. On June 16, the colonists received word from England that the hated Stamp Act had been repealed. Following the crisis, the rangers returned to the garrisons on the colonial frontiers. But all was not well for the rangers.

General Thomas Gage, the new commander of British troops in the American colonies, had, since January 1766, considered disbanding the rangers and using other regular units in their place. In February 1767, after being assured that he had this authority, Gage ordered the Georgia Rangers to be discharged on March 31. Although the rangers were not officially disbanded until October 1767, there was no further military use of these units after the announcement of Gage's order.

1773

In September 1773, Governor Wright ordered the raising of a troop of rangers "to keep good order amongst, and for the protection of the Inhabitants in the new ceded Lands above Settle River." He didn't mention to the government in England that he had raised this unit. A force of 6 officers and about 70 rangers was authorized. By November 1773, all of the officers (Captain Edward Barnard, First Lieutenant Thomas Waters, Second Lieutenant Edward Keating, Third Lieutenant Timothy Barnard, Quartermaster John Stuart, Sr., and Surgeon Francis Begbie) were commissioned. Once again, Georgia Rangers returned to the colonial frontiers, this time to continue to range between garrisons, but also to enforce the law by apprehending "all Horse Thieves, Vagrants and other Disorderly persons." Most of the rangers worked out of Fort James, near Dartmouth.

The rangers paid for their own uniforms and weapons, but were given horses. The following is a description of these uniforms from a newspaper of the period; the uniforms included "a Blue Coat faced with Red and a Red Jacket and Blue Cloth Boots as spatterdashes made to fit the Leg edged with Red and Gartered with Black strap and Buckle to wear occasionally and Breeches either Blue Cloth or Buckskin also a good Fussee, a Putteau, a Black Leather shot Pouch and Belt of the same Edged with Red also a good Powder Horn."

The rangers' only military action was against Creek Indians in the vicinity of Sherrill's Farm in Ogeechee, from late December 1773 to late January 1774. During this period, most of the rangers worked in conjunction with local militia to restore order. Following this action, in March, the Colonial Committee of the Commons recommended that three companies of rangers be raised, but no action was taken on this recommendation.

Governor Wright also used the rangers, as he had in the past, in some ceremonial duties, escorting dignitaries on special occasions. In June 1775, Captain Barnard died and was not replaced. As their authority from the governor diminished, so did the rangers' strength, until March 1776, when the troop ceased to exist.

GORHAM'S RANGERS

In 1743, the North American colonies were fighting the Spanish along the southern border between Georgia and the Floridas, and the French and Indians throughout the northern colonies and in Canada. King George's War was in full swing. The French used the area in the vicinity of Fort Saint Frederic, located near Crown Point, New York, as a staging area to conduct a series of hit-and-run raids throughout the northern New England area. Initially the English did little to stop or retaliate for these raids. In Nova Scotia, the governor dispatched a request for assistance to a friend in the Massachusetts colony, Captain John Gorham. Nova Scotia was having troubles from both its Indian tribes and Acadian settlers and there was no military force available to the governor.

Gorham rounded up a company of rangers, most of them Mohawk Indians, and headed north. His younger brother, Joseph, was a member of this company. The British called the unit the Nova Scotia Ranging Company. Gorham's ranger unit went to Annapolis Royal (also called Port Royal), Nova Scotia. The unit's first action was to attack "rugged coastal areas, which had considered themselves safe from attack." The rangers came in on two boats, surprising the French, who had not expected any attack, least of all from the water.

Late in 1744, the French launched an unsuccessful attempt to capture Annapolis Royal. Part of the forces that held the position and threw back the French assault included the rangers. In April 1745, William Pepperrell gathered a 4,000 man militia army in Massachusetts to attack the French fort at Louisburg. This fort guarded the approach to the St. Lawrence River and was located on Cape Breton Island in Nova Scotia. Gorham's Rangers were specifically recruited to accompany Pepperell's force and took part in the 45-day siege of Louisburg. On 16 June, the fort and what is described as "the greatest concentration of cannon in North America" fell to the English attackers. Following this, the only major battle in the war fought in North America, Gorham and his rangers continued to defend Nova Scotia, "operating by water and land to extend English authority." Within about three years, Gorham had recruited two more companies to join his original force.

In 1746, the rocky, foggy coast of Nova Scotia foiled an attempt by the French to make a grand assault against Annapolis Royal. This was the last major activity of King George's War in the Nova Scotia area. In October 1748, peace among the warring countries was settled by the Treaty of Aix-la-Chapelle. By virtue of their overwhelming presence, the English retained control of Nova Scotia, except for the strategic fort at Louisburg. In a move they would regret later, they returned the fort to France.

By 1749, following the treaty, Gorham's company (now called "Gorham's Rangers") was accorded a singular honor.

They were made part of the regular British Army. This was an honor not given lightly to colonial units. As a consequence of this action, the rangers became royal soldiers and were no longer viewed as provincial troops or militia. The distinction, to the rangers at least, was only in their bragging. At about the same time, Joseph Gorham received a commission as a lieutenant in the ranger company commanded by his brother.

During the following year, an advertisement appeared in the *Boston Weekly News Letter*, a prominent New England newspaper, seeking volunteers for what were called "the Independent Companies of Rangers now in Nova Scotia." Lieutenant Alexander Collender was Gorham's recruiting officer for this particular period and his "office" was at the Sign of the Lamb in the South End. At this same time, two other rangers companies were raised. One of them was known as the "English Rangers," and was commanded by Captain William Clapham. The other company was commanded by Captain Francis Barteleo.

During the next seven years, the rangers continued their patrolling activity without becoming involved in any major engagement or particularly noteworthy activity. During one fight, in March 1750, the English Rangers and a company of regulars reinforced Gorham's Rangers in a battle with Indians in the vicinity of the St. Croix River. In September of the same year, Gorham led another amphibious attack, this one in the vicinity of Chignecto. There were several bitter battles between the rangers and Indians in this area during the next year. In December 1751, John Gorham died of smallpox while in England. His brother Joseph, now a captain, became the ranger company commander.

There are several descriptions of what Gorham's Rangers wore, but generally this included canvas or linen pants (the rangers preferred wool or buckskin if they could get them), leggings made of two layers of wool cloth, coats of the same color as the leggings, sleeveless short jackets, long-sleeved waistcoats, and blue bonnets. Colors were usually dark but with blue cuffs and lapels. Some of the rangers also wore blue skirts to keep warm when moving by boat.

In 1755, several English victories in Nova Scotia (including the so-called "velvet siege" at Fort Beausejour on 16 June and the capture of Fort Gaspereau the next day without a shot being fired) gave them virtual control of the area, except for the fort at Louisburg. This was firmly controlled by the French and stayed that way until July 1758. Joseph Gorham and his rangers returned to fight again at Louisburg, this time in the army of Major General James Wolfe. The victory later that month was one of several key battles that turned the tide against the French the following year.

Wolfe was so impressed with Gorham's Rangers at Louisburg that he took them with him the following year when he attacked Quebec. During the intervening period Wolfe, who generally held ranger units in low regard (as did most European officers), used Gorham's company to counter raids by the French and their Indian allies. Wolfe went so far as to issue notices to his enemies that each of their raids would result in a retaliatory operation by Gorham's force of rangers. The rangers were very busy in late 1758 and 1759. Gorham's was one of six ranger companies that fought in the Quebec campaign, but he appears to have been the most efficient commander. Although Wolfe was killed during the battle, the French were defeated, effectively ending their power in North America.

Other English commanders knew of the performance of Gorham's ranger company at Quebec and used the unit as the nucleus of various task forces during the remainder of the fighting in Canada. Two years later, Joseph Gorham was commissioned a major in the regular English Army, something that not even Robert Rogers was offered.

Between 1761 and 1764, Gorham's command extended beyond his own ranger company, incorporating several other ranger units (sometimes called independent companies, light infantry, and even the "North American Rangers").

In 1762, Gorham's Rangers were part of the brief expedition to Havana. Upon his return to New England, Gorham began another recruiting drive to fill his ranks. In May 1763, in the major battle of the coda of the French and Indian War, known as Pontiac's Rebellion, warriors from seven Indian tribes (the Ottawas, Ojibwas, Potawatomis, Hurons, Shawnees, Delawares, and Eries) lay siege to Detroit. Gorham's ranger company was one of the many units rushed to the area to help lift the siege. Also participating in this fight was a little known unit of rangers, the Queen's Royal North American Rangers, led by Captain Joseph Hopkins. In September the English broke the siege and the following month Pontiac agreed to end the fighting.

Early in 1764, Gorham's Rangers were disbanded and Joseph Gorham returned to live in Nova Scotia. He died in 1790.

ROGERS' RANGERS

Probably the most well-known ranger organization in early American history is the one raised, trained, and led by a New Hampshire woodsman named Robert Rogers. Rogers and his companies of rangers fought on various fronts throughout most of the French and Indian War, sometimes alongside ranger units of other men, such as Joseph Gorham and Joseph Hopkins.

The origins of the French and Indian War involved: disputes between the English and French and Spanish over colonization of North America; trading with and among the Indians; religious persecution of Roman Catholics and other religious groups in Nova Scotia and other parts of North America; decades of broken treaties with the many Indian tribes by the English, French, and Spanish; encroachment on Indian tribal lands by the various colonists; and the Indians' response to this by fighting back.

The fighting began in 1754 over attempts by the English to build a fort at the "forks of the Ohio," the junction of the Allegheny and the Monongahela and the Ohio rivers. The French viewed this as an attempt to push them out of the Ohio area and cut into their lucrative trade agreements with the local Indian tribes. Fighting spread from there. The period was marked by shifting interests, alliances and treaties among the different sides. Treaties with various Indian tribes were entered into and broken with ease and arrogant disregard. This war, as had several before it, melded into a far larger European war in 1756, a war that pitted Britain, Prussia, and Hanover against

France, Austria, Russia, Saxony, Sweden, and Spain. The European phase is called the Seven Years War.

In the spring of 1755, Robert Rogers volunteered to accompany the forces of William Johnson in a campaign against the French at Fort Saint Frederic, near Crown Point, with a unit he had recruited. The unit was originally recruited to serve as engineers and be part of a New Hampshire provincial regiment. Because Rogers, who had only recently "beaten" a charge of counterfeiting, a crime that carried hanging as its ultimate penalty, and branding and ear cropping as lesser penalties, had signed up men who "were well versed in the lore of the woods gleaned from trapping beaver, hunting and pursuing Indians," the unit was given the name "Rogers' Rangers." Rogers' lieutenant was a close friend of his, John Stark.

The English campaign of 1755 centered around the disastrous attempts of Major General Edward Braddock to capture Fort Duquesne, now a French fort at the "forks of the Ohio." Braddock had failed to heed the advice of several colonial military officers. He insisted on using European tactics and on building a road to his objective over which he could move his army. His lack of security on the move, and even while stopped, was especially troublesome. At one point, during a road ambush by Indians, his troops foolishly moved *from* protected spots along the side of a road and formed a cluster *in the middle of the road*! Braddock also did not believe in using scouts.

As a consequence of Braddock's defeat, many of the Indian scouts supporting Johnson's thrust to Crown Point, deserted. Johnson turned to Rogers for reconnaissance support. On 24 March 1756, Governor William Shirley of Massachusetts, impressed with what he had heard about Rogers and his rangers, commissioned him to raise an independent company of 60 rangers, "consisting of individuals skilled in woodcraft and marksmanship." These rangers were to find routes for an army to move, scout out the dispositions of the enemy, and conduct raids against selected targets. The unit was to receive pay from royal funds.

Rogers spent the latter part of 1756 putting his unit together and conducting periodic reconnaissance in the vicinity of Lake George. Beginning in September of that year, he made it a

Major Robert Rogers (Artist, Thomas Hart, London, 1776).

practice to take a few regular officers along on patrol, always under his supervision. He was well aware of the low opinion most British regular officers held of provincial troops, but he hoped to at least open their eyes a little. The officers who went "on party" usually returned with complimentary comments about the rangers.

In January 1757, Rogers led a patrol consisting of four ranger companies; two were his and the other two were companies raised by Captain Humphrey Hobbs and Captain Thomas Speakman. Five days into the patrol the rangers were ambushed by a French and Indian force as they were attempting to determine where that force was. The rangers were unable to withdraw until after nightfall. At least seven rangers were killed, including Speakman, whose head was put on a spike and displayed in an Indian village, and several others were wounded. Following this action, the other two ranger companies were put under Rogers' command.

In April, Rogers and three companies of rangers were to accompany a British force to Nova Scotia as part of the command that would attack the French fort at Louisburg. However, when the British heard of the French victory at Fort William Henry, these plans changed. As a result of the surrender terms, two companies of rangers at the fort were dissolved, one commanded by Richard Rogers, Robert's brother, and an independent ranger unit under Captain Jonathan Ogden.

It was at about this time that Rogers formulated a document which is a milestone in ranger tactics and, in slightly different form, is still used by U.S. rangers today. This document is variously called Rogers' Rules of Discipline or the Standing Orders of Rogers' Rangers. Regardless of what it is called, it is an interesting and unique document because of its simplicity and foresightedness. Rogers believed in realistic training for his new recruits and for all his rangers. He instituted frequent live-fire exercises and rehearsed patrol activities. Another tactic that Rogers taught his men was fire-and-maneuver; that is, while one part of the unit is moving to a different position, one or more other parts provide covering fire. Rogers taught his rangers the advantages of using terrain in their tactics and how to recognize key terrain features. He also preached the necessity of cover and concealment in all ranger operations.

Rogers' Rangers generally dressed in comfortable frontier clothes, made of fringed buckskin trousers, long-sleeved long jackets or hunting shirts (trousers and shirts were brown or green in color), with soft shoes for warm weather but not cold, leggings, and bonnet caps. Weapons included muskets, knives, and hatchets, with the usual cartridge boxes and powder horns.

The rangers continued to harass French forces in the Lake George, New York area. Their patrols concentrated around Fort Carillon at Ticonderoga and Fort Saint Frederic. Although the rangers brought back information that these forts were relatively lightly held, the English elected not to attack. As the weather grew colder and it began to snow regularly, most of the English units went into their regular "winter quarters." Rogers' Rangers, however, continued to operate as they did every winter, using sleds, snowshoes, and ice skates when necessary to move.

One such winter mission, in early 1758, is among the best known of Rogers' unit. At the end of February, Major Israel Putnam, commander of the Connecticut Provincial Rangers, was sent to scout the area around Ticonderoga. On 10 March, four days after Putnam's Rangers returned, Rogers and 180 of his men set out to patrol the same general area. Included in his force were eight regular British officers who were "on party" for this mission. On the fourth day out, near Bald Mountain (now called Rogers' Rock), the rangers spotted a party of about 90 Indians and Canadian militia, and set an ambush. Only after the rangers sprung their ambush did Rogers learn his mistake. He had not attacked the main body but an advance vanguard for a force of about 700. The ensuing battle lasted for over three hours and 125 rangers were killed, plus 4 of the regular officers. Most of the survivors were wounded.

For several months afterwards the French believed that Rogers was dead. They had found several items of clothing and a copy of his commission in the debris of the battlefield. Rogers was not dead. It did, however take Rogers four months, and several forays against the French in May and July, to bring his rangers back to strength and to renew the damage done to his unit's reputation. On 6 April, Rogers was promoted to the rank of Major.

The following March, the rangers were again on patrol near Ticonderoga. The weather was even more severe than the previous year, with temperatures below zero. This time the rangers moved at night, hoping to arrive undetected. They discovered no enemy forces in the valley near the fort and conducted a thorough, though hasty reconnaissance and prepared to return. At midnight, 7 March, Rogers sent part of his frostbitten force back to prepare fires at a rendezvous point at Sabbath Day Point on the Connecticut River. The following morning the rangers surprised a wood-chopping party of about 40 French soldiers, killing four and taking seven as prisoners. The French at Fort Carillon heard the shooting and sent a force out to discover what was happening. For the next 21 hours Rogers and his rangers fought a running battle, eventually moving to the campsite of the party that had departed the previous night. Rogers sent some of his rangers for sleds and the scouting party eventually returned safely.

By May 1759, Rogers' Rangers included ten companies, three of them entirely made up of new recruits. Between then and late July, the rangers were heavily involved in the siege of

Fort Carillon, carrying out several special raiding missions. Finally, the British force captured the fort.

THE ST. FRANCIS RAID

In September, Rogers was ordered to take a force of 200 rangers from Crown Point, to the Abenaki Indian village of St. Francis, located about 45 miles from Montreal, "to chastise those savages with some severity." Rogers had wanted to raid the village for almost four years, and was finally given the mission. On the way to St. Francis, the rangers traveled through mosquito-infested swamps, hung their hammocks in trees, and crossed the fast moving St. Francis River by forming a human chain. Early on the morning of 5 October, 22 days after departing Crown Point, the rangers reached their objective. They attacked the village a half-hour before dawn. When the battle was over, at seven o'clock that morning, the rangers had killed more than 200 Indians and set fire to the village. On the return trip to Crown Point, the French and Indian forces pursued the rangers "like a hive of angry hornets." At one point, Rogers allowed his officers to persuade him to divide his force, a move he hoped would give them all a better opportunity to find food. The move only weakened each party. At least 50 of the fleeing rangers were killed in the running battle that followed. Eventually, Rogers returned to his base at Crown Point.

During 1759, several of Rogers' companies served at the battles for Louisburg and Quebec. At Quebec they conducted at least 22 separate scouting missions and raids. These companies served the army of General Wolfe. Rogers, however, did not take part in these actions.

Rogers' Rangers had the reputation of being unruly and unmanageable. Their reputation was well-deserved, but one that Rogers attempted to control by insisting on firm discipline. When recruiting prospective rangers, he made it clear that they were "subject to military discipline and the articles of war."

DETROIT MISSION

In the months following the St. Francis raid, many of the ranger companies were disbanded and their members discharged. By the end of the year, only four companies were still active. At the end of March 1760, however, the rangers' strength was again at eight companies. Over the next few months, the rangers conducted several successful raids, including one at Ste. Therese in June. As before, Rogers' companies served in several widespread areas. In September, Rogers was ordered to the Detroit area. He took at least one company of rangers with him, possibly two. His orders were "to take *actual* possession of Detroit, Fort Michelmackinac ... and other western outposts *formally* ceded to the English after the fall of Montreal."

On the way to Detroit, Rogers' party was blocked by an Indian force led by an Ottawa named Pontiac. Pontiac ordered Rogers and his men out of the area. Rogers refused. A standoff ensued and lasted overnight. In the morning, Rogers and Pontiac conferred again and agreed to terms. The ranger force continued to Fort Detroit, where Rogers sent a note to the commandant ordering the French to leave the area. Eventually, on November 29, Rogers took possession of Detroit. His mission to take the forts in the upper peninsula area was stalled by early winter storms. The forts were not taken until the following spring by another unit. Rogers' only loss during this campaign was one ranger who drowned.

On January 1761, Rogers' Rangers were disbanded at Fort Pitt. Those rangers companies that did not accompany Rogers to Detroit were sent back to Crown Point. In September 1760, they were disbanded and the men returned to their prior units. One small force of 20 rangers, under the leadership of Lieutenant John Butler, had been sent on missions to take outposts in the "wilderness of the Illinois country." This small band was mustered out of service in late January 1762.

During Pontiac's Rebellion in 1763, Rogers was once again in service. Although no longer in command of the rangers, he was involved in the siege of Detroit, where he made the acquaintance of Captain Joseph Hopkins and his ranger company. Rogers later served in another ranger unit, this one also in an English army. During the Revolutionary War he attempted to enlist in the American army and was even interviewed by one of his former ranger officers, John Stark. But Washington was suspicious of Rogers and refused to grant him a commission. Rogers then formed and led the Queen's Rangers, a British unit. He died in 1795, in England, broke and alone.

BATTALION OF 60TH (ROYAL AMERICAN) REGIMENT

Despite the well-documented disdain, even contempt, with which European officers, schooled in classical tactics, held colonial ranger units, there were several instances of the provincial tactics being used by regular units. For example, Lieutenant Colonel Thomas Gage formed "light infantry" units that essentially adopted the formations and tactics of ranger companies.

Gage realized early that classic tactics did not fit into the local geography (which required moving through heavily forested areas with few, if any, roads) and were not effective against the French and Indians. He also discovered that European tactics required the troops to carry more equipment than was necessary for wilderness fighting. Gage had uniforms made of less heavy material for his light infantry and insisted that their weapons consist only of what they could carry, relying less on artillery and mortar support. Since the barrels of standard infantry muskets reflected sunlight and could easily give away his troops' position, Gage ordered them to be subdued. He also adopted the idea of wearing leggings to save wear and tear on trousers and legs when moving through the brush.

Gage, always looking for an opportunity to get promoted, recommended that a 500-man regiment of rangers be formed, with him as the commander. This regiment would replace the rangers commanded by Rogers. A regiment was authorized but was not very successful, and Rogers continued to command his rangers. After the French and Indian War, the British dropped the idea of a light infantry regiment and decided instead to have one company of light infantry in each regiment of foot.

BOUQUET

Lieutenant Colonel Henri Bouquet had probably the most significant influence in recognizing and adapting ranger tactics to larger than company formations. Bouquet was a Swiss soldier-of-fortune serving in the English army and was very selective about who he allowed in his unit. Not every "applicant" was accepted, and those who were accepted were continually evaluated. He insisted on a training program that required stamina, memory, and a knowledge of different formations.

Bouquet, apparently taking notice of Indian capabilities, required that his men be able to run for long distances while carrying their equipment. He devised and trained his men to take up different tactical formations from a marching position and even while running. These formations were not the moving-fighting ones either. Some required his soldiers to disperse quickly. Bouquet developed a set of signals that he used to train his soldiers, making it simpler and quicker to spread the word on the movement he wanted them to execute.

He also taught his soldiers standard European tactics, both so they could execute them and recognize them if employed by an enemy, thus helping them to understand what may be about to happen. Most interesting of all his teachings was that he required his soldiers to shoot from both the kneeling and prone firing positions, in addition to the standard standing one. These positions, however, proved difficult to execute with the musket of the day, which was difficult to reload.

Bouquet was authorized to recruit a battalion of "light infantry" to be part of the 60th (Royal American) Regiment of Foot. This battalion was to operate principally in the western Pennsylvania area. In 1758, it got its first chance.

During that summer, Brigadier General John Forbes was appointed to conduct the campaign against the French at Fort Duquesne, at the "forks of the Ohio." His army set out in late July, taking a road that ran "through Pennsylvania instead of the old road coursing through Virginia that had been developed by Braddock." When they were still almost 100 miles from Fort Duquesne, Bouquet was placed in command of one column, which consisted of his light infantry battalion and several hundred other troops. Bouquet thought that he could capture the fort with his own column without relying on the much larger main column.

He ordered an attack that failed miserably. Almost 300 of his column were killed or captured. Forbes arrived at Bouquet's headquarters on 23 September. Eventually, negotiations with Indians in the area resulted in a separate peace with them.

When the French found out about this peace, they panicked and abandoned Fort Duquesne to the English.

On 10 February 1763, the Treaty of Paris was signed ending the French and Indian War in North America (and the Seven Years War in Europe). After the end of the war, several Indians tribes, led by Pontiac, the Ottawa chief, continued to fight, and attempted "to regain control of the Ohio Valley." Bouquet, now a colonel, and his provincial light infantry were sent to the site of their previous battle, now renamed Fort Pitt.

Bouquet departed from Carlisle, Pennsylvania on 25 July. He hoped to reinforce Fort Ligonier first, because it "contained provisions for the relief of Fort Pitt." The light infantry arrived at Fort Ligonier on 28 July. By now, the Indians had learned of Bouquet's presence and left Fort Pitt, hoping to force his light infantry to fight their larger force. Bouquet departed Fort Ligonier, bound for Fort Pitt. On the morning of 5 August, near Bushy Run, a creek just east of Fort Pitt, the Indians attacked Bouquet's advance guard. In a short time, the provincial unit was surrounded. Bouquet signaled for a maneuver and his unit opened files, trying to make the Indians think they were about to retreat. The Indians moved in and were met by troops closing in from the flank. The Indians cut short their fight, but attacked the unit later that day when it returned to Bushy Run. Again, Bouquet's unit dispersed the Indians and continued on to Fort Pitt without further incident.

On 3 October 1764, Bouquet took a force (which included his light infantry) to the vicinity of the Muskingum River, near Lake Erie, to conduct several peace conferences with the Indians in that area. The Indians released many prisoners following the successful completion of these conferences on 18 November. Ten days later, Bouquet and his force arrived back at Fort Pitt and, in continuation of the peace process begun earlier, released the Indian prisoners held there. This was the final act in Pontiac's Rebellion, the "Indian component of the French and Indian War."

QUEEN'S RANGERS

On 11 December 1761, Captain Joseph Hopkins, a veteran of the fighting with Braddock in 1755, received a letter in London that authorized him to raise a company of regular rangers. His unit was to have 2 lieutenants, 1 ensign, and 100 rangers, 30 more than the "American Establishment" standard. He sailed soon after and arrived in New York in May 1762. Hopkins set about recruiting his unit, the Queen's Royal American Rangers. He had five months to raise his company. It was the custom in the English army during this period that when units were "raised for rank," as the Queen's Rangers and most of the other independent companies raised at this time were, the only expense to the government was for the weapons of the soldiers and for their subsistence. Recruits were required to be five-feet two-inches tall, be at least 18 years old, but no older than 40, and be in good physical condition. Hopkins' Rangers would be reviewed by a senior officer and accepted into the service before any officer's commission was dated.

Abraham Cuyler and James Bain were his two lieutenants and signed on almost at once. Hopkins recruited Ensign Marvin Perry soon after. Hopkins recruited in Maryland and Pennsylvania and, by the end of July, he had 80 rangers in his company. In accordance with a custom of the period, some of these were taken from local jails. The company first assembled in Philadelphia, then moved by ship to Nutten Island, New York, where it was inspected and accepted into service.

The company was to be used in Detroit. The main body, under Cuyler, set out on 3 August. Hopkins and a small detail, including Bain, one sergeant, and one corporal, remained behind to complete the roster of recruits; they still needed about 15 more rangers. In short order, Hopkins had not only made up his shortfall, but had recruited several more rangers in addition. When he saw that it would not be difficult to raise more, Hopkins wrote and asked for authority to recruit "three or four hundred" more rangers and that he be promoted to the rank to major. His superiors turned down the request. Disappointed, Hopkins set out to join the main body.

TREATMENT OF DESERTERS

On 18 October, Cuyler's detachment arrived in Detroit and Perry's just four days later. Hopkins came later in the month. There was little for the rangers to do in Detroit at this period. Eight of the rangers deserted. Six of these were returned by Indians for the reward. They were tried by court-martial and sentenced to death by hanging. They were pardoned, however, on the condition of their good future behavior. Rarely, were recruits hanged for their first desertion offense and only occasionally for their second! Soon the rangers received orders to leave Detroit and return to winter quarters at Fort Niagara. At this post, the rangers had to provide 26 men daily for fatigue detail and 14 more (including a sergeant and a corporal) to the guard detail. As a result of the heavy work, the rangers received additional clothing to replace what was worn out. Although each ranger was supposed to replace his clothing at his own expense, Hopkins paid for their clothes.

On 13 May 1763, the rangers set out for the return trip to Detroit. As they progressed slowly to their destination, the rangers were unaware that Indians had already made at least one attack on the fort at Detroit. On 29 May, the Queen's Rangers were attacked at dawn by a force of more than 200 Ottawa Indians. Nineteen rangers were killed, 2 wounded seriously, and 21 were taken prisoner. Three of the prisoners later escaped as they were being rowed past Detroit. The remaining rangers made it safely over land to Detroit.

During one attack on the fort, Hopkins and 20 rangers ambushed the Indians and chased them for half a mile. Throughout the summer more fights continued and ten more rangers were killed. Hopkins wrote for permission to recruit additional rangers, but was again turned down. In September, Hopkins' senior commander received letters ordering the Queen's Rangers to be disbanded. Their duty at Detroit had been successful, but a treaty was to be signed and the rangers were not needed any longer.

Those rangers who wanted to remain in the army would be transferred to infantry units, the 80th Regiment at Detroit or the 46th Regiment at Niagara. The officers were to be placed on half-pay unless the commander at Detroit required their services. He did not. All administrative matters concerned with disbanding the rangers were not completed until 4 December 1763.

In April of the following year, Hopkins returned to London to settle an accounting problem. Hopkins was threatened with being thrown out of the army after 14 officers accused him of cheating his own men. One of these 14 officers was Robert Rogers. While problems existed about the Queen's Rangers accounts, it was unlikely that Hopkins was thrown out of the army. While in London, he tried to sell his half-pay captaincy to raise money to settle with the Pay Master General. He could not have done this if he had been thrown out in disgrace. Eventually, the matter was settled and Hopkins left England in disgust.

In November of the same year, Hopkins accepted a commission in the French Army as a lieutenant colonel and was later promoted to colonel. In 1775, he requested permission to return to America to join in the war, but he was told he could do so only as a private citizen and not as a French officer. Hopkins died in Paris on 10 November 1776.

The American Revolutionary War had several ranger units on both sides. The experiences, training, and tactics of the early rangers formed the basis for these newer formations.

PART II

REVOLUTIONARY WAR

INTRODUCTION

The Revolutionary War produced three significant changes in special operations or elite forces: 1) the size of the unit, 2) the use of the long rifle, and 3) the guerrilla tactics used by some of the units. The second was a product of the times and had a significant effect on operations, while the third helped to shape the nature of special operations to the present time. The Revolutionary War period started about 1775 with attacks on British patrols.

For the most part, the units up to this point were called "Rangers" and operated in company size strength of 50 to 150 men per company. The trend to larger units occurred during the French and Indian War, specifically with Rogers and Bouquet. This was partly because overall commanders decided to use ranger units in standard formations rather than using them to conduct raids and gather intelligence about the area and the enemy. Over the years, special units have frequently complained that they had to fit themselves to the mission, instead of higher headquarters using them as they were intended. Commanders, on the other hand, use what they have at their disposal to accomplish their mission. Rogers normally used multiple companies when he needed more men for a particular operation, while Bouquet's unit, although not defined as a "ranger" unit by its operations but based on the training it received, was organized and fought with the battalion (or multiples, as needed) as the basic unit. The use of larger units was not the standard during the Revolutionary War, but it continued, in particular in some of Daniel Morgan's later organizations. This was also evident with the partisan bands that fought under Francis Marion and Thomas Sumter. Indeed, Sumter's force was so large that, by mid-July 1780, Cornwallis estimated the strength of this "militia army" at 1,500.

Larger units should not be perceived as a negative. It was easier for the generals of this period to coordinate operations in more than one area if they could rely on units larger than company size that were commanded by a capable leader who could perform irregular missions. These generals, especially George Washington as the commander-in-chief, also relied on a Continental Congress to pay for these units and to promote deserving soldiers. This latter task was not always easy, as seen by the appointment of Gates in the southern department when Washington wanted Greene.

The long rifle was introduced into America in about 1700 by immigrants from Switzerland. As one historian put it, "The hard necessity of life on the American frontier called for economy in powder and lead, so such a small-calibered weapon of great accuracy was needed." This rifle was at least five feet long. Its ball weighed about one-half an ounce. The ball from a smooth bore musket, the typical military weapon of the British Army, had an effective range of about 50 yards and a maximum range of about 125 yards, while the ball of a long rifle could hit and kill a man at 250 yards. Virginia rifle makers improved on the early Swiss designs so that by the 1770s, the rifle was superior to all others. And yet, despite its increased accuracy and range, the rifle did not become the standard military weapon for some time.

The riflemen of Morgan's Rangers developed a method that helped them reduce the time it took to reload. Typically, the lead ball used in a smooth bore musket is about the same diameter as the barrel. The rangers, however wrapped their smaller bullet in a greased patch of buckskin or linen, and pushed it down the barrel with a ramrod until it came to a stop on top of the powder charge. The patch increased the size of the bullet. When fired, the wrapped bullet cleaned the bore of any residue left from the previous shot as it traveled out of the barrel. This tightly packed ball also increased rotation from the rifling grooves, improving the speed and accuracy of the ball as it left the weapon. As the ball left the barrel, the patch dropped off.

Because of the tactics used by most armies of the time, the long rifle was not immediately accepted as a standard military weapon. These tactics were best exemplified by regular units of the British Army. The long rifles had two disadvantages when compared to the regular military musket of the day—they did not have a bayonet stud and they took almost twice as long to load than the musket. The slowness cut down on its rate of fire. A third disadvantage was that the small caliber ball or bullet had less stopping power.

The bayonet figured prominently in British tactics. These tactics required absolute discipline coupled with constant drilling, so that the maneuvering of large units in rigid formations on the battlefield was almost choreographic. This kind of maneuvering, even in modern armies, is not something that comes naturally or without a lot of practice. The musket was designed for "disciplined volley firing." And when the formations came closer to the enemy, the bayonet was used. A well-trained, well-disciplined army, like the British Army, was an awesome sight in operations of the day. The fledgling American Army could not hope to fight and win this kind of war. It did not have the luxury of time to achieve this level of training and discipline nor did it have enough experienced sergeants who could conduct the necessary drills. The Americans, therefore, had to rely on what was at hand to fight, the long rifle and irregular tactics.

The irregular tactics employed, especially in the South Carolina campaign of 1780-81, were far superior to those used by earlier ranger units. In fact, Marion and Sumter are predecessors of modern American tactics such as those employed by the Alamo Scouts on Luzon in 1945, by the OSS in France in 1944 and Burma in 1943 through 1945, as well as in the techniques of today's Army Special Forces and Navy SEALs. For the most part, South Carolina partisans fought on their own terms and then disappeared into their surroundings. The partisan military philosophy was "... to keep the British off balance. We aren't strong enough to beat them in open battle, so we'll make life miserable for them. If we can't drive them out with a single blow, we'll wear them down." They also had the support of the local population, at least that part not still loyal to the British king, and they coordinated their operations with their higher command rather than just operating independently. The partisans were critical to winning the war in South Carolina and elsewhere.

MARBLEHEAD MARINERS

John Glover was a prominent businessman in Marblehead, Massachusetts. He owned several sailing and fishing ships, but became a fisherman and sailor before finally enjoying the fruits of his labor. In early 1775, when the Marblehead militia regiment was reorganized into a minuteman unit, as a result of the recent "take-over" of local political strength by the Whigs, Glover became a lieutenant colonel. He was the third ranking officer in the regiment, but later commanded it. This unit was the core of the 14th Continental Regiment. The 14th Regiment, although an Army unit, is included in this special operations history not for any army mission it performed (though these were significant) but because at two vital junctions in the Revolution it served as a navy special boat unit, a predecessor of similar modern units.

Soon after its reorganization, the Marblehead regiment conducted frequent drills, at least four times a week. The majority of the men were sailors and fishermen. They had spent most of their lives fishing, contributing to the principal trade in the Marblehead-Salem-Beverly area. The frequent drills were necessary to acquaint the men with the military manual of arms and discipline. Each soldier in the regiment, by order, provided his own "Fire arm and bayonet in good order & equipt with thirty Rounds of Cartriadges & ball, a pouch & Snapsack ..."

Because ammunition was scarce and the British Army was attempting to gather up all that was available, all training was conducted on a "dry run" basis. To conserve ammunition, most of the regiment also boycotted local game shooting.

In late April, Jeremiah Lee died and Glover took his place as regimental commander. By 16 June, the unit was sworn into service as the 23rd Regiment, with a strength of 505 officers and men, divided into 10 companies. On 1 July, the Continental Congress recognized the regiment as the 21st, now part of the American Army. This regiment moved to Cambridge, Massachusetts as part of George Washington's command. In mid-December, the regiment returned to Marblehead and Glover began recruiting new members to take the place of those whose enlistments expired at the end of the year. On 1 January 1776, Glover formed his command anew, this time redesignated again as the 14th Continental.

Although an infantry regiment, the uniforms of the 14th came from the same sea traditions as its men. Enlisted soldiers wore "blue jackets, white shirts, breeches, and caps." The coat had leather buttons and the trousers were tarred, a seafaring custom to waterproof them. At some point red lapels and blue stockings were added to the uniform. Officers wore "white jackets, breeches," and were issued broadcloth to make shirts. Individual weapons were a mix from the period: old muskets, "ordinary Cambridge" guns that had been issued when the army was assembled in Cambridge, and new issue English muskets taken from captured British supply ships.

On several occasions before the American Army left New England for New York, Glover and his men guarded or manned ships at the direction of Washington. At Washington's request, Glover personally procured several vessels for the army to perform sea missions. On 20 July 1776 just before he took his regiment to New York, Glover read the Declaration of Independence to the mustered unit.

By the end of August the American Army was reeling from a defeat by the forces of General Robert Howe in the battle of Long Island. The 9,000 American troops on Long Island were established in a defensive perimeter in the vicinity of Brooklyn Heights. Instead of pulling his soldiers out of this perimeter,

Washington reinforced them on 28 August with three regiments. One of these was Glover's unit, which took its place in the line between Fort Putnam and Wallabout Bay. By the next morning the British were only 150 yards from the perimeter. Howe decided to conduct a siege. He knew the Americans had their backs to the East River and British ships controlled the water.

On the 29th a "drenching Summer storm arose," keeping the British ships away from the East River. Washington decided he would attempt to evacuate his army in the storm. At least ten flat-bottom boats, a sloop, and some other sailing vessels constituted Washington's amphibious "fleet." He passed word to his subordinate commanders that they would be relieved by reinforcing regiments during the night and that they were to have their units assembled and ready to move when notified. Washington called Glover and Colonel Israel Hutchinson, commander of the 27th Regiment, to his headquarters and told them his real plan. Their two regiments were going to ferry his entire army across the East River that night. He chose these units because of their seafaring backgrounds. By ten o'clock that night, the seafaring infantrymen were ready to go.

For the first two hours everything went well. The Marblehead Mariners operated in silence and without lights as they skillfully maneuvered their vessels between the Brooklyn and Manhattan shores. Around midnight the tide shifted to an ebb tide and a "contrary wind" came up. Sailing vessels could no longer be used and only rowed boats now moved back and forth. Later, when the wind shifted, the sailing vessels were used again. In just over nine hours, the sailors of the two infantry regiments moved Washington's entire army *and its equipment* to Manhattan, under the very noses of the British Army. Howe was stunned. One British officer wrote in his diary, "In the Morning, to our great Astonishment, [we] found they had Evacuated all their works ... without a Shot being fired at them ..."

Four months later Washington again tasked Glover's infantry regiment with an amphibious mission. This time the Marblehead Mariners were taking American soldiers *to* a battle. Earlier that month the British had chased Washington out of New Jersey. Then, unable to cross the Delaware, the British withdrew to winter quarters. Washington could see that the British defenses were unprepared for a surprise attack; he devised a plan for such an attack by four separate forces to converge on Trenton on Christmas night. Eventually, three of these forces were unable to perform their missions. Washington, leading the fourth force, was determined, no matter how desperate this gamble, to strike at Trenton. He hoped that Glover's sailor soldiers would pull him through.

Washington had arranged to collect several Durham boats for this operation. These boats "normally carried cargoes of iron, grain, and whisky." They were about 60 feet long, 8 feet wide, pointed at both ends, and drew between 24 and 30 inches when fully loaded. A regiment could fit on each boat. The Marblehead Mariners would have to row across to the east side and pole back to the west.

On Christmas night, as the operation began, a storm came howling along the river, dropping temperatures in the heavy wind. The water was already high and rough, with large chunks of ice in the fast-moving current adding to the dangers. As the night wore on, Glover's men and their boats became covered with ice, making each trip over and back more difficult. One of them said later, "The floating ice in the river made the labor almost incredible." Just before midnight it got worse - snow began to fall. Now the Marblehead Mariners could barely see through the white, blinding storm. But still they pulled their loads, straining arm and back muscles to move the boats and eyes to see where they were going. Finally, in the last loads, artillery pieces and Washington himself crossed the ice-laden river. Private John R. Russell was one of those who rowed the boat that carried the Continental commander-in-chief. At three in the morning, several hours behind schedule, all the troops were across and ready to proceed to Trenton.

The dawn strike caught the British and Hessian soldiers at Trenton asleep. Even after the hard night of rowing, Glover's regiment played key parts in the battle. Afterwards, they took everyone, plus almost a thousand prisoners, back across the river to the Pennsylvania side. On the very edge of exhaustion, the Marblehead Mariners completed their mission, the last they would perform. One captain in the regiment described the preceding 36 hours as "two Nights and one day in as violent a storm as I ever felt." On New Year's Day, the 14th Continental Infantry Regiment, the Marblehead Mariners, was disbanded; the enlistment of most of its soldiers was over. In just over four months this regiment had established a special mission legacy that is carried on by the special boat units of today's Navy.

MORGAN'S RANGERS

On 14 June 1775, more than a year before the North American colonies formally broke with England by issuing the Declaration of Independence, the Continental Congress issued a notice to form ten companies of riflemen, two from Virginia, two from Maryland, and six from Pennsylvania. Captain Daniel Morgan, a veteran of the French and Indian War, was specifically named by the Frederick County (Virginia) Committee to command the company to be raised locally. Morgan had fought in the company of Virginia Rangers commanded by Captain John Ashby. Within ten days, Morgan had gathered a force of 96 local marksmen, most of them already seasoned Indian fighters and hunters from their youth.

What distinguished Morgan's first company of rangers from most of the other colonial soldiers, and practically all of the regular British and European regulars of the day, was its use of the heavier long rifle. As with many ranger units of the past, Morgan's Rangers did not necessarily wear a uniform, but dressed in similar style clothes, such as fringed buckskin shirts, trousers, and leggings. A distinctive item that most of them carried was a large piece of stout cloth, dyed to "the shade of a dry or fading leaf." This was a multi-purpose cloth, often used as a blanket or for bedding. It was usually rolled and worn over one shoulder and tied down with a belt when not needed. To make it readily accessible for use, it was wrapped around and tucked under the belt. Their footgear was moccasin shoes, and most wore small hats with deer fur attached. The officers wore a red sash over their shoulders and round the waist. In addition to their rifles, the rangers carried tomahawks, scalping knives, canteens, bullet pouches, and powder horns.

In July 1775, Morgan's company arrived in the Cambridge area. In September, it became part of an expedition commanded by Colonel Benedict Arnold "to invade Canada by way of Maine," with Quebec as the first objective. Washington had decided to make Canada the 14th colony. Arnold appointed Morgan as the commander of three companies of rangers. The other two companies were from Pennsylvania. Morgan's mission on the march north was to be the column's forward reconnaissance force and flanking guard, especially to pick out portage points and to remove any obstacles blocking the roadway. "Roadway" is an overstatement, as the way north was by path that was partly cut by Morgan's Rangers as they moved in front of Arnold's column. By early November, the column had reached the banks of the St. Lawrence River, with just over 600 of the 1100 men that had set out six weeks before. The losses were from dysentery and other illnesses, exposure, drowning, and starvation. A unit under Lieutenant Colonel Roger Enos even turned back when they were more than halfway to the river.

During the battle of Quebec, the rangers conducted many scouting missions to learn the dispositions of the English forces. In the final fighting, Arnold was wounded. The remaining officers in his command, most senior to Morgan, insisted that Morgan take command. In the end, however, the colonials suffered heavy losses. Most of Morgan's Rangers, including Morgan himself, were taken prisoner. At the end of July of the following year, Morgan and the other prisoners were exchanged for British prisoners. The colonial soldiers, including only 25 of Morgan's original 96 rangers, were turned over to American authorities on 24 September 1776 at Elizabethtown, New Jersey.

By the end of the year, when his parole was completed, Morgan was promoted to the rank of colonel and placed in charge of a Virginia regiment. Washington recommended the promotion, based primarily on Morgan's performance during the Quebec campaign and specifically during the final fighting. Morgan sought out officers, including Christian Febiger, William Heth, Peter Bruin, Virginia marksmen, and enlisted soldiers from his ranger company to act as cadre for his new unit. Morgan then moved his unit, which had only 180 men, to join Washington at Morristown, New Jersey to oppose the expected British offensive. Once again, the other American troops called this new unit "Morgan's Rangers."

At the end of June, Morgan was put in command of a corps of light infantry, including his rangers. The corps had 500 especially chosen sharpshooters "outfitted in hunting shirts and leggins." Washington considered Morgan's unit independent and excused it from all routine duties in the Continental camp. Morgan's deputy was Colonel Richard Butler of Pennsylvania. In the corps' first encounter, near New Brunswick, it joined forces with two other units and pushed British forces, under General William Howe, back across the river.

In August, Morgan's corps was temporarily transferred to upstate New York, in the hope it could counter the intimidation of American troops in the area by Indians fighting in General John Burgoyne's army. Washington urged publicity of the arrival of Morgan's corps of "frontier riflemen [who] were skilled in Indian fighting methods." Once in the area, Morgan's Rangers were bolstered by the addition of 300 selected marksmen, armed with muskets and bayonets, under Major Henry Dearborn.

Morgan undertook aggressive reconnaissance of the progress of Burgoyne's movements, paying particular attention to the Indians and other scouts. This "attention" eventually caused Burgoyne to recall all of his scouts. On 19 September when Burgoyne began to make his move, Morgan's corps moved to a heavily wooded area to engage the approaching British. This move was to prevent Burgoyne from using artillery for support and to preclude him from executing any close order maneuver in the woods. A fierce fight broke out in the vicinity of Freeman's Farm. The tide of battle moved back and forth with each wave of attack and counterattack. Morgan's Rangers hid in trees and other high places and, from the standoff distance offered by their long rifles, killed as many of the enemy's officers as they could find. This tactic caused confusion in the British ranks and contributed to the day's success.

Between 7 and 17 October, Morgan's Rangers saw action on the left of the American line, mostly fighting in conjunction with Benedict Arnold's division. In one particular action of note during this fight (disputed by some historians), one of Morgan's Rangers, Timothy Murphy, an excellent marksman, killed General Simon Fraser as he attempted to rally British forces under attack. Finally, on the 17th, Burgoyne surrendered in the village of Saratoga. Soon after, France entered the war on the side of the Americans.

Washington immediately recalled Morgan to Pennsylvania because he was having problems with Howe's army. Here, Morgan met and befriended a French officer, the Marquis de Lafayette. Lafayette, with the rank of Major General, occasionally went on patrol with Morgan's Rangers. He was impressed with the rangers' ability to run for long distances "never halting for rest or nourishment." During one fight, in early December, Morgan's Rangers fought the Queen's Rangers, now commanded by British Major John Simcoe. Soon after, Washington took his army into winter quarters at Valley Forge.

The next spring a new American Army emerged, trained during the bitter winter by the Prussian task master, Baron Friedrich von Steuben. During the campaign leading to the victory at Monmouth, Washington had ordered Morgan to avoid engaging the British. However, the rangers still performed scouting missions, guarded key road crossings, and were used as sharpshooters to harass British formations. In the spring of 1779, when Morgan returned from a winter furlough, he discovered that a brigade was to be formed, comprised of units he formerly commanded. The brigade was to be a light infantry unit. Two officers were being considered for command, Morgan and Anthony Wayne of Pennsylvania. When Wayne was promoted to brigadier general and given the command, Morgan resigned from the army.

Wayne's brigade was now too large to be an effective "ranger unit" and fought in a more conventional manner. It was not, however, Wayne's last encounter with rangers.

Morgan returned to active duty in the summer of 1780 when he was promised he would be promoted to brigadier general. He served under General Nathanael Greene in the "Southern Army." He was commissioned to form a light corps and some of his former rangers, including Major Peter Bruin, returned to serve under him again. With this unit Morgan contributed a victory over the Legion of Lieutenant Colonel Banastre Tarleton at the Battle of Cowpens, which some say was the most significant military battle fought in North America. During this battle, Morgan instructed his men to find the British officers and kill them ("shoot for the epaulettes, boys"). Among the units that supported Morgan at Cowpens was a South Carolina partisan militia unit under Andrew Pickens. Morgan also employed a double envelopment maneuver that was as stunningly executed as it was unexpected by Tarleton. Several weeks later Morgan retired for medical reasons.

KNOWLTON'S & WHITCOMB'S RANGERS

Following the disastrous American campaign on Long Island in August 1776, army leaders decided to form a light infantry unit hoping that this would make a difference in future battles in the New York area. This happened at about the same time that Robert Rogers was recruiting men to fill his new unit, the Queen's Rangers. An officer from a Connecticut unit, Lieutenant Colonel Thomas Knowlton, who had distinguished himself on Long Island, was chosen to recruit and lead the new American ranger unit.

Knowlton visited various regiments from Massachusetts and Connecticut and recruited enough volunteers to form three companies. He chose experienced frontier fighters, especially good marksmen. Once organized, Knowlton reported his unit ready for missions. As with Morgan's company, these rangers were armed with the long rifle. As described before, the long rifle had no bayonet stud and was no good for hand-to-hand fighting. This proved deadly for Knowlton's Rangers in their first action.

In mid-September, Knowlton's companies conducted an enveloping maneuver of British Army positions at Harlem Heights in New York. Washington instructed Knowlton to conduct a night attack on the enemy's rear area. With the element of surprise on their side, the rangers performed well for a while. But they attacked too soon and, unfortunately, directly into the

British flank. The rangers were unable to hold off the much larger British force. They were eventually surrounded and suffered many fatalities. Knowlton was among the dead. Two months later, most of those rangers who had survived the battle of Harlem Heights were captured by a larger British force near Fort Washington.

At about the same time as the Battle of Harlem Heights, Major Benjamin Whitcomb raised two companies of rangers from volunteers among units then located in the vicinity of Lake Champlain. These rangers supported the American Army in the northern colonies, especially Vermont and New Hampshire, for more than four years.

PARTISANS

In 1779, the British attempted to split the war by concentrating the fighting in South Carolina. If successful there, they would then move northward. The initial plan was to capture the city of Charleston, which they had failed to do in 1776, due to mismanagement of their forces. A ranger regiment, the 3rd South Carolina (Ranger), raised the previous year by Colonel William Thompson, helped to defend Charleston. The regiment also fought in several other early engagements. It was mostly a dismounted unit; only about one-third of its force had horses. By 1780, the regiment was part of the Charleston garrison.

Three men, unlike in temperament but similar in their choice of tactics, came to the forefront during the campaign of 1779. They added a different dimension to the history of American special operations. This dimension was partisan (or guerrilla) warfare. To wage a successful guerrilla war, irregular military forces require the support of the civilian population, which can provide a base of operations and help them disappear from their enemies by blending into the surroundings. The three men, who sometimes supported each other, but mostly operated independently, were Andrew Pickens, Thomas Sumter (the "Carolina Gamecock"), and Francis Marion (the "Swamp Fox").

The British commander, Major General Henry Clinton, had more than 10,000 soldiers and a fleet of 5,000 sailors at his disposal. The Americans, commanded by Major General Benjamin Lincoln, had just over 5,000 troops, half of them regulars and the rest South Carolina militia. Lincoln made the mistake of trying to hold Charleston. The British blockaded the town with its fleet and, after a successful landing, closed all but the smallest escape route by coming in on "the Neck between the Ashby and Cooper rivers." Lincoln could not decide whether he should leave by Cooper River to join Brigadier General Isaac Huger's force at Monck's Corner. When Lincoln hesitated, Banastre Tarleton's Legion attacked Monck's Corner and closed off the escape route. On 12 May 1780, Lincoln surrendered Charleston.

Within a week, Francis Marion, a prominent lawyer, indigo farmer, and former commander of the Second Regiment of South Carolina Riflemen, who had fought in the first battle of Charleston, left the city with several others who had served with him, including his friend Peter Horry. They were attempting to link up with part of the American Army, commanded by Major General Jean de Kalb, that was heading south.

At the end of May, Tarleton's Legion defeated an infantry-cavalry force at The Waxhaws, near the North Carolina border. When their beaten enemy quit and asked for quarter, the Legion cut them down where they stood. Thus was born "Tarleton's quarter" and the beginning of his reputation as a butcher. The "soft underbelly" of the South was now open to the British, pointing the way North.

The British had come back to Charleston because those loyal to the king had promised that, if victorious, all of South Carolina would be their plum. The army soon established garrisons in Georgetown, Beaufort, Charleston, Camden, Rocky Mount, and a fort at Ninety-Six. In June, General Clinton returned to New York, taking about one-third of his force with him and transferring command to Major General Charles Cornwallis. As a parting friendly gesture, Clinton announced that all paroles were null and void, and all those under parole were to resume their status as loyal British subjects. Despite the apparent return of the rule of law, Cornwallis was unable or unwilling to prevent his soldiers from indiscriminate looting. Local Tories then engaged in a series of "property seizures, house burnings, and personal harassment." The rebels retaliated in widely scattered places. Angered by the retaliatory acts, Cornwallis sent his troops on reprisal missions.

When Tarleton, attempting to enforce Clinton's order, burned the house of Thomas Sumter, who had served with Marion in the Second Regiment, it drove Sumter to gather men around him who had similar grievances. They decided to fight the British rather than accept Clinton's offer to serve against the American rebels. In short order, Sumter launched two hit-and-run raids against British outposts in Rocky Mount and Hanging Rock, and then continued to hit outposts at river crossing sites, burning any ferries he found. Sumter's unit had the advantage of being mounted and could move faster than the usually larger yet ground-bound British forces that chased them. Their attacks, which "relied on surprise and quick action," were usually mounted from nearby forested areas. Their principal weapons were the long rifle and the smooth bore musket. Those partisans under both Marion and Sumter who carried muskets preferred loads with multiple pellets. This gave them the opportunity to hit several of the enemy using only a single discharge.

Another former militia colonel, Andrew Pickens, also became active at this time. Earlier in the campaign, in December 1779, Pickens had hanged five Tories as traitors. He later accepted Clinton's parole and eventually took the required oath of allegiance. But his change of heart did not last long. Pickens then formed his own guerrilla unit. He considered the destruction of property by British military units and Tories to be a violation of the protection he was promised before he had taken the oath.

THE SWAMP FOX

Elsewhere, in Hillsboro, North Carolina, Francis Marion and his small band of about 20, met with de Kalb, who was waiting the arrival of the recently appointed commander of the American southern department, Major General Horatio Gates. Marion's band consisted of men and boys, "some white, some black, and all mounted but most of them miserably equipped." Gates immediately ordered the army out on campaign. Once on

Francis "Swamp Fox" Marion

the move, he dispatched units to link up with Sumter and to move behind Camden. Marion and his men were sent toward the Santee River to destroy boats and ferries to keep Cornwallis from "escaping" from the area.

In carrying out his orders, Marion sent men to contact various militia units, extending Gates' authority to include them in his (Marion's) mission. Local supporters contacted Marion and told him of Gates' defeat at Camden. They said that on the night before the battle overdue supplies reached Gates' camp. Gates did not allow time for the food to be completely cooked because some of his advance elements made contact with Cornwallis. The resulting dysentery among the Americans further reduced the men facing the overwhelming force of British regulars and resulted in a hasty retreat. General de Kalb was killed. In a related action two days later at Fishing Creek, Tarleton caught Sumter's unit in camp. Sumter barely escaped.

Marion moved his unit to Nelson's Ferry on the Santee and jumped a British unit escorting 150 prisoners, mostly Maryland Continentals. They freed the prisoners. This action made Marion instantly famous throughout the colony, even throughout the South. He quickly disappeared into the coastal lowland areas, recruiting new men and planning his next raids. Marion was very familiar with the South Carolina swamps. During the French and Indian War, he was in a militia unit that fought extensively in the marshes and swamps near Charleston. He struck outpost sites, communications posts, and foraging parties, winning fights at Black Mingo and Tearcoat Swamp, and then faded back into the swamps. One trick Marion occasionally used was to send a small, mounted force toward the British. When fired upon, the force would turn and run in apparent retreat. If the British pursued the force, they were ambushed.

Marion eventually chose a spot on Snow Island as his base of operations. This was a fairly inaccessible area located on the Pee Dee River. Marion preferred to strike at night and then quickly move back to the swamps. Tarleton quit chasing him to again pursue Sumter, saying, "[T]he devil himself could not catch him."

THOMAS SUMTER

Sumter, despite the defeat by Tarleton, continued to attract followers. He beat off a cavalry attack at his camp on Broad River. Then he moved west to threaten the fort at Ninety-Six. When he heard that Tarleton was on the way, Sumter ambushed him. Both sides withdrew and each claimed a victory. Sumter, however, was wounded in the right shoulder and was put out of action for almost three months.

Although Marion and Sumter were successful in their guerrilla activities, both knew that their efforts alone were not enough to win in South Carolina. Cornwallis knew this also. He sent Major Patrick Ferguson on a west- and northward sweep to support his own move as he headed north for North Carolina. But Ferguson was aggressively pursued by the "over-mountain men" and began to retreat toward the coast. When he came to King's Mountain, he decided to make a stand. His opponents had rifles and Ferguson did not. His bayonet charges were useless in the wooded area. The battle was violent and, following Ferguson's death, many of his men received "Tarleton's quarter" after the fighting had stopped.

On 2 December 1780, Nathanael Greene replaced Gates. As Greene gathered his commanders, he decided to split his units, sending them in several different directions. He thought it would be easier for smaller forces to get provisions locally. He intended to make things as complicated as possible for Cornwallis. He dispatched Lieutenant Colonel Henry "Light Horse Harry" Lee to cooperate with Marion on the coast. Daniel Morgan, recently recalled to active duty and promoted, was sent toward Ninety-Six.

Tarleton was also on the move and, on 17 January he and Morgan's forces confronted each other "at a place where a Loyalist named Hiram Saunders had been accustomed to rounding up his cattle" near the Broad River. The place was called the Cowpens. Morgan believed that Tarleton was overrated and he had a plan to take advantage of this. He put his force with the Broad River at its back, effectively cutting off any retreat. He placed his militia under Andrew Pickens 150 yards out in front of his main line. In front of them was a select group of Southern riflemen with instructions to fire, aiming for officers, until pressed and then to retreat into the line held by Pickens. This line was to fire three volleys and retreat by the left flank to an area behind the main line and hidden from view by the terrain. Their horses were tethered in this area. Morgan had a mounted infantry force in reserve to be used to cover his flanks.

In the battle, the operation went according to Morgan's plan. Pickens' line got off two volleys and pulled back. As the British sensed a rout, they moved quickly forward, losing their organization. Morgan ordered one last volley by Pickens' men as they came even with his main line. They turned and fired the volley. Then Morgan ordered his main line forward in a bayonet charge to pin the British force in place. The American "cavalry" then swept into the British flanks and rear. Again, "Tarleton's quarter" was given to the British. Ninety percent of Tarleton's force was killed or captured while Morgan lost 12 killed and 60 wounded. At least one historian believes that Morgan's tactics at Cowpens are the model for modern day principles of tactical defense in depth. Morgan promoted Pickens to Brigadier General that same day.

For Marion and Sumter, the remainder of the war in South Carolina consisted of many independent actions, such as raids on supply and communications lines, and on isolated outposts. Their mission was to disrupt the British rear areas while Greene kept Cornwallis from going after the partisan units by busily pursuing him. The activities of each were coordinated to cause maximum disruption of British plans and operations. In the final battle in South Carolina, Marion used a ruse to convince the British commander of a besieged Charleston to surrender the city. Marion made the British think that his unit had been reinforced by two corps, led by Lafayette and Anthony Wayne. Eventually, Marion and Sumter were also promoted to brigadier general and their units, and that of Pickens, joined with portions of the main American army.

It would be a long time before partisan units were formed again. In fact, the use of ranger units between the end of the Revolutionary War and the Civil War was very spotty and they were usually employed to perform a specific mission.

PART III

POST REVOLUTIONARY PERIOD

INTRODUCTION

The early years of the new United States were tumultuous, as the states and citizens adjusted to a central, Federal government. The continuing suspicion of a standing army guided efforts to keep the army small, perhaps even smaller than necessary, and usually "out there," on the frontier. The feeling at the time was that an army could be called up from the citizenry if and when it was needed.

It was needed soon. The urge to expand, to find "elbow room" as Daniel Boone once said, caused problems with the Indians because it was their land that was the target of this expansion. This was not a new problem. It had existed from the earliest colonial venture by the British and had not gone away. It erupted again and continued to be the cause of wars for the first century of existence under the Constitution. As the western boundary of the United States expanded, whether by war, purchase, or treaty, the army built forts and other outposts on that boundary. At various times, until the 1830s, the army or local governors raised ranger units and called upon them to patrol the area around and between these forts. When war broke out, rangers again conducted scouting and reconnaissance missions for the army. The rangers also performed another of their traditional missions, the raid, with great effect.

The most notable change to ranger organizations during this period was that rangers were "brought in" to the army more than in the past. With the exception of the Texas Rangers, ranger units were now part of the army, subject to all the rules and discipline of the service as well as to the "bounty" of the army - that is, government issue uniforms, equipment, and weapons or payment to purchase them. The latter was a holdover from British Army custom but did not last long in the U.S. Army. This change, in bringing the rangers into the army, did not occur quickly and was not consistently applied, especially concerning the Texas Rangers during the Mexican War. Training in ranger tactics generally meant light infantry training, the same as during the French and Indian War and the Revolutionary War. There was an obvious need for light infantry tactics (even if employed by mounted troops) because the army usually faced a mobile enemy, the Indians, who struck quickly and quietly. Size of ranger units during this period varied as it had in the past, with the typical basic unit established as the company. However, despite this organizational concept, rangers still acted in smaller groups to be more effective.

Several prominent military commanders of this period used rangers to great advantage. During the War of 1812, Andrew Jackson used rangers to conduct scouting and raiding missions. During the Battle of New Orleans they conducted night harassment operations against outposts and sentinels. Several years later, when he fought against the Creek Indians, Jackson again used rangers to scout and raid. During the Mexican War, other military leaders, including Zachary Taylor and Philip Kearney, used rangers. The Texas Rangers were used to scout, provide escort for supplies, raid, and harass. The Mexican War involved many young army officers who would become the leaders of both the Federal and Confederate armies during the Civil War. Many of them learned the concept of ranger operations during the Mexican War and used them later against each other.

The Texas Rangers have, and deserve, a history of their own. They fit into this narrative because of the operations they conducted during their first 30 years and, later, when the army used rangers from Texas and Arizona as scouts during the Indian Wars in the southwest. Between 1901 and 1909, the Texas Rangers and the Arizona Rangers were among the pre-eminent law enforcement organizations in the country. But the reputation and practices of the Texas Rangers evolved from their activities as a military force. They employed the concept of "an eye for an eye" brutally at times. An example of their exploits from their military period occurred during the occupation of Mexico City. The U.S. Army had problems with local hoodlums who killed, on average, one soldier every day. When a Texas Ranger was killed, a force from Hays' Regiment entered the roughest section of Mexico City and retaliated for the one death by killing 80 hoodlums. The killing of soldiers quickly ceased.

However, the Texas Rangers' most significant contribution to special operations was not their ferocity or brutality, but their adaptability. Up to this point rangers were most effective in forests and wooded areas. Texas was mostly "vast open plains" where the Comanche Indians were about the best "light fighters" in North America. The rangers came up with new tactics, based on the enemy and terrain. They improvised equipment, making it better suited to the war they were fighting. The Texas Rangers also had a significant impact on weaponry. It was a ranger captain who first saw and employed the five-shooter revolving pistol sold by the Patent Arms Manufacturing Company of Paterson, New Jersey. Another ranger captain recommended to the revolver's inventor, Samuel Colt, that it could be more effective if it fired six shots. Thus, one legend helped create another.

During this early frontier period, ranger units operated much as they had in the past. Some changes in organization, weapons, and tactics, were implemented that would carry over to future special operations units.

WOOD-RANGERS

The Treaty of Paris in September 1783 ended the Revolutionary War, but the British maintained a presence in America. The British still manned garrisons in the old Northwest Territory and traders still worked with local Indian tribes. The period of "peace" after the treaty included more war with some of those Indian tribes. The United States made several attempts to dictate peace but the Indians were unwilling to agree, realizing that to agree to peace meant leaving their land. Two tribes in particular, the Shawnee and the Miami, continued to conduct hit-and-run raids in Ohio and westward.

In 1787, Congress enacted the Northwest Ordinance. This legislation federalized the Northwest Territory, an area now encompassed by Ohio, Michigan, Indiana, Illinois, Wisconsin, and upper Minnesota. Congress thus authorized armed units of militia and, later, the regular U.S. Army to police these lands, keeping or bringing order among the American settlers and the Indians. Several military expeditions were sent in to settle the continuing violence. But the leaders of the Shawnees (Blue Jacket) and Miamis (Michikinkwa or Little Turtle, as the Americans called him) led better trained and better disciplined forces. The Indians also had a better scouting system and they chose where and when they would fight. President Washington appointed Major General Anthony Wayne to command a 1,000-man force to fight the Indians in the Northwest Territory. He took this action because of two major defeats at the hands of Blue Jacket and Michikinkwa, in October 1790 and November 1791. The Indians defeated forces commanded by Josiah Harmar and Arthur St. Clair.

Wayne began recruiting his army in April 1792 and established a camp on a site about 20 miles from Pittsburgh. Wayne was familiar with the ranger and light infantry training programs established by Robert Rogers and Henri Bouquet during the French and Indian War and believed that their techniques were sound. He used them to train and discipline his own army. He also collected as much intelligence as he could about the military tactics of Blue Jacket and Michikinkwa. Wayne concluded that the type of war the Indians were least suited to fight was a war of attrition. This, he decided, was the kind of war he would fight.

In addition to the ranger and light infantry training he established for his army, Wayne also selected between 20 and 30 of his best men to act as "wood-rangers" for the Army. They would be his "eyes and ears," keeping him informed of Indian movements. These wood-rangers operated in teams of two or three. The ranger commander was Captain William Wells, Wayne's "Captain of Spies."

Wayne was satisfied with the condition of training of his army by the spring of 1793 and set out on his expedition. At about the same time, a peace commission was meeting with the Indians in an attempt to settle the war. The government withdrew its previous insistence that these Indians were a conquered people and offered to relinquish any claims to lands north of the Ohio River except in certain areas. Payment was offered for the areas excepted. Wayne was aware, before the peace commissioners were, that the talks were in vain. An Iroquois Indian, an agent of his wood-rangers, passed information that the Shawnee and Miami would eschew the recognition and money of the United States, asking "because you have at last acknowledged our independence, we should for such a favor surrender to you our country?" Wayne decided to attack immediately, even though he knew that at the time (September 1793) the Indians were at their greatest strength, since the hunting season was recently over.

He found that his supply lines had been sabotaged and was unable to attack. One rumor was that this was deliberately done by Wayne's second in command, Brigadier General James Wilkinson. By the following May, Wayne's supply line problems persisted. Blue Jacket and Michikinkwa decided to repeat their previously successful tactics by attacking Wayne's supply trains, drawing the soldiers after them, and then ambushing the soldiers when they left their forts.

The first attack, at Fort Recovery, was foiled when a Chickasaw scout in the employ of the wood-rangers learned of it and alerted the soldiers. Artillery dispersed the Shawnees, led by Blue Jacket and Tecumseh, killing between 20 and 30 of them.

As Wayne extended his westward movement he built a new fort, Fort Defiance, in an area the Indians had recently left. The Indians held a counsel of their leaders and decided to attack Wayne's army in an area opposite the rapids of the Maumee River, an area filled with deep ravines and trees that had recently been blown down by a tornado. The Indians called the place Fallen Timbers. Once again, the wood-rangers learned of the plans and warned Wayne. He moved his army to a spot a few miles from Fallen Timbers and waited. He waited for three days, until 20 August.

Wayne based his waiting tactic on what he had been told by his wood-rangers. They reported that the Indians usually did not eat before a major fight, believing that this added to their ferocity and aided their reflexes. Wayne knew that the Indians had expected to fight him the first day and had, therefore, fasted the previous day. By the 20th, some of the Indians had left camp to find food and those who remained were weakened because of their fasting.

The first Indian assault, against an advance line of mounted militia, successfully drove the soldiers back and panicked the front line of infantry. Wayne took control of the situation and immediately ordered an assault on the Indians. Wilkinson did not obey the command, saying later he had not heard the order to attack. Two other regiments, commanded by Colonel John Hamtramck, responded at once, closing with bayonets and scattering the Indians. Three days later, on the same ground as the abandoned village of Kekionga, Wayne established and built Fort Wayne. Within five months, Blue Jacket and Michikinkwa agreed to discuss a peace settlement.

RUSSELL & COFFEE'S RANGERS

In August 1795, peace came to the Northwest Territory when the Shawnee and Miami Indian tribes finally signed the Treaty of Greenville. The Indians signed over lands northwest of the

Ohio River and the British agreed to leave American territory (although this did not require that they depart Canada). All along the western frontier of the United States, small groups of rangers continued to patrol. Their mission was as it had been when rangers were first organized - to move between forts and outposts, reporting on Indian movements and intentions. Beginning in about 1805, the army brutally put down several Indian uprisings. This kept the frontier in a state of turmoil.

In January 1812, as war with England seemed imminent, Congress authorized the president to raise ranger companies. The western frontier of the United States, generally along the Mississippi River, was "almost completely undefended." The British, taking a lesson from the French in the previous century, encouraged the Indian tribes in the west to attack settlements there. Five companies of rangers were recruited in the Ohio, Indiana, Illinois, and Kentucky territories and, soon after, two additional companies were raised. In 1813, an additional ten companies of rangers were authorized and raised. These ten included four raised in Indiana, three in Illinois, and three in Missouri. They were authorized in place of a regiment of infantry that had been planned. Rangers provided their own horses, weapons, equipment, and rations. Pay for mounted rangers was one dollar a day, three times the normal pay for soldiers.

These ranger companies were identified, over the years that they were active, in a wide variety of ways. Although they were members of the Regular Army, they were usually singled out and referred to as Rangers, United States Rangers, the Regiment of Rangers, and even the Corps of Rangers. By the following year, the 17 ranger companies had been consolidated into 10, with a total force of just under 1,100 men.

The Federal government expected the various territories and states along the frontier, especially those on the Mississippi River, to build a series of block houses and forts at strategic points. The mission of the rangers was to patrol the areas around and between these strong points. The ranger companies operated independently rather than as a larger force. As a consequence, lieutenants and captains commanded these companies. A total of 10 captains and 41 lieutenants were on the Army's rolls as ranger officers. The "senior" ranger officer was Captain

Andre Piere, although Colonel William Russell was theoretically the overall commander of these independent ranger companies.

Russell did not believe that it was possible for the companies to guard the entire frontier. He devised a plan to take advantage of the widespread locations of the ranger companies and to convince the Indians along the frontier that a much larger force than actually existed guarded the area. Russell rotated the companies in and out of areas always making certain that the rangers watched the critical lines of communications as much as possible. On more than one occasion rangers conducted long range expeditions into what was considered hostile Indian territory to collect intelligence for the army.

The story of rangers during this period is told in mostly small, not very well known battles. These battles were almost all part of the War of 1812. The battles, with one major exception, took place in the old Northwest Territory or Canada. The battles were at: Pimartam's Town, Illinois (on Lake Peoria) in October 1812; at the Mississippi Rapids near Campbell's Island, Illinois in July 1814; at Malcolm's Mill in Canada during November 1814; and, several months after the "final" battle at New Orleans, at Fort Howard, Wisconsin in May 1815.

The most significant contribution the rangers made during the war was with Major General Andrew Jackson in the south. Jackson and his rangers were fighting against two enemies, the British and the Creek Indians. According to Army records these were separate campaigns in two different wars. The rangers who supported Jackson were mostly from Tennessee and were commanded by Colonel John Coffee.

In his fight against the Creeks, Jackson derived his authority from the Tennessee legislature, which had authorized him $300,000 to raise an army and avenge the attack at Fort Mims by the Upper Creek Indians (also called the Red Sticks). Other Creeks fought with Jackson and were called the Lower Creeks or White Sticks. Coffee recruited a force of mounted Tennessee woodsmen and Choctaw Indians to be scouts and guides for Jackson's army.

Despite early victories at Tallashatchee and Talladega, Jackson's army slowed down because of the departure of soldiers on short-term enlistment and a high desertion rate. Finally, however, in March 1814, at Horseshoe Bend on the Tallapoosa River, Jackson's army met and nearly obliterated a force of 900 Creeks under Red Eagle.

Later, from December 1814 to January 1815 at New Orleans, Jackson continued to rely on Coffee's mounted rangers to provide intelligence on British movement as well as to conduct raids. The rangers' equipment, included long knives, tomahawks, long rifles, and was similar to equipment used in earlier periods, such as in Morgan's first company. A favorite tactic of these rangers was to "pick off sentinels" and then slip away quietly.

In 1815, the U.S. Army disbanded all regular ranger companies. Several states, including Pennsylvania, Michigan, Ohio, Illinois, Missouri, and Louisiana, raised state volunteer and militia companies of rangers to supplement troops of the Regular Army. These rangers continued to conduct patrols, particularly on the northern frontier of the United States, and watched the British and Indians in the area, especially since they each carried on an active fur trade with the other.

FLORIDA RANGERS

Just before the end of the War of 1812, the British built a fort in the Spanish colony of Florida on the Apalachicola River near Prospect Bluff. After the war, the British left and Seminole Indians and a group of fugitive slaves took over the fort. The states of Georgia and Alabama perceived the fort as a threat to open navigation of the Apalachicola, Chattahoochee, and Flint rivers, and asked the United States for help in policing the area.

In July 1816, Andrew Jackson dispatched a force of about 270 regulars and Coweta Creek Indians, commanded by Colonel Duncan L. Clinch, to attack the fort at Prospect Bluff. Clinch's force, including four boats, surrounded the fort and blew it up, killing more than 300 of those inside, including the families of the Indians and escaped slaves. Clinch gave most of the captured weapons and ammunition to the Creeks, a move that inflamed the Seminoles. Frequent incidents along the border followed, culminating in a battle near Fort Scott, in November 1817.

FIRST SEMINOLE WAR

A local Seminole leader warned the army command at Fowl Town not to enter his village. The commander attacked and burned the village, killing five Indians. Nine days later, the Seminoles retaliated by ambushing a group of soldiers and their families. The First Seminole War had begun.

In March 1818, Jackson sent a force of 2,000 regulars, volunteer militia, and White Stick Creeks, under Major Thomas Woodward, back to the former British fort at Prospect Bluff. The American force rebuilt the fort and named it Fort Gadsden. Jackson used the fort as his base of operations to conduct attacks against the Seminoles. On one particular pursuit, Jackson's men chased a band of Seminoles out of villages near Mikasuki. The Indians fled to nearby Saint Marks, a fort and town owned by the Spanish. When the Seminoles learned that Jackson was still after them, they fled Saint Marks. In a violation (and in apparent disregard) of Spanish sovereignty, Jackson invaded Saint Marks on 7 April.

Two days later, Jackson left Saint Marks for Suwanee Town, to the east. Along this march, Jackson attacked a Seminole village on 12 April and took 100 prisoners, including a 14-year-old named Osceola. Jackson pressed on to Suwanee Town, although several small fights slowed his progress. When he finally arrived, he learned that the Seminoles had departed. Jackson took two British officers prisoner and, later, hung one of them along with a trader captured at Saint Marks. On 20 May, Jackson captured Pensacola, another Spanish town, causing further diplomatic embarrassment for the United States.

During these battles, Jackson recruited two companies of rangers to patrol the area between the Apalachicola and Mobile rivers. Volunteers for these two ranger companies came from militia units from Georgia and Tennessee. Each company was commanded by a captain (named Boyle and McGirt) and included two lieutenants and about 70 rangers. One medical specialist, called a "surgeon's mate," was assigned to support both companies.

By October of that year, Boyle's company was conducting operations in support of the 4th Infantry Regiment, commanded by Colonel William King. The rangers served as advance scouts for King's unit. Early that month, King ordered Boyle to patrol in the vicinity of the Yellow River. Boyle assembled his company and picked 22 rangers to accompany him. They departed immediately by boat to patrol their assigned area.

On the 6th, the rangers found some evidence at a river crossing site that a party of Seminoles had recently used the site. For two days the rangers tracked the Indians. On the third day, near Choctawhatchy Bay, they discovered their prey to be a group of about 25. Sensing that he still had the element of surprise on his side, Boyle ordered his rangers to attack. The short fight ended after the rangers killed four Indians and captured several more, suffering no casualties themselves.

Boyle apparently forgot the teachings of Robert Rogers because he chose to stay for the night where he had fought. The next morning, just before dawn, another group of Seminoles attacked him and his rangers. At the first sound of incoming fire, half of the rangers fled. Boyle rallied those who remained and beat back the attacking Indians, killing three and taking more prisoners. Boyle and one of his rangers were wounded in the fight, but neither seriously.

On the 13th, Boyle and his rangers returned to Pensacola with their prisoners and the scalps of the seven Indians. King was pleased and sent a letter to Jackson telling him of the results of the patrol. Shortly afterwards, Boyle and his company were sent back to the same area, based on reports that between 40 and 50 Indians were still in the area.

Two things are particularly noteworthy in Captain Boyle's patrol. The first is the ability of his rangers to pursue the Seminoles for almost three days and remain undetected. The Seminoles were among the "most woods-wise of the North American tribes." The second is where the patrol took place. Boyle and his rangers pursued the Indians on water and over land, through what is now part of the Ranger Training Camp near Eglin Air Force Base, Florida.

In 1819, realizing that it could not defend its territory there, Spain ceded Florida to the United States. Immediately thereafter the area was flooded with new settlers. However, the war with the Seminoles was far from over. At least two more wars would be fought, the second between 1835 to 1842 and the third from 1855 to 1858. During the Second Seminole War, Osceola, Jackson's former prisoner, led the Indians. A series of U.S. Army officers, including Clinch, Winfield Scott, and Zachary Taylor, tried to win the war but failed. Taylor and his successor, Colonel William J. Worth, relied on some of the same ranger tactics that had been used successfully during the First Seminole War. Although large scale resistance tapered off, it did not end. Osceola's capture, in violation of a flag of truce, and death in an army prison did not end this war either. Eventually the Army declared victory and quit the battlefield.

TEXAS RANGERS

In 1821, soon after gaining its independence from Spain, Mexico decided that the best way to deal with the threat posed by hostile Indians against their settlers in Texas, *Tejanos*, was to induce more people to live there, including Americans. To that end, Moses Austin began bringing Americans to colonize the area. Austin died before his idea was fulfilled, but his son, Stephen, carried on his work. Two years later, in May 1823, the younger Austin employed ten men to act as rangers and paid them with his own money.

The early rangers were to protect the settlers from thieves, outlaws, and Indians. After several forays against Indians, the Mexican government ordered Austin and his Americans to let soldiers of the Mexican Regular Army be brought in from central Mexico to handle the situation. However, little was done. Instead, Americans landowners established a force of between 20 and 30 rangers. Each landowner sent one ranger to perform one month of duty for every half-league of land he owned. The rangers provided their own horses and weapons. They "fought under no flag, wore no uniform, and in practice observed no prescribed length of service (only the captains were paid)."

On 17 October, 1835, the American "permanent council" passed a resolution to determine the direction of the Texas Revolution. This resolution set the strength of the corps of Texas Rangers at three companies, with three officers and 55 rangers in each company. Rangers were paid $1.25 per day for "pay rations, clothing, and horse service." They had to furnish their own horse, saddle, bridle, blanket, and 100 rounds of ball and powder. The first commander of the rangers was Major Robert M. Williamson. The rangers' mission was to guard the western part of Texas from invasion by Indians.

THE TEXAS REVOLUTION

The Texas Revolution (2 March - 21 April 1836) provided little action for the Texas Rangers. One company led by Captain George Kimball went "to assist the besieged defenders of the Alamo and shared their fate." Later the same month, Captain John Tumlinson's rangers rescued the son of a woman who had escaped from the Comanches. The mother told the rangers where the Indian camp was located. The Rangers raided the camp just in time to prevent the boy from being killed. In June, Captain Isaac W. Burton and 20 rangers scouted the area along the Gulf Coast for any approach by Mexican forces. The rangers captured three boats with supplies worth about $25,000. In commemoration, Burton's rangers were named "Horse Marines."

Between 1836 and 1840, the rangers were stretched to cover the vast frontier that was Texas. Mostly, wherever the rangers were, the Comanches were not. In May 1839 Captain John Bird and 35 of his rangers followed 27 Comanches into a trap sprung by over 200 more Indians. Seven rangers were killed, including Bird. The rest held off the Indians with their rifles until the Comanches left. The nature of the war became more brutal. The number of atrocities committed by both sides escalated. The year 1840, which included the Great Comanche Raid and the Battle at Plum Creek, was particularly bloody. After that year, the supremacy of the Comanches was on the down-swing. The Comanches were skillful mounted archers, but were more effective at close range. In addition to his bow, a Comanche warrior usually carried a long lance and used it effectively. To counter the Indian tactics, the Texas Rangers learned to shoot in relays, since it took time to reload their long rifles. It was especially difficult to reload while on horseback.

At this time, a young ranger captain, John C. Hays, took an interest in ranger weapons. A purchase of some Colt Paterson five-shot pistols by the Texas Navy precipitated his interest. Hays realized that the revolver designed by Samuel Colt could also be valuable to his rangers. He arranged for a supply of pistols to be transferred to his company. He insisted that his rangers shoot accurately, not just fire a lot of shots. One training device consisted of two man-sized posts placed upright in the ground, 40 yards apart. Rangers had to ride at the posts at full speed, firing their rifles at the first post, then drawing and shooting their pistols at the second. Within two months most of his rangers were putting their pistol shots in the center of the posts.

In addition to pistols and horses, rangers of this period carried a mixed lot of equipment, much of it personalized, and borrowed from whatever struck their fancy as being useful. Clothing included bandannas, spike-rowelled spurs, and gourd canteens. Spanish saddles and Mexican blankets comforted man and horse. Eventually, many rangers carried one or two Colt revolvers tucked in a waist belt, a tomahawk, and a long knife. This knife was used "to prepare game, perform camp chores, and serve as the main eating tool. It doubled as a fighting knife as necessary." The rangers even adopted Comanche tricks of tracking and field-craft.

WAR WITH MEXICO

The United States annexed Texas on 20 December 1845. War with Mexico followed. Brigadier General Zachary Taylor had been preparing for it since the previous July. He had moved his forces from Louisiana to Texas and recruited a force of Texas Rangers to operate in front of his own forces. At first he could not pay them. Several companies were activated but only for short periods of enlistment. In April 1846, after these companies left and before any major actions had been fought, Taylor called on the state for more ranger companies. This time, a soon-to-be legend stepped forward and raised a company of two officers and 91 rangers. This ranger was Captain Samuel H. Walker.

The first mission given to Walker and his rangers was to determine if a makeshift fort near Matamoros, surrounded by a larger Mexican force, would be able to hold out until Taylor could return with much needed supplies. Walker and six rangers conducted the mission. They made their way through the Mexican lines under cover of night and contacted the commander of the fort. They left on another reconnaissance around the fort and went back inside. Before dawn, the rangers returned to Taylor. Walker told the general that the fort would hold and it did.

Eventually, two regiments of Texas Rangers joined Taylor's army during 1846, comprising a shifting number of companies that volunteered for periods varying from three months to a year. Although Taylor referred to them as the 1st and 2nd Mounted Rifles, they were called a variety of names, not all of them included the term "rangers." The rangers called their units the Eastern or Western regiment. The 2nd Regiment named its companies by number, while the 1st used the county where each was raised as the company name. Taylor often sent the rangers on scouting missions, both short and long range. They escorted prisoners and supply equipment. When Mexico City was finally taken, they were the only unit able to keep the peace. The activities of the Texas Rangers during the Mexican War are too numerous to detail. One more example, from a mission by rangers led by Captain Ben McCulloch, will stand to show why the Americans respected them and the Mexicans feared them.

RANGER BEN McCULLOCH

While on a reconnaissance to check a route to Cerralvo, a force from two companies (McCulloch's and Captain Richard A. Gillespie's) heard that two Mexican military officers they were seeking would attend a *fandango* in Punta Aguda. The rangers waited until night. After the party started, they approached the town and sent out scouts to circle the town. The sentries were posted at strategic spots to block the exits from town. Only when they were satisfied that no one could get out of town, at least alive, did the remaining rangers approach the town square. The village dogs were barking loudly, announcing the approach of the rangers, but the music and singing drowned out the sound. One minute was all music and dancing, then the rangers moved out of the shadows into the light of the square.

After some initial screaming and running around by the local Mexicans, the rangers urged the crowd to continue dancing while they looked for their prey. When they learned that the two Mexicans were not in town, the rangers joined in the dancing and drinking. Just before three in the morning they departed, many of them sleeping in their saddles.

The rangers performed many legendary acts during this war and were involved in most of the key battles. Walker even had time to encourage Samuel Colt to redesign his pistol into a six-shooter. Several companies of so-called rangers from several states, including Georgia, Pennsylvania, Indiana, Missouri, and even California, were raised during the Mexican War. These units, however, served in cavalry or infantry roles. Further west, in New Mexico, a company of Laclede Rangers, from St. Louis and commanded by Colonel Stephen W. Kearny, and a company of Chihuahua Rangers, commanded by a Captain Hudson, scouted and conducted counter-guerrilla operations to help secure the victory at Santa Fe on 18 August 1846.

POST MEXICAN WAR

After the war, at least six companies of Texas Rangers were on duty to keep watch for and fight both the Indians and roving bands of Mexican bandits. In 1854, several ranger companies were again attached to army units but only for a short time. After that, they reverted to state control. From that point on, the Texas Rangers' mission was keeping the peace and law enforcement. During the Civil War, the Confederate Army raised units of Texas Rangers, but these were cavalry units, by their tactics and employment, not rangers. For brief periods until almost 1890, Texas Rangers and Arizona Rangers conducted scouting and reconnaissance missions for the Army. Their principal mission was no longer military. Now it was frontier protection for their respective state and territory.

MOUNTED RANGERS

From April to September 1832, the United States fought the Sac and Fox Indian tribes in the Black Hawk War. Not surprisingly, this war was fought about land. Black Hawk, who was the chief of the two tribes, became increasingly frustrated over what he thought were violations of a treaty that gave the United States title to 50,000,000 acres of land. Black Hawk thought that the treaty "conveyed nothing more than hunting rights."

In April, he led a band of 2,000 (called the British Band of the Sacs and Foxes) east of the Mississippi and back onto traditional tribal lands. After burning one Indian village, a force of 1,500 men pursued the main Indian party but did not find them. The regular army commander co-opted two battalions of militia, commanded by Majors Isaac Stillman and David Bailey, and sent them to scout in advance of the main force, looking for the Indians under Black Hawk. Stillman's unit camped near the Kyte River and got very drunk. Black Hawk, attempting to settle the matter, sent emissaries to Stillman's camp but they were chased away.

Black Hawk decided to launch a suicidal attack on the militia unit. The drunk soldiers panicked and ran. Forty lightly armed Sac and Fox Indians sent a 275 man unit on the run, killing about 50 of them. This "battle" became known as Stillman's Run. Soon after, the Indians killed 15 settlers in an attack on a farm at Indian Creek. These two battles prompted the United States to commit 800 more regular soldiers and a hastily formed company of rangers, under Major Bogart, to assist the largely militia force that had gathered to fight Black Hawk. The rangers were, once again, to conduct patrols in northern Illinois. One of the short term militia soldiers who was called up at this time was a Springfield lawyer named Abraham Lincoln.

Throughout July and August Black Hawk was chased by a mounted force led by Major Henry Dodge. Eventually, after the Indians were reduced to about 500 by starvation, Black Hawk assembled what was left of his band at the junction of the Bad Axe and Mississippi rivers, intending to cross to the west. At this point the army, under Dodge and his commander, Major General Henry Atkinson, arrived and a battle ensued. The Army was helped by a nearby steamboat, the *Warrior*, which was loaded with soldiers that carried a six-pound gun. About 200 Indians made it across the Mississippi. Black Hawk was taken prisoner later, after being turned in to the army by members of the Winnebago tribe. On 19 September, another treaty was concluded. The Indians ceded a strip of land 50 miles wide along the "entire length of Iowa's Mississippi River frontage." This amounted to 6,000,000 acres.

The Army had had no cavalry units on active service since 1815. After the Black Hawk War, Congress authorized the army to raise six companies of mounted rangers, hoping they would be a match for the mounted Indians on the country's frontier. The Army chose Major Dodge to command these companies, based on his performance against the Sac and Fox Indians (these six companies were not the same rangers that fought against Black Hawk), and to conduct the following missions: two companies were to range the frontier of Illinois and Wisconsin, three companies were stationed at Fort Gibson, and the last company was posted to Fort Leavenworth. Each company had four officers, 14 sergeants, and 100 rangers. Recruits came from Arkansas, Missouri, Illinois, and Indiana. Few of these rangers, including the officers, had previous military experience. The companies at Fort Gibson supervised the resettlement of Creek, Cherokee, Choctaw, and Delaware Indians into the Indian Territory. The company at Fort Leavenworth conducted a patrol to Santa Fe and back, accompanying a "trader's caravan" on the way west.

The mounted rangers in Dodge's command enlisted for one year. Each ranger furnished his own horse, weapon, clothing, and equipment. The rangers also paid for their horses' forage. In late 1832, Washington Irving accompanied a training patrol from the company commanded by Captain Jesse Bean on its reconnaissance of the Arkansas and Cameroon rivers. Irving later wrote a book, *A Tour of the Prairies*, in which he described his experiences on this patrol. Bean, it seems, was still training his rangers and many of the experiences on this patrol (lost weapons, hunger, horses ridden to death) became object lessons in his training.

In December 1832, Dodge's command, the Battalion of Mounted Rangers, became a Corps. This meant the rangers were now a separate branch of the army. When the rangers' period of service was approaching its end, the Secretary of War contemplated whether to continue the unit's service. He was pressured almost from the time the rangers were formed to replace them with a uniformed regiment of dragoons. He eventually decided to disband the rangers in favor of a dragoon unit for the following reasons: the ranger battalion was more costly than a similar-sized dragoon unit (the rangers were paid twice the usual army pay); the ranger organization was inefficient, with too many men in each company and no formal battalion staff; the period of service, one year, was too short. Finally, cavalry tactics needed to be preserved.

Rather than correcting the deficiencies he saw in the ranger battalion by reorganizing them, putting them in uniform, and lengthening their term of enlistment, the Secretary of War opted to disband the organization at the end of its period of service. It was not the first time such an action was taken and it would not be the last. During this decade, a young instructor at the U.S. Military Academy was teaching the tactics that, to this point, were associated with ranger organizations. The instructor was Dennis H. Mahon.

PART IV

CIVIL WAR PERIOD

INTRODUCTION

During the Civil War more than 400 Union and Confederate military organizations called themselves "ranger" units. In the Federal Army, units from 15 states used this name. In the Confederate Army, ranger units were formed in all 13 secessionist states. It is difficult to address every unit within this work. But only a handful of these units on each side fit the definition established for selection. For example, Company D, 4th Virginia Cavalry Battalion was known as the Little Fork Rangers, though they were simply a cavalry unit.

To narrow the pool, five organizations have been selected which closely represent the elite nature of special operations forces and their missions. The casual reader will recognize at least three such units, Andrew's Raiders, Morgan's Raiders and Mosby's Rangers.

Another equally important aspect of the Civil War organizations is how the belligerents viewed them. Officers in each army had experienced war in the first half of the century but they did not agree on the use of special operations forces. In fact, disagreement existed within each army, a condition which has not changed much in the last 100 years. Commanders, both past and present, have good arguments supporting their positions.

Generally, Civil War special operations forces conducted scouting, reconnaissance, and raiding operations, the traditional "bread and butter" of special operations forces of the period. At least one of those included here, the Andrews raid, fits the broad definition of a direct action mission. The "organization" was put together for a single operation of strategic value and was conducted behind the lines. Interestingly, the operation was led by a civilian, probably because he was familiar with the area, knew the train schedule, and was known in the area as a Southern sympathizer.

One of the units, Morgan's, started as a conventional cavalry unit. In fact, it existed for almost four years prior to the war and formed the nucleus of his famous raiding unit. Some of Morgan's early operations were small force raids, while others were traditional cavalry operations. His unit is included here because of the less conventional missions it performed.

Two of the Confederate units were organized as a result of the Partisan Ranger Act, a piece of legislation passed by the Confederate Congress on 27 March 1862. The act was a hotly contested issue before it was passed, while it was law, and even after it was repealed two years later. It brought fame to such military leaders as Turner Ashby, E.V. White, John B. Imboden, Harry Gilmor, Kincheloe, O'Farrell, and others. Proponents of the act believed that partisan warfare was acceptable because it was conducted by soldiers whose battlefield was, more often than not, behind the lines. Additionally, partisan warfare had traditions in the South, especially in South Carolina during the Revolutionary War. To Southerners those men were, and still are, military heroes. Those who opposed the Partisan Ranger Act believed that these units were unnecessary and that it was sneaky or illegal not fighting toe-to-toe with the enemy. Others believed that such units drained the resources and best people from conventional commanders engaged directly with the enemy. Since the act also gave all members of Partisan Ranger units a share of whatever they captured, others said that the units only attracted criminals and outlaws. These sentiments were echoed by Federal and Confederate officers alike. Some

Federal commanders hung captured members of Partisan Ranger units, stating that the rangers were nothing more than outlaws. In retaliation, some ranger organizations, including Mosby's, retaliated by hanging captured Federal troops, especially those of units that had hung the Confederate rangers. Many rangers and other guerrillas, when taken prisoner, had their records marked prohibiting their parole or release. As a result, some of Mosby's and McNeill's rangers, as well as others, languished in military prisons until the end of the war. When the Partisan Ranger Act was repealed in April 1864, only Mosby's battalion and McNeill's company were permitted to continue operating.

Another item worth mentioning is that several Federal and Confederate units elected their own officers. The elections varied from unit to unit. In Mosby's unit, elections carried little weight. He told his men who the officers were and that they could either vote for them or not vote at all. In special operations units of the Civil War, the commanders were not elected, although unit members voted for replacement commanders. McNeill, as was John Gorham, was succeeded by a relative, in this case a son.

As in previous sections, the terms company, squadron, or battalion are not consistent in size. Neither McNeill's company nor Means' company contained more than 60 men. Three of the units operated generally in the same area and knew of one another. Means, Mosby, and McNeill's units operated in the northern Virginia area, Means usually from the Harpers Ferry area, Mosby in the eastern Shenandoah Valley, and McNeill in the western valley area and in West Virginia. Their operations were not confined to just Virginia. Each was active in Maryland and Pennsylvania. Morgan, however, commanded troops that operated in a ten state area during the course of the war.

ANDREWS' RAID (Federal)

For almost a year, James J. Andrews had led a double life. Each "side" in the Civil War thought he was a staunch loyalist and friend. Few knew that he was one of the most valuable spies in the Federal service. On the evening of 5 April 1862, in Shelbyville, Tennessee, Andrews listened to a plan to steal a locomotive in the vicinity of Big Shanty, Georgia and run it north to Chattanooga, Tennessee attempting to destroy stretches of track behind the two towns and to burn certain bridges. The goal was to make that particular railroad line useless for the reinforcement of Confederate Chattanooga. The following morning, three Ohio regiments, the 2nd, 21st, and 33rd, chose volunteers for this operation. Thirty men were selected on the basis of their demonstrated courage, resourcefulness, and discretion. Two of the 30 had previous experience with locomotives, one as an engineer and the other as a master mechanic.

Later that day and the next, some of the volunteers met Andrews and briefly discussed the mission. All of those selected were to travel in civilian clothes. Those who did not have suitable clothes borrowed or bought them. On Monday night, 23 men met Andrews on the Wartrace road, outside of Chattanooga. Andrews explained the plan, including the need for the men to travel in small groups, posing as Southern sympathizers. Andrews told them to be on the train for Marietta leaving Chattanooga the following Thursday at five in the afternoon. During their trip south, it rained heavily and steadily. This slowed the travel of several groups of raiders and they had to delay their departure plans a day. They did not arrive in Marietta until Friday night, the 11th.

The following morning Andrews briefed 17 of his raiders in his hotel room. The first scheduled stop north of Marietta was Big Shanty, where the passengers would take a 20 minute stop for breakfast. The crew would also eat there, at Lacy's Hotel. The hotel was on the east side of the train and a camp with three or four Confederate regiments was on the west side. Andrews and Knight, the former engineer, would check the engine and uncouple the rear half of the train. Once on their way, they expected to follow the train's schedule in order to have a clear track.

As the train, pulled by the locomotive *General*, left the Marietta station, two of the raiders had been left behind, unknown to the others. Porter and Hawkins had not been called in time at their hotel. In Big Shanty, all of the passengers left the train and, almost as easily as Andrews had predicted, the raiders disconnected the rear half of the train and boarded the front, in a closed box car. After a few anxious seconds when the engine died, but was quickly restarted, they were on their way. They had stolen a Confederate train!

But the raiders had not counted on William Fuller, the conductor of the train. His immediate thought was that Confederate army deserters were responsible and that they would probably leave the train puffing on the tracks a mile or so out of the station. Fuller and two other railroad employees began running after the train. Fuller was partially correct. The train *did* stop in a mile or so but only so the raiders could cut the telegraph lines and pile nearby ties across the rails. While they were stopped Andrews told his men, "When we've passed one more train the coast will be clear for burning the bridges and running on through to Chattanooga ..." The train started up and kept going until it was north of Allatoona. It stopped again so the raiders could take a rail out of the line. This stop took longer than Andrews had expected. When the rail was ripped free, he ordered it stored on one of the box cars. Just past the next bridge, they spotted a branch line with a small locomotive, the *Yonah*.

Behind them Fuller kept running until he found a handcart. Fuller suspected that the raiders were not army deserters but "Yankee spies." As he and the others came upon the *Yonah,* they reached a downhill slope. They didn't see the missing rail until it was too late and the cart overturned. But Fuller was not hurt in the accident and immediately took over the small engine and continued chasing the raiders.

At Cass, the raiders stopped once more to take on water and wood. When they arrived in Kingston, they had a delay of 35 minutes while waiting on a siding for a priority ammunition train heading south to go through. The raiders waited another 10 minutes for the second section of the train. William Pittenger, one of the raiders, said, "The wait for the extra freight was agonizingly long." He described the race against time in which they were engaged as "grand and terrible." But the delay, Andrews thought, had caused some suspicion in the minds of the station crew. Soon after they started, the raiders stopped again to cut telegraph lines and leave ties across the tracks. After more than ten miles they stopped again to remove another rail. It was during this stop that the raiders heard the pursuing engine. Wilson, another raider, thought to himself that "the destruction of a bridge was the only thing that would save us and to do this we had to outrun them." In Kingston, Fuller had commandeered another locomotive, *William B. Smith*, and continued his chase and gained each time the raiders stopped. By now, Fuller had recruited several others. When they came to obstructions on the tracks everyone jumped off and helped in the clearing. When they reached the gap in the track, Fuller left the locomotive and began running again.

At Adairsville, the raiders once again had to slow for a southbound train which was delayed. Andrews decided to take a chance and left without waiting for the overdue train. After they cleared the town, Andrews ordered full speed. His gamble paid off. When they reached Calhoun the overdue train was on a siding. They slowed for the station, then pulled out.

Before Fuller reached Adairsville, he encountered yet another train, pulled by the *Texas*, going south. When he explained what had happened, those on the train allowed him to take it over and he went after the raiders in reverse. In Adairsville, he shunted the cars onto a siding and then continued north, with the locomotive still running in reverse.

Andrews figured that he still had to make seven more stops to cut telegraph wire, lift rails, and burn several bridges. One of these stops would also be for more wood and water. At their first stop, on a curve of tracks, the raiders had to cut their work short when they heard the sound of the pursuing *Texas'* whistle. Before setting out, they managed to loosen and lift one rail. When Fuller approached the loose rail, he was travelling fast.

He didn't see it until it was too late. In a flash, however, he realized that he could make it because the bent rail was on the inside of the curve and a train running at high speed through a curve would throw its weight onto the outside rail. With a jolt, the *Texas* continued the chase. Up ahead, Andrews could see that the train behind was still coming so he had his raiders uncouple the last box car, sending it careening back along the tracks.

When it approached, Fuller quickly reversed his locomotive and connected it to the errant box car. He continued after the raiders. Up ahead, the raiders began dropping ties onto the track. This slowed the chasers, because they had to clear the track as they went. The raiders began to pull away slowly. Then the raiders set another box car loose and slowed Fuller even more. But only for a little while, until he shunted the extra box cars off onto a siding near Resaca. One of the men with Fuller said later, "Andrews at this point was more anxious to escape than to destroy bridges." At Tilton, the raiders stopped for water but Fuller had pressed on behind them. As he passed through Tilton, Fuller dropped off one of his crew with orders to get a telegraph message off to Chattanooga, warning them what was happening. By now it was raining. On the other side of town, Fuller noticed that the telegraph line was cut. He knew his message would not get through. He pressed on after the raiders.

At the tunnel just south of Ringgold, Andrews thought he would gain time. He believed Fuller would slow down, suspecting an ambush in the tunnel. He was correct. In the meantime, the raiders attempted to set fire to the last box car, but they didn't have an easy time of it. When the damp wood failed to catch fire on the third try, the raiders' hopes of setting fire to the last bridge at Chickamauga failed as well.

Andrews knew that there was no use in continuing. He put the train in reverse and ordered all the raiders off. He told his men to head west across the mountains to what he hoped were friendly lines. After his raiders jumped, Andrews sent the *General* back toward the chasing Fuller. But even this last effort failed. The *General* met the *Texas* before it could gather any forward speed.

Eventually, all of the raiders, including the two who were left behind in Marietta, were caught. Andrews and seven others were hanged as spies. Fuller attended Andrews' execution, saying afterwards, "He died bravely." The rest were sent to prison without a trial. In October, eight of the raiders escaped and eventually reached Federal lines. The remaining six were paroled in March 1863. On the 25th of that month they went to Washington, where they met with the Secretary of War. The Secretary told the raiders, "Congress has ... ordered medals to be prepared on this model, and your party shall have the first to be given ..." These six and the eight others who survived were the first to receive the new decoration, the Congressional Medal of Honor. Later that afternoon, the raiders met President Abraham Lincoln. Soon after, the survivors of those who had been hanged also received the same medal.

LOUDOUN RANGERS (Federal)

The neighbor against neighbor nature of the Civil War in certain parts of the country led to friction that escalated into violence. Kansas and Missouri are a perfect example. Less perfect is Loudoun County, Virginia. In this area, not all of the citizens supported secession. Among the most well-known was Samuel C. Means, a prominent businessman. Local Confederate supporters confiscated Means' business, forbade him to return to Loudoun County, and set traps when they heard he was in town. For a short time, Means acted as a scout for Federal units in the Maryland-Virginia border region. Then, in May 1862, Means was commissioned in the Federal Army and received instructions from the Secretary of War to raise a cavalry company that would be called the Loudoun Independent Guards. When the unit was mustered into service in June, at Harper's Ferry, "Guards" was changed to "Rangers." Means had no trouble recruiting 50 men in Loudoun County for his company.

On the morning of 27 August, a Confederate cavalry battalion attacked and trapped a portion of the company in a church in Waterford. After the third offer of surrender, the rangers agreed to terms. Two rangers were killed, seven wounded, and 19 taken prisoner, but the prisoners were immediately paroled. Soon after, Means moved his unit to Catoctin Furnace. In the next several weeks, the small company conducted several raids and then relocated to Harper's Ferry. When the town was attacked on the night of September 14, Means and his rangers, leading a cavalry force of 2,000 troops, fled Harper's Ferry under the cover of darkness. Along the way, Means suggested a raid on a target of opportunity - an ammunition convoy bound for General Longstreet. This raid was a success.

The rangers reassembled near Ellicott's Mills in Maryland and Means made a side trip to Baltimore to obtain more horses. Following the battle of Antietam, in which it played only a small part carrying messages, the ranger company scouted the area between Monocacy and Shepherstown. When McClellan crossed the Potomac at Brunswick at the end of October, the rangers served as guides for the Army and then went into winter quarters at Point of Rocks, Maryland.

Throughout the winter the rangers moved often and continued to conduct raids between moves. On one such raid, in late January 1863, they took several prisoners. During the winter, Means recruited more rangers. On a raid in March, 12 rangers left the column "to call on some lady friends." When they returned, Means locked them in a local jail. He then "gave them a severe lecture on military discipline," and released them. On a raid at the end of March, the rangers stopped at a still-house and filled their canteens with whiskey only hours old (it was still warm!). They returned to camp happy, but with some difficulty. During April, the rangers conducted scouting operations and carried dispatches in the Winchester-Berryville area of Virginia.

In June, small parties of rangers attempted to locate the northward movement of Lee's army. Operating once again from Harper's Ferry, the rangers kept track of the Confederate forces as they marched into Pennsylvania. The rangers returned to Ellicott's Mills and remained there until late July. On their next assignment, the rangers requisitioned horses from the Maryland-Virginia border area. While on this mission, Means sent several rangers into Loudoun County on a conscript mission. Some of the rangers doubted Means' authority to do this, but they didn't argue. Not surprisingly, very few "recruits" were found.

During a raid in Loudoun County, in August, the rangers captured several Confederate prisoners, 30 horses, and assorted weapons and equipment. In late September, while at Harper's Ferry, Means' received authority to recruit three new companies. The companies were now designated A through D. Still, they were not large companies. Companies A and D had about 30 rangers, and B about 50. Soon after, the rangers returned to the Winchester area to patrol and scout in the direction of Port Royal, Virginia.

On 18 October, another Confederate attack on Harper's Ferry caught the Federal forces by surprise. A ranger lieutenant formed his men and they attempted to shoot their way out. Thirteen of the 30 rangers made it out but the remaining were wounded and taken prisoner. In late October, a raiding party of 20 rangers captured a handful of prisoners and supplies near Leesburg. Among the prisoners was a general from the Confederate Quartermaster Department.

In November, one of the ranger company commanders, Michael Mullen, was captured. Soon after his transfer to Camp Parole, near Annapolis, Maryland, where he was to be exchanged, he died. At the end of the month, Means consolidated companies B, C, and D to form Company B. He appointed Captain James W. Grubb as the commander of Company B, with a company strength of 60 rangers. In January 1864, the rangers returned to Point of Rocks for winter quarters. In late March, Means was ordered to consolidate his ranger battalion (two companies) with the 3rd West Virginia Cavalry. He refused, stating that the rangers had been "recruited for special service," subject to his orders only, and that these instructions came directly from the Secretary of War. The Secretary of War supported his version, but Means resigned from the army in April. His senior lieutenant, Daniel M. Keyes, became the new unit commander and was promoted to captain.

On 16 May, both ranger companies attacked an element of Mosby's Confederate Rangers and took three prisoners. This was at least the second time that Mosby's command had come off second best to the Loudoun Rangers. On the return trip, Mosby's men struck back but the Loudoun Rangers repulsed them and took four more prisoners. The following day, about 150 rangers from Mosby's battalion attacked the Loudoun Rangers in camp. For the next several months the two units raided each other, with no serious inroads made by either command. During the battle around Frederick-Monocacy, the rangers were attached to a unit of Illinois cavalry but saw little action.

The rangers next raid was at Aldie, in Virginia, in late August. They encountered a Virginia cavalry unit en route and took three Confederate prisoners. Later, the rangers ran into a civilian who was suspected of collecting supplies for the rebels. When they searched him they found $3,000. They confiscated the money and took him prisoner.

From then until the end of the Civil War, the rangers operated mostly out of Harper's Ferry. They conducted various scouting and raiding operations, and occasionally encountered Mosby's Ranger battalion. In late March 1865, Keyes broke his leg and had to leave the army. Lieutenant Edwin R. Gover took his company and Grubb assumed command of the battalion. Just before the end of the war, the rangers succeeded in killing a notorious guerrilla, John Moberly, who had eluded them for almost two years. On 30 May, the Loudoun Rangers were mustered out of service at Bolivar, West Virginia.

MORGAN'S RAIDERS (Confederate)

John Hunt Morgan was a veteran of the Mexican War, rising to the rank of captain. In 1857, in his home state of Kentucky, he organized the Lexington Rifles, a militia unit that, in September 1861, formed the core of the 2nd Kentucky Cavalry Regiment. Most of the members of the Rifles were from prominent Kentucky families. Although Kentucky was slow to become involved in the Civil War, it later provided men to both sides. Morgan's unit stole rifles from an armory and fled south, where they were sworn into service on 23 October. Initially a company, the unit had four officers. Morgan was the captain and the lieutenants were Basil Duke, who was married to Morgan's sister, James West, and Van Buren Sellers.

Within a short time two other companies were added. Morgan now commanded a squadron. His first operation was a small raid in Nashville before the battle of Shiloh. After the battle, he led a five-company raid, but a Federal attack dispersed his command. Neither failure dampened Morgan's spirit for operating behind Federal lines. By mid-June 1862, he had been promoted to the rank of colonel and commanded the 2nd Kentucky Cavalry Regiment, 876 men strong. Many of his men rode Denmarks, at the time among the best American saddle horses, and carried cut-down Enfield rifles. George St. Leger Grenfell, an English soldier-of-fortune who joined Morgan's unit, drilled Morgan's men endlessly on foot and on horseback. On 4 July, Morgan set out from Knoxville, Tennessee on his first big raid. He was going back into Kentucky.

After a brief skirmish at Tompkinsville, Kentucky, one of Morgan's men tapped into a telegraph line and learned of the disposition of Federal troops in the area. Morgan would use the technique on most of his operations. They struck first at Lebanon, where they captured almost 200 Federal troops and destroyed stocks of food, guns, ammunition, and clothing. Near Lexington Morgan split his force to destroy railroad bridges and tear up track. Skirting the city of Lexington to avoid a large Federal force there, Morgan fought a battle in Cynthiana that left eight of his men dead and 28 wounded. During the operation, he captured 300 horses, a supply of weapons, and had destroyed Federal military supplies and equipment. He returned to Tennessee by a more easterly route, completing the raid in 24 days. He had also recruited more than 300 new men for his unit.

The following month, Morgan's Raiders were in the vanguard of Bragg's grand plan to cut Federal supply lines and "liberate" Kentucky. They first hit at Gallatin, where they destroyed almost 30 railroad cars, a water station, two bridges, and wrecked one of the two tunnels at Tunnel Hill. It was during this raid that "Morgan's neckties" achieved notoriety. His men tore up railroad track in several places, heated it until it was hot, then wrapped the track around nearby trees. The effect resembled a necktie. When Bragg ordered Morgan to meet him in Lexington, Morgan insisted that his men dress in their finest uniforms and parade into town. But it was a short-lived triumph. After Bragg declined to fight Buell at Munfordville, Morgan's unit acted as a screening force for the main Confederate army fleeing south to Tennessee.

In December, the raiders, now over 1,200, raided a Federal storehouse at Hartsville and captured supplies and over 2,000 prisoners. On the 13th, Confederate President Jefferson Davis personally promoted Morgan to brigadier general and Duke to colonel. Before the end of the month, Morgan's command included seven regiments. He immediately took his army on a "Christmas raid" into Kentucky, moving up through the west central part of the state and circling back to the east by a different route. This raid was markedly different from those in the past since it was much more difficult to hide or even maneuver a force of 4,000. A severe snow storm hit the force just before the end of the month and Morgan decided to head back to Tennessee. His army had taken more than 2,000 prisoners and destroyed a "vast quantity of enemy supplies" while losing only two killed and 24 wounded. Despite the extensive destruction to the railroads, trains were running between Lexington and Nashville by 1 February 1863.

Throughout the harsh Tennessee winter of 1863, Morgan planned what many consider his most significant operation, the so-called "big raid." He decided to conduct a raid in the states north of the Ohio River, destroying Federal supplies and attacking "his favorite whipping boy," the Louisville & Nashville Railroad. Bragg told him not to cross the Ohio, and to stay in Kentucky. On 2 July, Morgan set out. He was barely on his way when he encountered Federal troops and fought a two-hour battle at Tubb's Bend, suffering 71 casualties, the first of many he would have on this operation. From there, Morgan headed directly for the Ohio River, where his advance party commandeered two steamboats. After crossing into Indiana, the raiders burned one of the boats. At first, Morgan found little resistance but, within a day, more than 8,000 men were mobilized to fight the raiders. Morgan hit several railroad targets and even considered going to Indianapolis to free 6,000 Confederate prisoners held there. Instead, he turned east and headed for Ohio. En route, Morgan's men looted, burned, and stole beyond their officers' ability to control them. Duke wrote later, "I could not believe that such a passion could have developed...among any body of civilized men." By now Federal troops were pursuing Morgan and his raiders. Although he later ordered it returned and the thief court-martialed, the theft of valuable "coin-silver jewelry" from a Masonic lodge reflected how little control Morgan had over his men. Once in Ohio, Morgan divided his force. He sent part south, while he continued east, skirmishing with local Federal troops and attacking railroad targets. Thievery and plundering worsened. When Morgan attempted to cross into West Virginia, he encountered the fight of his life at Portland. He was lucky to escape with only about one-quarter of his force. Duke was taken prisoner. By now, Morgan was hunted wherever he went. Eventually, on 26 July, Morgan was captured. Some consider the spot where he was captured to be the northernmost point reached by Confederate troops during the war.

Morgan was sent to the Ohio State Penitentiary in Columbus, where he held a reunion of sorts with Duke and others from his command. On 27 November, he and six men escaped. By Christmas he was in Columbia, South Carolina with his wife. He still had to face Bragg for disobeying orders. Although Bragg did not court-martial Morgan, he continued to hint at one and tried to block Morgan from getting another command. He was not successful.

In Georgia in late April 1864, Morgan raised another unit, comprised of many men from his old command. He even led this unit on a long raid back to Kentucky, taking (some said stealing) several thousand horses and robbing at least one bank. Morgan had lost control of his unit. In the end, although they had taken thousands of prisoners, Morgan had nothing to show for the operation. He had no horses, many casualties, and had suffered a black eye to his reputation.

On 3 September 1864 a Federal soldier shot and killed Morgan while he was visiting friends in Jonesboro.

McNEILL'S RANGERS (Confederate)

The first military unit John H. "Hanse" McNeill raised and commanded was a cavalry company in Missouri. This company took part in three of the principal engagements in that state, at Carthage, Wilson's Creek, and Lexington. Soon after the last fight, Federal troops took McNeill and his youngest son, Jesse, prisoner. By the early summer of 1862, both had escaped and returned to the family's original home, Hardy County, Virginia.

McNeill went to Richmond to affirm his previous commission as a captain. While there, he received authority to raise a company of partisan rangers. By 20 September, McNeill had raised a sufficient force to attempt a reconnaissance. He led his rangers to the area of New Creek, West Virginia, conducting a thorough scout of the area and capturing several pickets. Soldiers of the garrison pursued the rangers, who eluded detection. On the 24th, the company was mustered into service as Company I, 1st Regiment Virginia Partisan Rangers, commanded by Colonel John D. Imboden. The regiment was a "conglomeration of infantry, cavalry and artillery."

The rangers accompanied the unit on only one operation, the Paw Paw raid. The unit was then designated as Company E, 18th Virginia Cavalry. Then, in early 1863, the rangers broke from the 18th Cavalry to operate independently as McNeill's Rangers. Until his command became independent, McNeill continued to take part in operations of his parent unit.

Taking a core of 17 men from Company E, McNeill began recruiting for his own company. He even placed advertisements in local newspapers, requesting men who were "fond of active duty under a brave, daring, sagacious and skillful leader." While he was filling his ranks, he assisted other units in raids, particularly in February against a Federal wagon train that had just completed a foraging expedition. By the middle of April he had 55 men in his company. He and his son were the unit captain and senior lieutenant and the other two lieutenants were Isaac Welton and Bernard J. Dolan.

In an early April raid near Burlington the rangers netted 25 horses and a dozen prisoners. By this time, people in Virginia began to recognize McNeill's name, based on just a few daring operations. Later that month, the rangers were part of a very large operation aimed at destroying railroad bridges. McNeill's company, with other units, succeeded in capturing the garrison at Oakland, Maryland where the Baltimore and Ohio line crossed the Youghiogheny River and "speedily reduced [the bridge] to smoldering ruins." It was one of 16 bridges destroyed during the operation.

Before Lee took his army north in June, McNeill conducted a raid on a Federal wagon train in the Winchester-Berryville area, capturing more horses and prisoners. During the Gettysburg campaign, McNeill's Rangers conducted scouting operations on the flanks of the Army of Northern Virginia as it moved north, making side raids at targets of opportunity. They did not take part in the battle at Gettysburg but acted as flank security for the Confederates when they retreated south after the battle. They also conducted various scouting and foraging missions. Back in Virginia, the rangers spent a week operating in the western Shenandoah Valley before taking some time to refit.

After a brief rest, they again struck at supply trains and isolated Federal detachments. The rangers captured numerous horses, weapons, equipment, and men. Additional recruits came to the company during this period. In November, the rangers moved to western Virginia to observe the movements of Federal forces. On the 16th, they raided a wagon train near Burlington. The following month Federal forces attempted a two-column advance into the Shenandoah Valley that divided Confederate units and pushed them further south. McNeill's Rangers were among several units that struck back. The rangers attacked the Federals' flanks and rear, and fought in a desperate holding action until General Jubal A. Early arrived to turn back the Federals.

In early 1864, even as the Confederate legislature looked at the question of disbanding partisan ranger organizations, McNeill's Rangers continued to strike at supply convoys and at isolated Federal units. During April, McNeill faced two court martial trials, one concerning proper dispersal of public property and funds, and the other for harboring a deserter. He was acquitted in each trial. On the 21st of that month, the Confederate Secretary of War, under authority granted by the Congress on 17 February 1864, repealed the Partisan Ranger Act, disbanding all such units except Mosby's and McNeill's.

In May, McNeill conducted his most significant operation to date, a raid on the railroad stations at Piedmont and Bloomington, in northwestern Virginia, where vast railroad supplies were stored and many machine shops were located. The rangers, in lightning attacks, destroyed seven machine shops, nine locomotives, and more than 100 loaded railroad cars. Additionally, six more locomotives were set at full speed and sent down the tracks to eventual wreckage. In less than an hour, more than $1,000,000 in Federal property was destroyed. On the 10th, the rangers lured Federal cavalry into a trap set by Imboden's brigade. The rangers captured eight supply wagons and an ambulance. For the rest of the month, McNeill's Rangers harassed outposts in Hardy and Hampshire counties.

During that summer, the Federals launched another campaign to push the Confederates from the Shenandoah Valley. The rangers, however, continued hit-and-run attacks at isolated Federal forces and supply wagons. The raids only increased the Federals' vigilance and made the work of the rangers harder. On 2 October, McNeill planned a raid on an isolated unit near Mount Jackson. But it ended in tragedy. McNeill was mortally wounded. Although he did not die until 10 November, his son, Jesse, became the new commander. For a short period, McNeill's Rangers operated in the eastern Shenandoah, where Mosby and his battalion of partisan rangers had enjoyed much success.

In late November, before Jesse McNeill could shape his command, the rangers became the target of Federal forces. The Federals warned local citizens not to harbor or help the rangers. On the 27th, the rangers attacked a force that was looking for them, then faded into the night. Subsequently, they attacked the recently rebuilt shops and rail storage area at Piedmont, laying waste to it for the second time in seven months.

For the next two months, Lieutenant Welton served as the acting commander while McNeill recuperated from a serious leg injury. The harshness of the winter reduced the size and number of the ranger operations. Meanwhile, the Confederate Army made another attempt to consolidate McNeill's Rangers out of existence. The success of the next raid stopped this attempt. Acting on intelligence gathered during a scouting mission by Sergeant John B. Fay and Ranger Cephas Haller, the rangers crossed the Potomac into Maryland in late February 1865 and rode to Cumberland. Moving past several Federal picket lines and using the password and countersign they had forced from a prisoner, the rangers entered the homes of two Federal generals. The rangers captured the generals and returned safely to their lines with Federal forces in hot pursuit. Even Mosby was impressed with the rangers' daring. "This surpasses anything I have ever done," said Mosby. "[T]o get even with you boys, I've got to go to Washington and carry Abe Lincoln out." It was "one of the most thrilling incidents of the entire war," recalled General John B. Gordon, years later.

On 30 March, the rangers mounted their final attack on a railroad depot and derailed a train. Less than two weeks later, the war was over and the rangers were disbanded.

MOSBY'S RANGERS (CONFEDERATE)

The limited military experience of John Singleton Mosby, a lawyer who entered the Confederate Army as a private, did not prepare him for the brilliant two years he served as commander of a Partisan Ranger Battalion in the Army of Northern Virginia, where he became known as the "Gray Ghost." In that capacity, he was the only colonel in that army who reported directly to Robert E. Lee. "Grumble" Jones made Mosby his adjutant, promoting him to Lieutenant. When Fitzhugh Lee, whom Mosby hated, took command of the unit, Mosby left. J.E.B. Stuart wanted Mosby in his cavalry command and made him a scout. It was Mosby who scouted and subsequently led Stuart's famous "ride around" McClellan's army near Richmond in 1862. Later, when McClellan turned his command over to Burnside, Mosby watched the ceremony while hiding in some trees a short distance away. On 30 December 1862, Stuart gave Mosby nine men and authorized him to conduct winter guerrilla activities in Loudoun County.

From this humble beginning, Mosby built a battalion, the 43rd Virginia Cavalry. Over time it fielded more than 2,000 rangers, but never exceeded 300 at any one time. Mosby had definite ideas about how to conduct his unit's operations. Several believed that his ideas were not encumbered by a West Point education, one which focused on Napoleonic tactics. Mosby read voraciously on a variety of subjects. He knew the history of the Scottish Highlanders and the South Carolina Partisans. As a boy, he marveled at the exploits of Francis Marion. Mosby's most special quality was his ability to communicate his vision of ranger operations to his men. He developed unique training and operations techniques that were ahead of his time. Mosby's military philosophy is best summarized in two of his writings: "A small force moving with celerity and threatening many points on a line can neutralize a hundred times its own number" and "The military value of a partisan's work is not measured by the amount of property destroyed, or the number of men killed or captured, but by the number he keeps watching." His aim was "to weaken the armies invading Virginia by harassing their rear." His tactics were based on speed, mobility, and surprise - as one historian put it, "thrust before parry."

Mosby's men carried at least two Colt revolvers, and several even carried extra loaded cylinders. Contrary to popular belief, they did not use rifles or swords. He taught them to shoot with both hands by having them practice shooting at a tree stump while riding at a full gallop, a similar technique to that employed by John Hays of the Texas Rangers. Mosby's Rangers did not wear uniforms when on operations, although most wore a gray shirt or pants, or both. His men had the best equipment and clothing available - all of it taken from the Federal Army. Mosby was the ultimate planner and never acted on impulse. Even though he rarely used his entire command for a single operation, he knew that every day of the war one of his rangers was making life miserable for the Federals somewhere.

FAIRFAX COUNTY RAID

In his early operations, Mosby captured almost twice as many men as he had in his unit "and more than double as many horses." He conducted raids on Federal scouts and patrols. On 8 March 1863, he carried out one of his most daring operations. He had gathered intelligence on the area around Fairfax Court House, VA for several weeks, planning what appeared to be an impossible mission. After gathering his men together, he told them what the mission was. Under the cover of darkness and with a force of 29, Mosby's Rangers rode through several Federal units and arrived at the courthouse, ten miles behind the lines. Taking five rangers with him, Mosby captured a soldier guarding the headquarters of Brigadier General Edwin H. Stoughton and entered the general's house. When a lieutenant came down the stairs, Mosby stuck a pistol in his ribs and told him to lead the rangers to the general. Stoughton was asleep in bed. Mosby walked to the bed and shook the general awake. "General," he said, "did you ever hear of Mosby?" The sleeping Stoughton answered, "Yes, have you caught him?" "He has caught you," Mosby replied. The rangers helped the general and his aide get dressed and quickly left the house. For an hour the rangers searched the town for another person that Mosby expected to find. He was not found, but the rangers rounded up 32 prisoners and 58 horses. The rangers left and returned to the safety of Centerville, skirting several Federal camps on the return trip.

When President Abraham Lincoln heard of the raid he reportedly indicated more concern for the loss of the horses than the General and said, "I can make Brigadier generals, but I can't make a horse."

PSYCHOLOGICAL IMPACT

Mosby's raid into the thick of Federal lines sent a message to Richmond *and* to Washington. The psychological effect was felt in the Federal Army for more than six months. Several reports told of soldiers taking planks from railroad bridges around Washington, to preclude cavalry, especially Mosby's, from sweeping into Washington and taking Lincoln. When Stuart heard of the raid, he promoted Mosby to captain.

Col. John Mosby,(Confederate), Courtesy National Archives.

Fairfax Court House, VA, 1863

In early July, while the battle of Gettysburg raged, Mosby, now a major, accompanied Stuart in his wide-ranging reconnaissance north of the advancing Army of Northern Virginia. Stuart praised the rangers in his report, saying "Mosby was particularly active and efficient. His information was always accurate and reliable." During the next year, Mosby continued to attack and harass the Federal rear, capturing supplies, equipment, horses, and prisoners. He had become a painful thorn in the side of the Federals. Eventually, following an attack on a wagon train near Berryville, Sheridan commissioned a 100-man unit under Richard Blazer to "clean out Mosby's gang."

On 23 September 1864 six of Mosby's Rangers were captured in Front Royal by an element of George A. Custer's command. All six were summarily executed, either shot or hung, without a trial. As ranger William T. Overby was hoisted on a horse, he said, "Mosby'll hang ten of you for every one of us." The Federals hung a placard on Overby that said the same fate awaited all of Mosby's men. After the incident at Front Royal, Mosby (now a colonel) wrote a letter to General Robert E. Lee, telling of his intention "to hang an equal number of Custer's men whenever I capture them." Lee authorized the action. In his writings after the war Custer denied that this unit was his. However, Mosby believed that it was and acted according to his belief.

GREENBACK RAID

Early on the morning of 14 October, Mosby and his rangers attacked and stopped a Baltimore and Ohio passenger train near Kearneysvile. Among the captured items were a satchel and a tin box belonging to two Federal Army paymasters who were aboard the train. The satchel and box were filled with greenback bills, totaling $173,000. Later Mosby wrote a letter to Federal authorities clearing the paymasters of suspicion that they had stolen some of the money.

On 6 November, Mosby gathered 27 prisoners from Custer's unit, and made them draw lots to see who would be executed. Three were hung and three were shot. But not all of them died. Three of the prisoners survived. Five days later, Mosby sent a letter to Sheridan explaining what he had done and why. He concluded by saying that any prisoner he took in the future would be treated well unless "some new act of barbarity" forced him to act otherwise.

Mosby's Rangers continued to attack Federal rear areas for the duration of the war. Many Federal officers, Grant included, believed that Mosby had been responsible for Lincoln's assassination. Although a former ranger was one of the plotters, Mosby had nothing to do with it. But traps were set to capture him when he surrendered his unit. On 21 April 1865 Mosby gathered his command at Fauquier and disbanded the unit rather than surrender.

PART V

POST CIVIL WAR

INTRODUCTION

A few special operations forces were formed during the years between the end of the Civil War and the onset of World War II. Up to the end of the 19th century, the Army fought Indian Wars across the western part of the country. The Navy was beginning to develop steel ships and large fleets, thanks to the writings of Alfred T. Mahan, and knew how influential sea power could be. The frontier was still open and the United States continued to acquire territory.

As the army had done in earlier wars, it turned to the Indians themselves to perform scouting missions against the western plains Indians, taking advantage of intertribal and intratribal antagonisms. Civilian scouts also worked for the army on a contract basis. They were often hunters and trappers who were familiar with the various Indian tribes in a given area. The insignia of the Indian Scouts, crossed arrows, lives on in modern times, as a symbol of the special operations branch of the Army. It was first used by the 1st Special Service Force in World War II and now.

The major foreign wars of the last half of the 19th century in which the United States fought were the Boxer Rebellion in

106

China and the Spanish-American War. The Navy and Marine Corps figured prominently in both, while the Army's involvement was mostly in Cuba. Special operations forces, as defined earlier, were not used during this period. It is important, however, to highlight a military force, known as the Rough Riders, that foreshadowed a recruiting technique that would later be used by the Office of Strategic Services, the Central Intelligence Agency, and the Navajo Code Talkers of the Marine Corps. In the past particular leaders raised or recruited their own forces from a civilian population base or from within the service. What the Rough Riders, and particularly the two leaders of the unit— Leonard Wood and Theodore Roosevelt— did was to recruit portions of the population that had special abilities. They sought people that they believed were best qualified for adventurous active service. As it happened, the recruiting campaign was widely publicized and the unit drew many prominent people. In one aspect, this was a straight-line continuation of what ranger leaders in the past had done. It was also what the OSS, CIA, or Marines would do in the future by recruiting active service personnel, civilians, and even former service people, who had certain skills or placements - whether by specific qualification, business position, or family connection. In another aspect, this set the stage for what is known today as the selection stage for filling special operations forces.

After the turn of the century, in the Philippines, another operation was being planned that is weaved into the fabric of special operations history. A 33-year-old brigadier general named Frederick Funston, who had earned his commission and promotions by combat actions, described an idea he had to General Arthur MacArthur. Funston wanted to lead a patrol, consisting of Filipino loyalists and several American soldiers, into the headquarters of Emilio Aguinaldo, one of the prominent rebel leaders. The "cover story" would be that those Filipinos were rebels. They had taken several VIPs as prisoners and wanted to present the prisoners to Aguinaldo. The group landed on a remote beach and trekked through the jungle for a month. When they reached their destination the plan worked flawlessly. Because of the audacity and the success of the operation, some believe Frederick Funston led the Army's first Long Range Reconnaissance Patrol (LRRP).

During World War I, two events occurred that would have a far reaching impact on modern special operations forces. Both were planning events for behind the lines operations by American forces and were proposed at about the same time.

In September 1918, two young lieutenants, John R. Eddy assigned to the 4th Infantry Division and Edward G. Sewell assigned to the 91st Infantry Division, sent a memorandum to the Assistant Chief of Staff G-3 (Plans and Operations), First Army. They proposed that division-level ranger companies be formed using Indians drawn from the American Expeditionary Force. At the time, about 2,500 Indians were in the war theatre. The lieutenants believed that the rangers could "quietly work through and beyond the lines of the enemy," mapping German dispositions and gathering other useful intelligence. They could also "locate enemy snipers, observation posts, and machine gun positions." Because of their abilities as night-fighters, the rangers could conduct patrols, guide patrols, and serve as advance (that is, long range) reconnaissance parties.

One month later, General John J. Pershing listened to a proposal from his staff aviation officers, Colonel Billy Mitchell and Mitchell's assistant, Major Lewis Brereton. Pershing wanted a plan to attack German troop concentrations that were threatening AEF units. Pershing expected a massive air bombing strategy but Mitchell told him that sufficient bombers would not be available until the following spring. Instead Mitchell proposed air lifting the U.S. 1st Infantry Division, "in one great air armada," flying them behind the lines to Metz, and then dropping the division by parachute. The aviators insisted that the air assets available at the time could keep the Americans supplied. Pershing was skeptical but he authorized Mitchell to continue planning his airborne raid.

Both plans came too late in the war to be implemented. By raising the concepts, the ideas for employing special operations forces and providing an effective means of delivering them to the battlefield were kept alive. In the next world war, both ideas would bear fruit.

INDIAN SCOUTS

On the morning of 25 June 1876, while preparing to "crush" the Sioux at Little Big Horn, one of Lieutenant Colonel (formerly General) George Custer's Indian Scouts warned him that "we'll find enough Sioux to keep us fighting two or three days." Instead, Custer underestimated his enemy's strength and overestimated his own. Had the audacious cavalry commander listened to his trusted Scout, he might have lived to fight another day. But he didn't.

Few elite units in the history of the United States military have stirred the imagination like the Indian Scouts. Wild, deadly, courageous, and fanatically loyal, the Indian Scouts served as reconnaissance troops and guerrilla fighters for the Army in its attempt to subjugate the hostile Indian tribes of the Great Plains and Southwest Territories during the brutal Indian Wars of 1866-1890. In addition to providing an invaluable service in capturing such notable chiefs as Sitting Bull, Crazy Horse, Cochise, and Geronimo, the Indian Scouts also tracked down cattle rustlers and outlaws, patrolled the nation's southern border, served as reservation police, and later led General John "Blackjack" Pershing in his punitive expedition into Mexico in pursuit of the elusive bandit and revolutionary Poncho Villa. The Indian Scouts remained an active Army unit until their deactivation in 1943.

Although Indians had been used as scouts by the military since colonial times, it wasn't until 1866 that a Congressional act, General Order 56, authorized the Army to enlist up to 1,000 Scouts into Federal service. General Samuel R. Curtis had effectively used a 75-man company of Pawnee Scouts to quell Cheyenne and Sioux uprisings in 1864 and, following the Civil War as clashes between settlers migrating west and Indians escalated, the Army reluctantly saw the need to recruit the "hostiles" into their own camp.

RECRUITMENT OF SCOUTS
Enticed by a renewable six-month enlistment, a weighty $13 per month scout pay, military benefits, and by the chance to

exact revenge on their ancient tribal enemies, volunteers for the Indian Scouts came from nearly every Great Plains tribe. Hearty warriors from the Apache, Opat, Navajo, Yagui, Pueblo, Walapais, Yaupais, Mojave, Pima, Maricopa, Arikaras, Crow, Sioux, Cheyenne, Shoshone, Pawnee, Negro-Seminole, and others quickly offered their services.

EQUIPMENT

Outfitted in a standard issue Army blue shirt and overcoat, and armed with a Spencer carbine, Colt pistol, and a tribal weapon of their choice, the rest of the Indian Scouts uniform was as varied as the men. Apache Scouts, who spoke little to no English, distinguished themselves from hostile Apaches by their red headbands and often carried a tribal lance into battle. Other Scouts, such as the Pawnees and Cheyennes, armed themselves with tomahawks.

GENERAL GEORGE CROOK

"Nothing will demoralize the hostiles so much as to know their own people are fighting in the opposite ranks," said General George Crook, a brilliant yet slobbish-looking Indian fighter, who enjoyed great success using the Indian Scouts during his Winter Campaigns from 1872-75. Crook sought out the wildest Apaches he could find and fueled their bitter intratribal hatred of their Apache brothers. During that time, his tenacious Scouts haunted the legendary chief Cochise and shadowed his every move across the unforgiving deserts and rugged mountains of the Southwest into Mexico. Later, during the Apache breakout of 1885, Crook was again put in command of Apache Scouts and ordered to locate and apprehend Geronimo.

Although Crook's Apache Scouts were excellent horsemen, they preferred to travel on foot. The large, well-built Scouts were physically superior and better suited to the hardships of desert life than their white Army counterparts. At times Indian Scouts walked up to 85 miles a day under a searing sun and lived plentifully off the seemingly barren land. The Scouts normally operated 12-24 hours in front of the main body of troops but always maintained communications with the troop commander. With the exception of a few minor revolts, Indian Scouts were loyal to the death. A Scout named "Dutchy," reportedly tracked

Apache Scouts, U.S. Army Photo.

Three surviving Indian Scouts, 1943. (L-R) S. Sgt. Jim, Sgt. Delklay, S. Sgt. Kelsay. Jim & Kelsay were awarded Medal of Honor. DOD Photo.

his father, who, according to reports, had killed a white man. "Dutchy" returned with his father's head in a sack.

Ten of Crook's Indian Scouts, known only as Alchesay, Jim, Elsatsoosu, Kosoha, Chiquito, Machol, Blanquet, Kelsay, Nantaje, and Nannasaddie each earned the Congressional Medal of Honor for "Gallant conduct during campaigns and engagements with Apaches." Four Negro-Seminole Scouts were also awarded the Medal of Honor. Private Adam Paine earned his at Staked Plains, Texas in 1874, while Private Pompey Factor, Sergeant John Ward, and Trumpeter Isaac Payne distinguished themselves in battle at the Pecos River the following year. Earlier, on 8 July 1869, a Pawnee Scout named Coruxtechodish, also known as "Mad Bear," earned the Medal of Honor for his actions at the Republican River.

Today, 130 years after activation, the legacy of the Indian Scouts lives on. In 1942, the 1st Special Service Force, which considered itself a "spiritual descendent" of the Indian Scouts, adopted the arrowhead as the basis of its shoulder patch and the crossed arrows as its branch insignia. Ten years later the Army Special Forces modeled its crossed arrows insignia after that used by the Indian Scouts from 1890 to 1943. The Army later adopted the crossed arrows the branch insignia when it created a distinct Special Operations branch.

"We were recruited from the warriors of many famous nations," said one of the last surviving Scouts in 1946. "In a few years we shall have gone to join our comrades in the great hunting grounds beyond the sunset, for our need here is no more. There we shall always remain very proud of our Indian people and of the United States Army, for we were truly the first Americans and you in the Army are now our warriors. To you who will keep the Army's campfires bright, we extend our hands, and to you, we will our fighting hearts."

THE ROUGH RIDERS

"Oh, but we have had a bully fight!" exclaimed Colonel "Teddy" Roosevelt upon the return of his Rough Riders from Cuba following the United States' victory in the Spanish-American War. "I think the rank and file of this regiment are better than you would find in any other regiment anywhere."

As war fever with Spain swept across the United States in early 1898 over the sinking of the battleship *Maine*, in Havana Harbor, Congress authorized the formation of numerous volunteer units to meet the threat, including the First United States Volunteer Cavalry. Often called "Teddy's Terrors" and "Cavalry Cowpunchers," the unit was more affectionately dubbed "Rough Riders" by an adoring public. Although the colorful unit was in existence for only 133 days, it was to become one of most well-known units in United States military history.

Dr. Leonard Wood, a renowned Apache fighter and winner of the Congressional Medal of Honor, and Theodore Roosevelt, then Assistant Secretary of the Navy, used their considerable influence to gain command of the unit. Wood, a licensed physician and rugged veteran of several bloody campaigns in the Indian Wars was given the rank of colonel, while Roosevelt was posted as a lieutenant colonel.

The unit was to originally draw men from the Arizona, New Mexico, Oklahoma, and Indian Territories, but as soon as word spread, rugged adventurers from across the nation rushed to enlist. So many men wanted to join that Congress quickly raised the authorized size of the unit from 780 to 1,000 men.

The unit attracted men from all walks of life and all professions, including Regular soldiers, Texas Rangers, sheriffs and marshals, IRS agents, cowboys, actors, musicians, miners, hunters, and top Ivy League athletes from Yale, Princeton, Harvard and other colleges. It also drew volunteers from the Apache, Cherokee, Chickasaw, Choctaw, Creek, and Pawnee Tribes. Even Australian, Scottish, and English soldiers of fortune who had campaigned in Egypt, South Africa, and in southern China came to join up, lured by the thought of some "real action." In fact, so many applied that hundreds were turned away.

Some of the more well-known personalities that were accepted into the Rough Riders were Craig Wadsworth, the country's top steeplechase rider; Ben Daniels, marshall of Dodge City; Bob Wren and Bill Larned, the nation's top two tennis players; Dudley Dean, one of Harvard's best quarterbacks; Hamilton Fish, grandson of the Hamilton Fish who had served as Secretary of State under President Ulysses Grant; Frank Knox, who, during World War II, become the Secretary of the Navy; and many more.

Formed as a mounted cavalry unit at Camp Wood in San Antonio, Texas, in February 1898, the unit boasted some of the most expert horsemen and shooters anywhere. Adorned in their own unique uniform, consisting of sombrero-type campaign hats, canvas trousers, flannel shirts, and blue polka dot neckerchiefs, and armed with the finest weapons available, including the Krag-Jorgenson carbine and a long barrel Colt revolver, the units' training consisted mostly of drill, target practice, and long trail rides.

Unfortunately, the Rough Riders never got the chance to prove their cavalry skills. Due to the deplorable logistical situation in Tampa, the disembarkation point for soldiers leaving for Cuba, the Rough Riders had to leave their mounts behind and serve as dismounted cavalry.

After arriving in Cuba aboard the *Yucatan*, the Rough Riders were among the first U.S. troops to land at Daiquiri on 22 June 1898. They received their baptism under fire at Las Guasimas, a small village standing between U.S. troops and Santiago. Despite the oppressive heat and humidity, dense jungles, and ever-present threat of malarial fever, the Rough Riders fared well, losing only eight men with 34 wounded.

But it wasn't until 1 July that the Rough Riders earned their place in military lore. By now Roosevelt was breveted to colonel and put in charge of the regiment as Wood had replaced General Young who had fallen with malaria. The Rough Riders were assigned to support Regular Army troops in the assault of the hills overlooking Santiago.

Atop his horse "Little Texas," and armed with a pistol that had been aboard the battleship *Maine* when she was sunk, Roosevelt first led a spirited charge up Kettle Hill, which was heavily fortified by a series of earthworks and trenches. "If you don't want to go forward, let my men pass!" shouted Roosevelt to officers of the Ninth Cavalry, which the Rough Riders were assigned to support. Dressed in his special order khaki uniform from Brooks Brothers in New York City, the incorrigible commander led the charge on horseback under a hail of enemy fire. Both the Rough Riders and the "Buffalo Soldiers" of the Ninth Cavalry followed. Halfway up the hill Roosevelt encountered heavy barbed wire. He coolly dismounted and continued the assault on foot, inspiring his men to bravery.

Later, after Kettle Hill had been secured, Roosevelt and his Rough Riders were assigned to support Fifth Corps in its assault on San Juan Hill. Again, Roosevelt led his troops on foot. Three days later the hills guarding Santiago were securely in U.S. hands. The Rough Riders emerged as heroes despite suffering 490 casualties during the campaign. After arriving home on 15 August, Roosevelt was recommended for the Medal of Honor and became a national hero. Shortly thereafter he was elected

Theodore Roosevelt & Rough Riders, 1898. U.S. Army Photo

Governor of New York, and later became VicePresident under William McKinley. Following McKinley's assassination in 1901, Roosevelt became the twenty-sixth and youngest President of the United States.

Although the formation and training of the Rough Riders hardly qualifies it as an elite unit, especially since the unit was composed of mostly non-military volunteers, the overall quality of its men, both physically and mentally, must be considered as exceptional for the times as was the recruiting campaign, which was designed to get and keep the best and toughest men available.

PART VI

WORLD WAR II

INTRODUCTION

The Second World War witnessed the most dramatic change in the history of warfare. Technological advances in aircraft, ships, tanks, communications, and weaponry turned the art of war into a deadly science. Massive armies battled across three continents, while modern navies and air forces fought savage battles for control of the seas and the skies. Gone were the days when opposing armies faced each other on remote battlefields removed from civilians. It was total war, where non-combatants became inexorably intertwined into the bloody equation. Entire populations were caught in the middle of, and participated in, a brutal ideological and expansionist conflict. Factories, transportation hubs, power plants, communications centers, and even the hearts and minds of civilians all became prime targets.

Although the U.S. military favored conventional warfare, relying on mass and sheer firepower, it was not always feasible or practical. Conventional warfare could not easily be waged in the jungles of Burma, deep in occupied Europe, or on the far flung islands of the Pacific Ocean. To adapt to the myriad of land, sea, and air operations facing them, progressive military leaders broke tradition and created smaller, more specialized units to conduct a new brand of unconventional warfare.

The advent of the parachute, submarine, sophisticated communications equipment, and smaller, more powerful weapons were central to the success of the World War II elite units. It was now possible to insert and supply troops and agents deep behind enemy lines where they could organize internal resistance groups, strike at selected targets, and provide conventional commands with timely intelligence that would otherwise be nearly impossible to get.

At the heart of these elite units was a separate breed of soldier, airman, sailor, or marine. Most were volunteers who preferred the danger and excitement of special operations over the often routine duties of conventional soldiering. Physically and mentally above average, the men comprising World War II elite units were equipped with the latest weaponry and received the most extensive and sophisticated training in the history of the U.S. military.

Amphibious units, including the Alamo Scouts, Navy Scouts & Raiders, Underwater Demolition Teams, and Alaska Scouts, to name a few, landed on enemy shores before conventional invasion forces and performed beach and ground reconnaissance, obstacle demolition, intelligence gathering, and a host of other related missions.

In the skies, Air Commandos and Carpetbaggers inserted and resupplied agents and troops into hostile territory. When not conducting clandestine drops, the units performed numerous operations, including conventional bombing, air rescue, and propaganda warfare. Ground and airborne units, such as the Marine Raiders, Army Rangers, Merrill's Marauders, and the 1st Special Service Force, were created to strike hard and fast at the enemy's vulnerable points, while the OSS Jedburghs, Operational Groups, and Detachment 101 organized and instructed partisans and guerrillas on how to sabotage, harass, and resist the enemy in occupied territories. OSS agents, both men and women, performed some of the most dangerous and important work of the war deep in occupied territory. Many were civilians who were recruited for their particular skills and abilities.

World War II marked the beginning of modern warfare and witnessed the birth of better trained and dedicated elite special operations forces. The rise of these units, however, was not entirely by design. The military was rife with interservice rivalry which caused oversecrecy and duplication of effort, especially in the intelligence field. Military leaders often hesitated or refused to share information with one another. This prompted many branches to form their own elite units to collect the information they needed, sometimes information that was readily available from other sources. In some cases, both the Army and Navy had similar types of units, who were not aware of the other's existence, operating in the same general area gathering the same information. This was clearly a waste of manpower and resources, but it did produce a wider base of experienced personnel and a wellspring of knowledge for military planners to draw from during future conflicts.

ALASKA SCOUTS

In the fall of 1941, Colonel Lawrence V. Castner, an intelligence officer with the Alaska Defense Command, was convinced that war with Japan was imminent. He feared that the Alaska Territory, which was largely undefended, was ripe for the taking. Castner urged General Simon Buckner, commander of the Alaska Defense Command, to authorize the formation of an independent intelligence unit to locate and report on Japanese incursions, provide pre-invasion reconnaissance, and explore unknown parts of the Aleutian Islands and the coastal wilderness of Alaska. Buckner agreed and the Alaska Scouts were born.

Castner's primary concern was the security of the Aleutian Area. The Aleutians, consisting of a chain of some 150 rugged and foggy Alaskan islands, extend 1,200 miles southwest and northwest of the Alaskan Peninsula separating the Bering Sea from the Pacific Ocean. Castner, a graduate of West Point, had a high reputation to uphold, but he was equal to the task. His father had formed the Philippine Scouts at the turn of the century and was the first white man to explore vast areas of Alaska's interior between Cook Inlet and the Yukon River.

Officially formed as the Alaskan Defense Command Scout Detachment (Provisional), the unit was more commonly called "Alaska Scouts." To Castner's great displeasure, his unit soon earned the dubious nickname "Castner's Cutthroats." Rivaled only by Teddy Roosevelt's "Rough Riders" of the Spanish-American War, Castner's Cutthroats, which numbered only 68 at peak strength, was perhaps the most rugged, colorful, and distinct unit ever assembled. Men nicknamed "Bad Whiskey Red, Indian Joe, Waterbucket Ben, and Aleut Pete," only added to the unit's reputation.

At the nucleus of the Alaska Scouts were four hand-picked Regular Army volunteers who were familiar with the territory. Three came from the western states and one from Tennessee. Castner so trusted the judgment and abilities of these men that he allowed them to screen all newcomers to the unit. As the unit increased in size, adventurous outdoorsmen, dog team drivers, Aleuts, Indians, prospectors, trappers, big-game guides, and Eskimos from throughout the territory volunteered. All of them were expert survivalists who knew the country well. They could find food and shelter where it appeared impossible, and endure the blizzards, sleet, snow and ice, williwaws, fog, mosquitoes, sun, and humidity of an unforgiving arctic wilderness.

After a brief stay at Fort Richardson, the Scouts set up a training camp by a nearby river. The site had been an old "Fish Camp" and offered few luxuries. Clothed in a variety of uniforms ranging from buckskin to waterproof canvas to animal fur, the Alaska Scouts spent hours learning the finer points of scouting and patrolling, map reading, voice and Morse Code radio operation, hand-to-hand combat, marksmanship, and commando tactics. The lion's share of their training was spent on learning how to survive.

Formed to operate in three-to-five-man teams, the scouts trained to infiltrate by rubber boat, submarine, PBY flying boat, *bidarkas* (native boats), and various commercial craft. The toughened and fiercely individualistic Scouts also learned to rely on each other. Eskimo Scouts taught their fellow scouts how to survive in arctic conditions. They showed them how to build shelters, boats, fishing nets, snares, and how to construct snowshoes from available materials. Other Scouts taught which woods to burn, how to cross dangerous lakes and rivers, and to survive in the woodlands.

The Scouts' physical stamina was legendary. One Scout walked over 90 miles of frozen tundra in three days. As a testament to their survival skills, two Scouts lived off the land for ten months while stranded on St. Matthews Island, in the icy Bering Sea. The men not only staved off polar bear attacks and endured the tortuous elements, but completed their reconnaissance mission.

Early in the Aleutian campaign the Alaska Scouts conducted numerous patrols and performed a variety of duties. In June 1942 two Scouts observed and reported on the Japanese bombing of Dutch Harbor. Later, the Scouts helped evacuate and resettle native Aleuts from the Aleutian and Pribilof islands. They also performed reconnaissance missions, set up watch

Alaska Scouts on Attu with captured Japanese flag. U.S. Army Photo.

stations, and monitored Japanese activity on the western islands.

On 27 August 1942, the first of two teams of Scouts landed
by rubber boat on Adak Island. The following night the second
team landed. Together the teams combed the island. When they
discovered that the island was unoccupied, they signaled the
invasion force to land. The Scouts performed a similar mission
on Amchitka Island. On 12 January 1943, a detachment of men
went ashore despite 100 mile per hour winds and paved the way
for the landing of 2,100 troops and engineers.

The Scouts spent the next few months patrolling the islands
east of Attu, the Allies' next target in their advance through the
Japanese-held Aleutians. On 11 May 1943, the Scouts and a
company of men from the 17th Infantry Regiment landed on
Attu. They hit the shores at Red Beach in Holtz Bay and
protected the Northern Force, while another detachment of
Scouts, attached to the Southern Force, landed at Massacre Bay.
After fighting with and providing intelligence for the 7th Division throughout the action, the Scouts remained on the island
and performed additional reconnaissance and map-making duties. Later in mid-1943, the Alaska Scouts participated in the
invasion of Kiska. The Japanese, however, had abandoned the
island hours before the invasion.

By November 1944, with the Aleutian Campaign all but concluded, there was little need for the Alaska Scouts to continue their reconnaissance and intelligence operations. The unit was redesignated the 1st Combat Intelligence Platoon and spent the remainder of the war conducting search and rescue operations, mapping previously unchartered territory, and testing experimental equipment for cold weather use.

Although no record exists as to how many missions the Alaska Scouts performed between December 1941 and November 1944, only one man was killed in action, that occurring on Attu. Their commander gave the best testament to the Scouts' unique skills, physical toughness, and indomitable spirit under hellish conditions; "They have one thing in common," exclaimed Castner, "they're tough!"

The platoon remained an active Army unit until 1947, when it became part of the Alaska National Guard. It is still active today.

MARINE RAIDERS

Ten months before the Japanese attack on Pearl Harbor, the United States Marine Corps was experimenting with an elite amphibious commando force modeled after British commando units. Its purpose was to land on enemy beaches "generally thought inaccessible," launch raids with "surprise and high speed," and conduct "guerrilla operations for protracted periods behind enemy lines." The Marine Corps successfully tested the concept in early 1941 at a fleet landing exercise. Three Provisional Rubber Boat Companies were deployed for the exercise and had performed well enough to prompt Marine planners to continue the program.

On 6 January 1942, the 1st Marine Raider Battalion was formed at Quantico, Virginia under the command of Lieutenant Colonel Merritt A. "Red Mike" Edson. Within a month a second Battalion was activated under Lieutenant Colonel Evans F. Carlson near Camp Elliott, California, with Major James Roosevelt, the son of the President as his second-in-command. The now-famous battle cry of Carlson's Raiders was "Gung Ho," which is a Chinese phrase for "work together." In the 1st and 2nd Raider Battalions, the United States military had its first modern commandos. By the end of October 1942, two additional battalions of Marine Raiders were available for service in the Pacific.

In addition to basic Marine infantry skills, the Raiders received extensive training in the use of rubber boats. The boats, developed in the 1930's, became one of the primary tools of most commando-type units of World War II, both in the Pacific and in Europe. With the exception of specialized amphibious training, the Raiders were basically a highly-trained infantry battalion, but their reliance on speed, mobility, and shock effect, set them apart from regular Marine units. After nearly six months of advanced training, the first Marine Raiders were ready for action.

TULAGI

Nicknamed "Edson's Raiders," the 1st Battalion got its feet wet on 7 August 1942, landing on Tulagi, a tiny island 20 miles north of Guadalcanal. The landing beach was not defended and the Raiders quickly secured the beach and moved inland to wait for the main Marine landing force. After repelling four minor attacks that evening, the Raiders, along with men from the 2nd Battalion of the 5th Marines, secured the island the next day.

MAKIN ISLAND

As Edson's Raiders waited for action, Carlson's Raiders were busy in the Gilberts, some 1,000 miles northeast of Guadalcanal. On 17-18 August, two companies of the 2nd Battalion raided Makin Island in an effort to gather intelligence and divert enemy reinforcements from reaching Guadalcanal. Leaving Pearl Harbor on 8 August, aboard the submarines *Nautilus* and *Argonaut*, the Raiders reached the atoll on 16 August. Early the next morning, the Raiders boarded several rubber boats, and, despite battling a heavy surf and encountering mechanical problems with the boats' motors, most of the Raiders landed successfully. One boat containing nine men drifted away from the main body.

Over the next two days, Carlson's Raiders, one of whom was posthumously awarded the Medal of Honor, engaged in bitter fighting, killing some 350 well-entrenched Japanese, capturing the Government House, and destroying a seaplane base. But the cost was high. The Raiders, under constant counterattack and sustained sniper fire, lost 30 men killed. The nine men whose boat had drifted apart from the landing force had been captured and beheaded. Although the raid diverted some reinforcements from Guadalcanal, it also resulted in the Japanese fortifying a number of unoccupied islands that later had to be taken by American troops at a high price. It wasn't until 23 November 1943 that Makin Island was finally secured.

GUADALCANAL

Back at Guadalcanal, Edson's Raiders were preparing for their first real test. On 8 September, a combined force of Raiders and men from the 1st Marine Parachute Battalion conducted an amphibious landing behind enemy lines near Tasimboko. After raiding an abandoned enemy camp at Taivu, the Raiders learned that a 4,000-man Japanese force, commanded by Major General Kiyotake Kawaguchi, was planning to attack Henderson Field, some thirty miles to the west.

Edson and his force were immediately sent to shore up the field's defenses. By 13 September they were dug in on a ridge south of the airfield. That evening, the Japanese, who outnumbered the Raiders and Paramarines by two-to-one, mounted several frenzied attacks. In more than 10 hours of hand-to-hand combat, the Raiders, along with reinforcements from the 2nd Marines of the 5th Marines, beat back more than a dozen attacks. The next day, the beaten and broken Japanese force withdrew with over 1,000 dead.

The ridge, known as Bloody Ridge due to the high number killed and wounded, was renamed Edson's Ridge, by the Raiders in honor of their commander, who, during the ghastly day of fighting, had earned the Medal of Honor for extreme heroism. During the battle Edson ran over the battlefield and took command of the troops wherever the hottest action was. He even called in artillery fire on his own position. Another Raider, Major Kenneth D. Bailey, commander of C Company, was also awarded the Medal of Honor for his part in the battle. Despite suffering a terrible head wound and refusing to be evacuated, Bailey led his company in 10 hours of fierce hand-to-hand combat which claimed his life.

Meanwhile, on 20 September as the 1st and 2nd Raider Battalions rested, the 3rd Raider Battalion was formed in American Samoa, under Lieutenant Colonel Harry "The Horse" Liversedge. On 23 October, the 4th Raider Battalion was organized at Camp Linda Vista, California, under Major Roosevelt. Before the newly-formed battalions could get into the fray, Carlson's Raiders were back in action.

Continuing operations on Guadalcanal, Carlson's Raiders landed at Aola, on the northeast coast of the island and conducted a series of patrols and raids known as the "Thirty Days Behind The Lines." Beginning on 4 November, the 1st Battalion spent a month behind enemy lines patrolling, collecting information, raiding outposts, and setting up ambushes. During the extended patrol, Carlson's Raiders engaged the enemy in six separate actions and killed 175 Japanese troops, while losing only six men.

With the exception of an unopposed landing by the 3rd Raider Battalion on Pavuvu in the Russell Islands, on 21 February 1943, the Marine Raider Battalions saw little action until June 1943. The landing by the 3rd Raiders supported an Army landing on nearby Banika Island. In the interim, the 1st Marine Raider Regiment, commanded by Liversedge, was organized on 15 March, on Espiritu Santo, in the New Hebrides. Consisting of the four existing Raider Battalions, the 1st Raider Regiment was part of the New Georgia Attack Force, or Northern Landing Group, which eventually consisted of the 1st Raider Battalion and Army units.

NEW GEORGIA

As the 1st Raider Regiment was preparing for operations on New Georgia, the 4th Raider Battalion, now commanded by Lieutenant Colonel Michael S. Currin, got an early start. Landing at Segi Point, on 21 June 1943, two companies of Raiders prevented enemy occupation of the eastern part of the island. For the next 11 days, the Raiders slogged through hellish terrain and heavy downpours, fending off Japanese patrols. On 1 July the Raiders defeated the enemy in bitter fighting at Tetemara, which cleared the way to Viru Harbor, a key anchorage.

Meanwhile, on 30 June, the rest of 4th battalion landed at Oloana Bay on adjoining Vangunu Island, and established a beachhead for the Army landing force. By evening, the Raiders had repulsed several attacks and overrun the main enemy positions. The next day, the Raiders sunk three enemy supply barges. Following a couple weeks on patrol, the unit rejoined the battalion and prepared for the main assault along the north coast of New Georgia.

On 5 July 1943, the 1st Raider Regiment conducted an unopposed landing at Rice Anchorage on the north coast of New Georgia. The Raiders quickly moved southwest to block possible Japanese reinforcements from the south and west. Four days later they engaged the enemy at Enogai. After a day of heavy fighting, where 300 Japanese and 47 Raiders were killed, the regiment was augmented by the 4th Raider Battalion. The combined force then advanced toward Bairoko, a heavily-defended village guarding the approaches to Bairoko Harbor. On 24 August, after nearly a month and a half of heavy fighting and patrol action by the Raiders and Army units, the Japanese abandoned the village.

BOUGANVILLE

Four days later the 1st Raider Regiment left New Georgia and was effectively finished. Edson's 1st Battalion had lost 74 killed and 139 wounded, while Currin's 4th Battalion had suffered 54 killed and nearly 140 wounded or too sick for duty. Despite the losses incurred by the 1st and 4th Raider Battalions, two battalions of Raiders continued to fight in the Pacific. On 12 September the 2nd and 3rd Raider Battalions were placed under the control of the newly-formed 2nd Raider Regiment (Provisional). The regiment, under the command of Lieutenant Colonel Alan Shapley, had been created to coordinate Raider operations on Bouganville, the largest of the Solomon Islands. Bouganville was the site of several enemy airfields from which the Japanese could protect Rabaul, the principal Japanese stronghold in the Bismarck Archipelago and a major roadblock to General Douglas MacArthur's return to the Philippines.

On 1 November, the Regiment, along with Army and other Marine units, landed on Bouganville, west of Cape Torokina on Empress Agusta Bay. The 2nd Battalion, now commanded by Lieutenant Colonel Joseph P. McCaffrey, and the 3rd Battalion, under Lieutenant Colonel Fred D. Beans, spent the rest of the year defending the Cape Torokina area, conducting patrols, and consolidating the Northern Solomons.

On 11 January 1944, the Raiders left the island. With the final outcome of Bouganville in little doubt, Raider operations were turned over to larger Army and Marine units. By February, all Marine Raider units were disbanded.

The 2nd Raider Regiment was disbanded on 26 January 1944. On 31 January, the 2nd and 3rd Raider Battalions fell to a similar fate. On 1 February, the 1st Raider Regiment, along with the 1st and 4th Raider Battalions were all officially disbanded. For their work in the Solomons, Edson's and Carlson's Raiders were awarded the Presidential Unit Citation. Former Raiders from all the units were then reorganized into elements of the 4th Marines.

MARINE FORCE RECON

A year before the United States was thrust into World War II, the Marine Corps had already laid the groundwork for the formation of a small, highly-trained unit to land on enemy territory well ahead of conventional Marine landing forces and scout out enemy positions. Although the Marines had formed motorized Division Scout Companies in March 1941, the genesis of Force Recon sprang from the early efforts of Major General H.M. Smith in January 1942.

Smith called for the formation of an elite reconnaissance squad to work in conjunction with the Army, but the plan never materialized. Instead, a small "Observation Group" consisting of two officers and 20 men from various intelligence and infantry regiments, was formed at Quantico, Virginia, and attached to the 1st Marine Division. In January 1943, the unit expanded to six officers and 92 enlisted men and was redesignated the Marine Amphibious Reconnaissance Company. In April 1944 it became the Marine Amphibious Reconnaissance Battalion.

When the Navy formed the Amphibious Scouts and Raiders School at Fort Pierce, Florida, in August 1942, Force Recon personnel attended the training course and learned rubber boat handling, scouting, patrolling, raiding, demolitions, survival, and hydrographic and ground reconnaissance techniques. After training the men were assigned to four-man reconnaissance teams.

The first credited Force Recon mission was a month-long photo reconnaissance of Tarawa, Kuma, Buta Ritari, Makin, and Apamama Islands from mid-September to mid-October 1943. The operation was conducted by only one officer operating aboard the submarine *Nautilus*. The first beach/ground reconnaissance was performed on Apamama on 21 November 1943 by the Amphibious Reconnaissance Company. Operating from rubber boats, Force Recon teams, consisting of 68 men, landed on the island and gathered information on the Japanese forces there. Five days later elements of the 6th Marines landed on the island.

The unit performed much the same type of work as other reconnaissance units of the period. It conducted a variety of missions including beach marking, obstacle demolition, pre-invasion and post-invasion reconnaissance, and "mopping up" duties. The battalion also joined regular Marine combat forces ashore and fought as infantry. Their primary means of delivery was rubber boats, submarine, and flying boat. In over 180 missions the Amphibious Recon Battalions provided hydrographic and ground reconnaissance on Saipan, Tinian, Iwo Jima, and on numerous islands throughout the Pacific.

THE KOREAN WAR

At the outbreak of war in Korea, only the Reconnaissance Company, 1st Marine Division, was available for service. During the first year of the war the recon company operated in nine-man boat teams and conducted motorized reconnaissance missions. It also assisted UDT teams in behind the lines sabotage missions along the east coast of Korea. Over the next two years the company performed a myriad of duties, including amphibious and helicopter assaults, scouting and patrolling, rear and flank security, and various sniping missions.

After the war, Force Recon members expanded their capabilities and began training and working with UDTs and different methods of infiltration and extraction. In 1957 the First Force Reconnaissance Company was formed, and in 1959, the Second Force Reconnaissance Company was created. It was during that period that Major (later Lieutenant General) Bernard Trainor spent a year with the British Royal Marine Commandos learning commando reconnaissance techniques. Trainor took what he learned from the British and applied it to Marine Force Recon concepts. This included training in airborne operations, enhanced amphibious and air operations, and attendance at the Army Ranger School.

THE VIET NAM WAR

Although Force Recon units had been successful during World War II and Korea, it was in Viet Nam that they were finally recognized for their special capabilities. Force Recon units earned a reputation as one of the most deadly units of the war. From 1966 to 1971, Marine Force Recon, operating under the code name "Sting Ray," performed countless reconnaissance missions deep behind enemy lines near the Laotian, Cambodian, and North Vietnamese borders. Nicknamed "Green Ghosts" by the enemy, Force Recon teams called in devastating artillery fire on Vietcong and North Vietnamese Army positions. Using laser range finders and other high-tech equipment, Sting Ray teams inflicted "casualties on that enemy, whenever and wherever he was encountered."

Early in the war recon units were formed into 24-man teams and were used as raiding and screening units, but the larger teams were more easily detected and proved ineffective. The teams then reverted to their original World War II size, usually containing no more than 12 men. Most operated in five-to-seven man teams and were inserted into enemy territory by helicopter and exfiltrated in the same way. Each team carried two radios and was supported by two artillery pieces, and when necessary, by Marine aircraft and naval gun fire.

Each reconnaissance battalion also contained a 31-man scout-sniper platoon. One man, Carlos Hathcock, recorded 93 confirmed kills during the war. Many of the men trained at the MACV Recondo School in Nha Trang under the guidance of Army Special Forces.

Force Recon was the first and only Marine unit to ever conduct an airborne jump. In June 1966, during Operation KANSAS, a small Force Recon team parachuted in near Chu Lai. By November 1969, two additional Force Recon teams had performed a jump reconnaissance in Viet Nam.

POST VIET NAM

After the withdrawal of U.S. forces from Viet Nam in 1973, Force Recon was downsized, but it continued to perform important missions, including the evacuation of U.S. citizens from Cyprus and Lebanon in 1974, and from Cambodia and Viet Nam the following year. In 1983 a recon platoon was killed in the suicide truck-bombing in Beirut. Partly as a result of that terrorist act, Force Recon assumed a special operations role in 1985. Unlike other services, which had Delta Force, SEALs, and special air units to wage low-intensity warfare and to conduct special operations, the Marines were left out in the cold. But with its new role, Force Recon broadened its capabilities to include raids, hostage recovery, and classified amphibious operations in conjunction with the Navy. In 1988 surveillance-reconnaissance-intelligence groups were formed (SIRG) which utilized the latest electronic technology and intelligence gathering methods.

That same year Force Recon elements and Navy SEAL teams successfully raided oil platforms during the Tanker War in the Persian Gulf. Two years later Force Recon Companies were stationed along the Kuwait border during Operation DESERT SHIELD and performed fixed and mobile border surveillance. In preparation for the ground war phase, recon teams performed advance reconnaissance of the invasion routes. During Operation DESERT STORM, recon units called in artillery and air strikes on Iraqi armored divisions and were among the first units to enter Kuwait City after its liberation.

The new role also called for a higher degree of training. As a prerequisite, recon volunteers must be in excellent physical condition and pass an indoctrination course. They must also be able to complete amphibious reconnaissance, airborne, and diving training. This is in addition to specialized courses in sniping, scouting and patrolling, hostage rescue, weapons, survival, navigation, small unit tactics, and a host of other skills.

True to their original concept, Force Recon elements have served as the eyes and ears of the Marine Corps in the Pacific, Korea, Viet Nam, the Persian Gulf, and countless other areas. The evolution from simple scouting and patrolling to high-tech reconnaissance and joint covert operations has spanned over 50 years.

DOOLITTLE'S RAIDERS

During the dark days of April 1942, Japan's military juggernaut appeared invincible. While remnants of the U.S. Pacific Fleet licked its wounds in the months following Pearl Harbor, Imperial forces steamrolled through much of Southeast Asia, conquering Burma, Thailand, Malaya, and French Indochina in quick succession. In the Central and South Pacific, the situation wasn't any better. American outposts at Wake Island and Guam were overrun, followed by Japanese occupation of the Gilbert Islands. In the Southwest Pacific, the Japanese seized the Philippines, the Celebes, Borneo, the Bismarck Islands, and had footholds in the Solomons and New Guinea. From Java east to the Solomons, the enemy controlled a 3,000-mile front which directly threatened the security of Australia. But on 18 April 1942, "Doolittle's Raiders" shattered the myth of Japanese invincibility.

In late February 1942, 45 year-old Lieutenant Colonel James H. Doolittle was selected to lead the first strategic bombing raid on the Japanese home islands. Doolittle had earned a reputation during the 1920's and 30's as one of the world's top pilots, setting numerous speed and altitude records. The brilliant Doolittle, who held a doctorate degree in aeronautical engineering from the Massachusetts Institute of Technology, was the first pilot to fly across the continental United States in under 12 hours and the first Army pilot to fly by instruments. The meticulous leader was originally selected to study the feasibility of the project and to train pilots for the joint Army-Navy operation, which would be launched from the *Hornet*, the Navy's newest aircraft carrier. But Doolittle was determined not to be left out of the action. After several attempts, he finally convinced General Henry H. "Hap" Arnold, commander of the Army Air Corps, that he was the only man who could lead the mission. Arnold reluctantly agreed.

But first, Doolittle needed a select group of men, pilots, navigators, crew chiefs, radiomen, and gunners. One hundred and forty men from the 17th Bombardment Group stationed in Oregon, volunteered for the mission. Each man was handpicked for his bravery, experience, and skill. Beginning on 1 March the volunteers began training in secrecy at Eglin Field, near Pensacola, Florida. When the training was completed Doolittle retained only 80 of the best men for the mission.

Since the Army crews had never taken off from an aircraft carrier, nor had a B-25 ever been launched from one, the centerpiece of the special training was learning how to take off and land on short runways of only 700 to 750 feet with maximum loads. The pilots and crews also practiced low-level bombing with dummy and live bombs. Flight crews trained daily and learned how to conserve fuel and adjust their engines for maximum efficiency. Crews also cross-trained and learned the jobs of their fellow crewmembers. Since the planes would be launched over 650 miles from Tokyo, each plane had to be outfitted with extra fuel tanks. Some guns, armor, and other non-essential equipment was removed to reduce weight. The operation was so secret that even the radios were removed to prevent accidental disclosure. Remarkably, it wasn't until the crews were aboard the *Hornet* that Doolittle told them what their target was.

Although the Raiders were highly-trained, well-prepared, and had the best equipment available, many planners thought that the raid was suicidal. Despite the negative attitude surrounding the mission Doolittle and his men were determined to succeed.

Because of an encounter with a Japanese fishing boat the flight was launched prematurely by the Navy. At 8:17am on 18 April, Doolittle and his Raiders, consisting of 16 B-25 Mitchell bombers, took off from the *Hornet*. Doolittle took off first. Flying as low as 75 feet above the ocean to avoid enemy radar, the Raiders sped toward the Japanese heartland. Four hours later, Doolittle boldly flew over Tokyo at tree-top level amidst heavy anti-aircraft fire. Once over the target, Doolittle climbed to 1,000 feet and released four 500-pound incendiary bombs, which served as guiding beacons to his other Raiders. Within hours, all 16 planes had delivered their payloads on industrial centers in Tokyo, Yokohama, Kobe, Nagoya, and on the naval base at Yokosuka.

As quickly as the Raiders appeared, they were gone. The plan was for the Raiders to land at air bases near Chuchow, in China. But they weren't so fortunate. Their fuel exhausted from the long flight, eight crews parachuted into eastern China, while two made it deeper into the heart of the country before bailing out. Five crews crash landed behind enemy lines near Hang-chow. Of the 25 men who crashed-landed, three were killed. One crew, which experienced mechanical problems, landed in Siberia rather than bail out over the China Sea. Despite landing in "Allied" territory, the crew was detained by the Russians for over a year before they escaped across the border into Iran.

With the assistance of friendly Chinese troops and civilians, most of Doolittle's Raiders returned safely to Allied lines. Eight Raiders were captured and taken to Nanking, where they were severely beaten and tortured. Of the eight, three were executed, two by firing squad and one was beheaded. Another later died of sickness. The others spent the rest of the war in a prisoner-of-war camp.

Facing certain death if caught helping the American flyers, numerous brave Chinese hid the men from Japanese patrols, provided food and medical care, and transported them safely back to friendly lines. But they paid a high price for their friendship. Infuriated and embarrassed by the raid, the Japanese swiftly retaliated. In a savage three-month reign of terror in eastern China, Japanese soldiers razed countless villages and towns and slaughtered nearly 250,000 civilians.

Although the raid did not cause major damage, it created a firestorm within the Japanese military. The sacred Japanese homeland had been penetrated by foreign invaders causing a

B-25s taking off from the Hornet for Japan raid. April 1942. U.S. Navy Photo.

need for more military units to protect Japan itself. For the first time the Japanese doubted whether they could win the war. The raid also prompted Japanese naval planners to take a fateful military gamble. Fearful of more carrier raids on mainland Japan, Admiral Isoruku Yamamoto devised a plan to engage and annihilate the U.S. Navy at Midway. Instead of anihalation of the U.S. fleet, his own force was effectively destroyed during the battle.

In the United States, morale soared. Doolittle's Raiders captured the imagination of the entire country and restored hope of an Allied victory. The raid was especially uplifting because it followed on the heels of the humiliating surrender of American forces on Bataan and Corrigedor. For his part in the raid Doolittle was promoted to brigadier general, skipping the rank of colonel, and awarded the Congressional Medal of Honor by President Franklin Roosevelt. The rest of his Raiders were awarded the Distinguished Flying Cross.

PSYCHOLOGICAL OPERATIONS & CIVIL AFFAIRS UNITS

Unlike other units in this book, which either directly faced the enemy in combat or operated behind enemy lines in a clandestine role, Psychological Operations (PsyOps) and Civil Affairs (CA) units, by the sheer expertise of their troops and unique missions deserve recognition among America's elite warriors. Since most PsyOps and CA units operated at the detachment, battalion, and brigade levels, this narrative addresses the respective organizations as a whole.

The Intelligence section of the War Department General Staff created the Psychological Warfare Branch on 28 February 1942. On 4 January 1943, the Psychological Warfare Group was established and attached to the Office of Strategic Services (OSS). Under the overall direction of the OSS commander Major General William "Wild Bill" Donovan, the Psychological Warfare Group employed military and foreign affairs experts, scholars, psychologists, expatriates, and others to devise ways to weaken enemy morale and induce desertions. Nine months later, the Propaganda Department was created.

Over the next two years, PsyOps units conducted an active and subtle psychological war against Axis forces throughout Europe and Asia. To destroy morale, PsyOps units struck at the heart of the common soldier. Nothing was sacred. They appealed to the lonely, hungry, and cold enemy troops with promises of hot food and good treatment. On the other hand, PsyOps messages preyed upon their doubts, implying that their wives were being unfaithful and that the only way they could keep their loved ones was to bring a quick end to the war and to return home.

Early PsyOps strategies were crude compared to today's methods, but effective nonetheless. In a concerted effort aimed at the Germans, special air units, such as the Eighth Air Force's 406th Night Leaflet Squadron and others, dropped millions of propaganda leaflets, including the "Feldpost," the first German language newspaper. PsyOps radio broadcasters bombarded the airwaves with disinformation and half-truths and sowed the seeds of doubt in the minds of their enemies. Meanwhile, PsyOps teams roved the front lines in vans mounted with loudspeakers and urged enemy troops to surrender. Although the PsyOps units of World War II achieved mixed results against fanatical opposition, it undoubtedly saved the lives of countless American troops by eroding the enemy's will to fight.

In 1950, Brigadier General Robert A. McClure, the former head of the Psychological Warfare Section of the Supreme Headquarters in Europe during World War II, was named chief of Psychological Warfare. Two years later, on 10 April, a permanent Psychological Warfare Center was established at Fort Bragg, North Carolina, and became the home of the newly-formed U.S. Army Special Forces.

During the Korean and Viet Nam wars, PsyOps achieved mixed results. But in the 1980's the U.S. military leadership placed greater emphasis on PsyOps. During Operation JUST CAUSE in 1989, highly-trained PsyOps units parachuted into Panama with the invasion troops and immediately set up loudspeakers and took control of Panamanian television and radio stations. For days they urged Panamanian Defense Force soldiers to "cease hostilities" and for civilians to cooperate with U.S. forces. The PsyOps efforts were successful in minimizing the bloodshed. "We had a loudspeaker mounted on a tank," said a former member of the 4th PsyOps Group. "On Christmas morning we set up outside the building where we suspected that Noriega was hiding, and blasted rock music all day long. We knew that he hated rock n' roll, so to get under his skin we kept playing 'I can't get no satisfaction' by the Rolling Stones. We played it over and over again—real loud!"

But it was during Operation DESERT STORM that PsyOps enjoyed its finest hour. Working with coalition Arab experts, the 4th PsyOps designed numerous leaflets targeting specific Iraqi units. The leaflets, which were dropped by C-130 Talon aircraft, appealed to the Iraqi soldiers' sense of brotherhood with fellow Arabs fighting on the side of the Coalition Force. They urged the haggard Iraqi soldiers to "walk east towards Mecca" and to join their brothers in peace. Several leaflets instructed Iraqi soldiers how to surrender while others warned of the next days' air strikes. All this contributed much to the quick victory in the Gulf. According to one survey, 70 percent of Iraqi POWs reported that the leaflets had a direct impact on their decision to surrender.

CIVIL AFFAIRS

Early in World War II, the War Department General Staff realized that rebuilding the war-torn nation of a defeated enemy would be essential to maintaining a lasting peace. In May 1942, it established the first Military Government (Civil Affairs) school at the University of Virginia, to train soldiers to do just that. Other universities followed suit and began training soldiers as engineers, archivists, judges, public safety experts, teachers, and finance specialists in preparation for the duties of occupation. In March 1943, the War Department formally established a separate Civil Affairs branch to "Seal the Victory."

During the war, Military Government teams normally arrived with the occupation forces and immediately set about rebuilding the political and economic infrastructure of the occupied country. In Italy, Germany and Japan, Military Government teams assisted in denazification and demilitarization and restored civil administrative and judicial systems. The teams oversaw the construction of power plants and provided refugees with much needed food, shelter, and medical assistance. Military Government teams also were sent to North Africa, New Guinea, Okinawa, and the Philippines, where they performed the same function. All told, over 7,000 officers were trained in Civil Affairs.

Since World War II, Civil Affairs teams have served in Korea, Viet Nam, Grenada, Saudi Arabia, Kuwait, Turkey, Iraq, Guantanamo Bay, Somalia, Rwanda, Haiti and Bosnia. On 27 November 1990, all PsyOps and Civil Affairs were organized into the Civil Affairs/Psychological Operations Command.

NAVAJO CODE TALKERS

$\mathbf{T}$he idea of using Indians to speak their own language on military radios was not new. In World War I, an army unit, the 142nd Infantry Regiment, had used Choctaw Indians to pass messages. In October 1918, during the battle in the Argonne Forest, 14 Choctaws served as radio operators helping their regiment to coordinate tactical movements. The technique worked, but the Germans later found out how they were duped. During the period between world wars, Germans traveled to the United States to study the languages of many of the Indian tribes, just in case this tactic was used against them in the future.

But the idea that Philip Johnston proposed to the Marines in early 1942 was different from the technique used by the Army. Johnston was the son of missionaries and had grown up among the Navajos. He could speak the Navajo language fluently as a young boy. Johnston's idea was based on two significant differences from the previous use of Indian language as a code. First, Johnston knew that the Navajo language was not written. It was strictly an oral language and was difficult for adults to learn because it was a tonal language. This meant that no written reference or dictionary existed that a cryptanalyst could use to identify the language. Second, he proposed that a specific code be devised based on the Navajo language. This would further encrypt the message. The Canadian Army had tried to develop a code based on Indian languages but gave up because there were no words to describe such things as military vehicles (trucks, tanks, planes), units, or maneuvers. Johnston suggested assigning words to mean these things. For example, bird names stood for different types of airplanes, fishes were used for ships and boats, and the names of Navajo clans were used for military organizations. He also suggested that words could be spelled out using his code. This further complicated the job of an enemy cryptanalyst, since he would never know if a word was being transmitted or only a letter.

The Marines were skeptical but decided to give Johnston a chance to prove his idea. In March 1942, he conducted a test in

Washington, DC for planners at Marine headquarters. The Marine officers gave messages in English to one group of Navajos who translated them and radioed them in the Navajo code to a second group who translated them back to English - with no errors. The Marines were impressed. They authorized a special program to recruit appropriate candidate Marines on the Navajo reservation.

Those who were recruited had to take basic boot training, just like all Marines. After completing training, they were sent to signal school to learn the various methods of military communications, including "Morse code, semaphore signals...message writing, wire laying, pole climbing, and communications procedures ..." They trained on the equipment they would use in combat. Finally, they went to special training to learn and further develop the code they would use.

To maintain the secrecy of the code, the Navajos had to memorize it. The basic rule, that they could not write the code down and take it with them, was an iron-clad one, and was not broken during the war. Their special training course lasted four weeks. The first two weeks were spent in the classroom and the last two were under simulated combat conditions. The first group of trainees consisted of 30 Navajos. Twenty-nine successfully completed the course. Several of the code talkers from the first class stayed on to teach successive classes. Others went back to the reservation to recruit new candidates, while the remaining Navajos went to tactical units in the South Pacific, to take up their signal duties. There they would be joined by graduates from later classes. Johnston became the head of the training program. By the end of the war, 450 Navajo recruits went through the demanding training course. Only 30 did not complete it.

Several Marine officers tried to break the code by having it analyzed by intelligence experts, as well as by other Navajos. Nothing worked. The intelligence analysts said the messages "sounded like gibberish" and non-trained Navajos could not detect patterns or sense from the messages received. Despite their expertise, front line Marine commanders were still reluctant to use code talkers. At Guadalcanal and the Marshalls, many Marines who heard the code thought it was evidence that the Japanese were using American radios. Navajo code talkers were often mistaken for Japanese because of the similarity in their physical features. Eventually, one commander arranged a test which pitted the code talkers against a mechanical encoding-decoding device. The code talkers won and were used with more regularity.

As the war progressed, the size of the code expanded. This gave the code talkers alternate choices for words and letters to use, and several new terms. This made the job of Japanese codebreakers even tougher. Major General Alexander Vandegrift was the first division commander to realize the value of his code talkers and, in December 1942, he requested an additional 83 for his division. One early success that helped prove the value of the code talkers occurred when they were used as navy air communicators in November 1943, during the air war for Rabaul. Suddenly, the Japanese were no longer able to decode messages about air activity directed at their key island base. Within six days of the first use of Navajo code talkers, the air raids were so successful that the Japanese navy began to pull its fleet out of Rabaul harbor.

For the rest of the island-hopping war in the Pacific, the Navajo code talkers went wherever the Marines went. The Japanese continued to be confused by what they intercepted from American radio traffic. The Navajo code talkers were involved in every major Marine action in the last two years of the war. Soon, the code talkers were directing artillery fire, operating out in front of friendly lines, and gathering intelligence behind enemy lines. At least one team of code talkers worked with a Nisei, who would wander through Japanese camps at night and then pass on what he had learned to the Navajos. The Indians encoded the intelligence and passed it back to their headquarters.

The "code talkers' finest hour" was at Iwo Jima. They passed all traffic to and from the seaborne command post to the three division headquarters ashore. They directed naval gunfire support and close air support to the marines on the island. One officer of the 5th Marine Division said, in describing the first 48 hours of the invasion, "During that period, they [six Navajo code talker teams in his headquarters] sent and received more than

800 messages without an error." The code talkers even sent (and received) word of the capture of Mount Suribachi and the flag raisings there. Another marine officer said, after the island was secured, "Were it not for the Navajo code talkers, the Marines never would have taken Iwo Jima."

The code talkers were used again at Okinawa and even as part of the occupation forces in Japan. Some of them were later used in Korea and Viet Nam. The Army also used small units of Indian code talkers. The 180th Infantry Regiment of the 45th Infantry Division used Choctaw Indians and the 4th Signal Company, 4th Infantry Division, used Comanche Indians. The Comanches, first used during the D-Day invasion of France, also developed their own code.

None of this work by Indian code talkers was well known until about 1969, because the government considered the Navajo code classified. Since 1971, increased credit and recognition have been given to this special mission force as more is understood about how they were used and how effective they were.

DETACHMENT 101

"Few worse things can happen than to lose a battle because we didn't trust the fighting qualities of these Kachin," said Lieutenant General Joseph Stilwell, the American commander of the China-Burma-India Theater, speaking to Captain Carl Eifler, commanding officer of OSS Detachment 101. "You've been saying they're anxious to take on the Jap. This is their chance."

Detachment 101 was the major special operations success story of World War II. The 250 Army officers and 750 enlisted men of the Detachment recruited, trained, and led approximately 10,000 Kachin tribesmen in a highly effective unconventional war against the Japanese. At its peak, Detachment 101 was dropping 1.5 million pounds of supplies per month to agents and guerrillas in the field. The unit also conducted "morale operations," or black propaganda operations by producing fake leaflets ordering the Japanese to surrender.

Participating in two campaigns and six major assaults in Burma, the Kachin and other tribes working for Detachment 101 far exceeded Stilwell's expectations. The primitive Burmese tribesmen and their American agents killed 5,000 Japanese troops, captured 75 prisoners, destroyed 57 bridges and 272 enemy vehicles, and rescued 425 Allied airmen. Amazingly, the detachment suffered only 27 Americans and 338 natives killed.

Detachment 101 was created in April 1942 by order of William Donovan, head of the OSS. The Detachment's mission was to gather intelligence and conduct sabotage behind Japanese lines in Burma. Donovan selected Eifler, a hulking 250-pound former customs agent, to command the unit. Eifler, an energetic, courageous, and highly imaginative leader, had worked for years along the Mexican border ferreting out smugglers. This experience made Eifler uniquely qualified because in Burma, he and his fledgling unit would be doing the smuggling.

Before leaving Washington for the CBI Theater, Eifler recruited a small number of trusted men that formed the nucleus of the unit. He selected Captain John Coughlin, a former heavyweight boxer, as his executive officer. Coughlin in turn recruited Lieutenant William R. "Ray" Peers and others.

"We had four infantry officers, two engineers, three radio technicians, a watchmaker, a court stenographer, a Korean patriot, and an American who had been the advisor to...a powerful Chinese warlord" said Peers, describing the early recruits.

Following demolitions, hand-to-hand combat, weapons, guerrilla tactics, cryptography, and other training at Camp X, a British Special Operations Executive (SOE) camp in Canada, and at Camp B, an OSS training site on Catoctin Mountain in Maryland, the Detachment departed for Asia. Camp B eventually became "Shangri-La," President Roosevelt's favorite summer retreat. Later it was renamed Camp David by President Dwight D. Eisenhower.

Upon arriving at Stilwell's command with 21 men, Eifler met with Stilwell, and in October established a headquarters and training site at a British tea plantation at Nazira, Assam, in northeast India. Faced with the difficult language barrier and a shortage of supplies, Eifler initially had problems recruiting men for his detachment.

Drawing on volunteers from the Anglo-Burmese Army and Burmese refugees, including smugglers, professors, merchants, and assorted other types who had certain "skills" and a knowledge of English, and after procuring equipment from official and "unofficial sources," Eifler began training his agents. Each man underwent three months of tough training, including parachuting, intelligence collection, radio operation, infiltration and exfiltration techniques, unarmed combat methods, survival techniques, escape and evasion, and basic junglecraft. By December Eifler had three small teams available.

Detachment 101 did not enjoy immediate success. Despite its early failures, mostly due to a lack of established native contacts within the occupied areas, the unit learned from its mistakes and began recruiting greater numbers of native agents, which resulted in more intelligence for Stilwell. Pleased with their work, Stilwell directed Eifler to "expand" his operations with the Kachin tribesmen of northern Burma.

Capitalizing on the Kachin's bitter hatred of the Japanese, which was apparent by the natives' affinity for cutting off and drying the enemy's ears, Eifler's agents found a wealth of men to draw from and recruited Kachin to provide intelligence on Japanese activity. As the Detachment became more adept at operating in Burma, advance agents parachuted behind Japanese lines to recruit small bands of Kachin. After identifying friendly natives who were willing to help, Eifler sent in additional teams of agents to set up training sites and instruct the tribesmen in small unit hit-and-run tactics.

In December 1943, Peers replaced Eifler as commanding officer. Eifler had been suffering with severe headaches resulting from a head injury he received on an earlier mission. Coughlin was actually next senior in rank, but Donovan placed him in command of all OSS activities in Asia under Navy Captain Milton Miles, who also commanded Naval Group China or SACO. Upon taking command, Peers reorganized the detachment into area commands consisting of four regional armies and an operations element which traveled with Stilwell's headquarters.

Coinciding with the Allied offensive in Burma in February 1944, Detachment 101, now numbering some 3,000 strong and growing, transformed from an intelligence gathering unit into a viable guerrilla army. Operating in groups from 10 to 300, with some as large as 1,000, the unit's first large-scale operation was helping Merrill's Marauders on the assault of Myitkyina, an important enemy communications center and site of a hardened airstrip located near the Irrawaddy River bordering China.

During the operation the guerrillas, also known as the "Kachin or Jingpaw Rangers," provided information on Japanese troop activity, screened the Marauder's movement, and guided them through the Kumon mountains of northern Burma south toward their objective. The rugged and loyal Kachin also served as litter bearers and even provided their elephants to transport supplies and equipment. Once outside Myitkyina, the Kachin guided the assault force to the airfield. Meanwhile, other groups of tribesmen cut enemy communications between Myitkyina and the Japanese 56th Division, which would be used to reinforce the city.

On 17 May, the Marauders and Kachin from Detachment 101 captured the airfield, but Myitkyina remained in enemy hands until 3 August. Following the victory at Myitkyina, bands of Kachin ambushed the Japanese as they retreated along the Irrawaddy River. According to Brigadier General Frank Merrill, commander of Merrill's Marauders, "We could not have succeeded with the help of [Detachment] 101."

In the jungle the Kachin were unequaled. The ghost-like tribesmen ambushed the enemy and disappeared into the jungle, leaving the Japanese to their fate among the numerous pungyis and booby traps. Several Japanese prisoners said that they "so feared the guerrillas that they rated one Kachin equal to ten Japanese." A comparison of casualties between the Kachin and the Japanese attests to that belief. For every Kachin lost, 25 Japanese were killed.

During the remainder of the year the Kachin and Detachment 101 increasingly helped in the campaign in northern Burma. They provided 85 percent of the Tenth Air Force's bombing targets, rescued downed Allied airmen, and guided the Allies in their southern advance from Katha to Bhamo.

Throughout the first six months of 1945, Detachment 101, which had grown to 10,000 men, harassed the Japanese at every turn, particularly along the Burma Road, which was the Allies' vital supply link into China. Along the Hsenwi-Wanting section, Shan and Karen guerrillas accounted for nearly one third of enemy casualties.

Further south, the Kachin harassed enemy communication lines along the Taunggyi-Kentung Road which was the primary Japanese escape route into Thailand. During this time the Kachin engaged the Japanese at Lawksawk, Loilem, Mongkung, Heshi, Pangtara, and eventually at Rangoon on the southern tip of Burma. By the summer of 1945, the Kachin had driven the enemy from the area.

On 12 July the unit was disbanded. For their efforts, the Kachin were given captured Japanese weapons and a campaign badge. They were also awarded the Citation for Military Assistance, and presented with a "Kachin Ranger" shoulder patch. The Kachin then returned to their villages. Meanwhile, many of the remaining Americans and others, joined the OSS in China. In November 1945, OSS Detachment 101 was awarded the Presidential Distinguished Unit Citation.

ARMY RANGER BATTALIONS

Steeped in the tradition of America's early Rangers, such as Robert Rogers, Francis "Swamp Fox" Marion, and countless others, the Army Ranger Battalions of World War II bore great resemblance to their predecessors. Numbering six permanent battalions, the 1st through 6th, and the short-lived 29th (Provisional), the Army Rangers were modeled largely after British commando units and were designed to provide the Allies with a versatile, highly-mobile force which could attack with speed and surprise.

They performed some of the traditional Ranger missions, such as hit-and-run raids and intelligence gathering. This was the first time, however, that Rangers went into action outside North America.

Formed by Lieutenant General Lucian K. Truscott, Jr., the 1st Ranger Battalion was activated at Carrickfergus, Northern Ireland, on 19 June 1942, under the command of then Captain William O. Darby. Darby, a 1933 graduate of West Point, was the quintessential Ranger. Young, handsome, and highly intelligent, Darby did everything he asked his men to do and quickly earned the respect and admiration of his men and superiors.

Volunteers for the 1st Ranger Battalion came from American units stationed throughout Northern Ireland. Darby wanted men with athletic ability, endurance, and initiative; men who had some experience in judo, weapons, demolitions, and communications. He was also interested in recruiting volunteers who knew something about railroads and power plants, especially since they were the two things that his Rangers would be blowing up.

Following a grueling six-week training program at the British commando school at Achnacarry, Scotland, which emphasized physical fitness, armed and unarmed combat, infiltration by stealth, and aggressive attack, the Rangers received amphibious training with the British Royal Navy. After all the training was completed and the men selected, the Rangers were ready. But they would suffer an ignominious debut.

NORTH AFRICA

Following the debacle at Dieppe, on 19 August 1942, where 50 Rangers accompanied British commandos in a joint British-Canadian landing on French shores to test invasion techniques and German defenses, the Rangers conducted daring and successful raids at Arzew and Sened Station supporting the invasion of North Africa. Shortly thereafter, the battalion covered the withdrawal of American troops from Kasserine Pass through Feriana to the Dernia Pass.

Later in the campaign, the Rangers fought in the battle for El Guettar, opened the road at Djebel el Ank, and fought off numerous counterattacks near Kjebel Berda. By the conclusion of Operation Torch, Darby and the 1st Ranger Battalion had earned a reputation for toughness, one that would be tested to the limit in Italy.

ITALY

Following the 1st Battalion's impressive work at Arzew, Allied Headquarters requested the formation of another Ranger unit to operate from headquarters in preparation for Operation Overlord, the invasion of Europe. In December 1942, some of the original members of Darby's Rangers, along with volunteers from the 29th Infantry Division, formed the 29th Ranger Battalion (Provisional). The unit trained at Achnacarry, and was operational by fall 1943.

The 29th Rangers and British commandos combined on raids and reconnaissance missions on the Norwegian and French coasts. The most notable raid was the destruction of a German radar installation on Ile d'Ouessant, a tiny island off the Atlantic coast of Brittany. But on 15 October 1943, the provisional unit was deactivated in favor of permanent ranger units.

Between April and September 1943, four additional Ranger Battalions were activated. The 2nd (1 April) and 5th (1 September) Ranger Battalions were formed at Camp Forrest, Tennessee, while the 3rd (25 May) and 4th (8 June) Ranger Battalions were organized near Nemours, Morocco. Officers and sergeants from Darby's 1st Battalion served as cadre for the 3rd and 4th Battalions. During July 1943, three of the five battalions participated in the invasion of Sicily. On 10 July, Darby's 1st Battalion landed at Gela, and captured the city's port. They later stormed the fortress city of Butevia. At the same time, the 3rd Battalion assaulted enemy positions near Licata, and later captured Popo di Norco. After occupying the eastern half of Gela, the 4th Battalion repulsed several vicious enemy counterattacks and secured the beachhead, which was nearly lost in the first several days of fighting.

During the next few months of the Italian campaign, the three Ranger Battalions encountered heavy fighting. On 9 September the combined Ranger force assaulted Maiora, on the Italian mainland. After taking Chiunzi Pass against heavy odds and fighting off seven ferocious counterattacks, the 1st and 3rd Battalions joined conventional forces and pressed on toward Naples, while the 4th Battalion cleared the Sorrento-Meta area and reinforced troops at Salerno.

LTC. William O. Darby (center) Arzew, North Africa, 12 Mar. 1942, DOD Photo.

Darby's Rangers, Italy

Throughout November and into mid-December, the 1st, 3rd, and 4th Battalions engaged in heavy combat against the German Winter Line. Darby and his battalion, operating in the Venafro Sector, became embroiled in two weeks of bitter mountain fighting. Despite being heavily outnumbered, the Rangers captured the high ground and held on to it before being relieved.

Meanwhile, the 3rd and 4th Battalions faced similar opposition at San Pietro. The beleaguered Rangers of the 3rd Battalion, despite being surrounded and taking heavy casualties, fought their way to the high ground above the town and secured it until replacements arrived in early December. The 4th Battalion, however, found itself it deep trouble. After taking the high ground northeast of Ceppagna, while attached to the 45th Infantry Division, the Rangers attempted to advance further, but were stopped cold. They were finally relieved on 14 November.

Following the grueling and costly fighting of 1943, the Ranger battalions were given a much needed rest. Although these Rangers had seen some of the toughest fighting of the war to that point, they had compiled an almost unbroken string of victories. Anzio changed all that.

ANZIO

On 22 January 1944, the 1st, 3rd, and 4th Ranger Battalions landed at Anzio Beach. For the next eight days the Rangers encountered hard fighting and worked to widen the beachhead. On 30 January, in a daring night attack, the combined Ranger Force moved toward Cisterna. The 1st and 3rd Battalions reached the outskirts of the city undetected, but the 4th Battalion, which was approaching along the Anzio-Cisterna Road, was discovered and engaged by the defenders. This also alerted the German forces that the 1st and 3rd Battalions were in the area. The Germans, reinforced by a paratroop division and heavy tanks, quickly surrounded the 1st and 3rd Battalions and inflicted terrible casualties. Of the 900 Rangers who were trapped, nearly half were killed or wounded. With the exception of six men, the remainder were captured. On 31 January, the 1st and 3rd Ranger Battalions ceased to exist. Later, in April 1945, the fabled leader of Darby's Rangers was killed in an artillery bombardment in Italy, while Assistant Division Commander of the 10th Mountain Division. He was promoted posthumously to brigadier general. With his death, all vestiges of the 1st and 3rd Ranger Battalions were gone.

The 4th Ranger Battalion didn't fare much better. Realizing that the 1st and 3rd Battalions were surrounded, the 4th attempted to reach them the following day. After mounting a desperate attack against overwhelming odds, they were stopped cold at a road junction outside Cisterna. Decimated by their valiant attempt to rescue the other Rangers, the 4th Battalion had to be relieved. The survivors were distributed among the 1st Special Service Force or sent home. The unit was officially deactivated on 24 October 1944, at Camp Butner, North Carolina.

NORMANDY

As the Ranger Battalions at Anzio were fighting for survival, the untested 2nd and 5th Battalions were training for the upcoming invasion of Fortress Europe. In addition to standard ranger training, the 2nd Battalion underwent advanced amphibious training at the Navy Scouts & Raiders School at Fort Pierce and at selected camps in England, while the 5th received additional training in Scotland. Their D-Day mission was to scale the 10-story cliffs at Pointe du Hoc, four miles west of Omaha Beach, and knock out a battery of six 155mm howitzers guarding the landing beaches.

On D-Day, 6 June 1944, the 2nd and 5th Ranger Battalions landed at Normandy. Three companies of the 2nd Battalion were assigned to assault the battery, while the remainder of the Battalion landed with the 5th Rangers near Pointe de la Percee, three miles to the east. Using rocket-propelled ropes and rope ladders under withering enemy fire, the first Rangers reached the top of Pointe du Hoc within ten minutes. To their surprise, the guns had been moved. But by day's end the Rangers had located and destroyed five of the six guns. Some 160 of the 270 Rangers who assaulted Pointe du Hoc, were either killed or wounded.

On the beaches near Vierville, the 5th Ranger Battalion, along with men from the 2nd Battalion and 116th Infantry Regiment, encountered heavy fighting on their advance toward Vierville-sur-Mer and St. Pointe du Mont. After moving inland and along the coast, the Rangers spent the summer rooting the enemy from France, Belgium, and Luxembourg, on their eastward drive toward Germany.

THE PHILIPPINES

Halfway around the world in the steamy jungles of New Guinea, another Ranger Battalion was being formed for MacArthur's return to the Philippines. On 26 September 1944, the 98th Field Artillery Battalion was redesignated the 6th Ranger Battalion as part of Lieutenant General Walter Krueger's Sixth Army. With no standard Ranger training under

6th Rangers & Alamo Scouts on Patrol as they head for Cabanatuan
POW Camp on Luzon. Jan 1944. DOD Photo.

their belts, the men of the newly-formed 6th Rangers were put
through a crash course in preparation for their advance mission
in the Philippines.

On 17 October 1944, three days before the planned invasion
of Leyte, elements of the Rangers landed on Suluan,
Homonhon, and Dinagat Islands guarding the eastern approaches to Leyte. Once ashore, the Rangers attacked Japanese
troops, assisted teams of Amphibious Scouts in setting up signal
lights and beacons on Dinagat and Homonhon to guide the
invasion forces through the straits, and secured the islands
against enemy reoccupation. Within a month, the Rangers
moved to Leyte and assisted in operations there before joining
invasion forces heading for Luzon.

On Luzon barely two weeks, 121 Rangers, guided by two
teams of Alamo Scouts and supported by two Filipino guerrilla
units, attacked the Cabanatuan Prison Camp in Central Luzon.
In a daring night raid, which was one of the most well conceived
and perfectly executed operations ever performed, the 6th
Rangers liberated 513 prisoners of war and killed over 500
Japanese, at a loss of only two men killed. Following their
outstanding work at Cabanatuan, which earned them the Presidential Unit Citation, the 6th Ranger Battalion spent the rest
of the war conducting combat patrols and providing security.
After the Japanese surrender, the 6th Rangers traveled to

Kyoto, Japan, and performed occupation duties before being inactivated on 30 December 1945.

Back in Europe, the 2nd and 5th Ranger Battalions spent the last nine months of the war performing a myriad of duties. Throughout five major campaigns, the Rangers did what was asked of them and more. They supported conventional forces in combat, patrolled, performed military government duties, processed and guarded prisoners of war, provided headquarters security, and ultimately, pulled occupation duty. By war's end, the 2nd Battalion had reached Grun, Czechoslovakia while the 5th Battalion got as far as Reid, Austria. The 2nd Battalion was deactivated on 23 October 1945, at Camp Patrick Henry, Virginia. The 5th Battalion was deactivated one day earlier at Camp Miles Standish, Massachusetts.

Despite their status as elite, highly-trained units, the Ranger battalions seldom got the opportunity to showcase their abilities in the type of operations they were trained to conduct. Instead, because of American commanders' reluctance and misunderstanding of how to use such forces and relative inexperience with them, the Rangers were misused. They were frequently wasted as guards, thrown into mopping up operations, or mired in occupation duties. Worse yet, they were too often sacrificed piecemeal in operations more suited to conventional infantry units.

Although the Ranger Battalions' record is dotted with setbacks, it contains many extraordinary victories. In no way do the failures detract from the fighting spirit, tenacity, and dedication of the Rangers. Rather, it is indicative of the growing pains suffered by the Army in the maturation process of employing such elite units in a time when mass and firepower reigned supreme.

By 30 December 1945, all the Ranger Battalions had either been destroyed or deactivated. Five years later at the outbreak of the Korean War, the Rangers were back in combat.

ALLIED INTELLIGENCE BUREAU

MacArthur wanted nothing to do with the Office of Strategic Services. First, he had heard nothing good about the organization from his professional associates and friends. Second, and more important, if he allowed it to operate in his theatre, the Southwest Pacific Area, it would still report to and be controlled by Donovan. Donovan was in Washington - and he did not work for MacArthur. That pretty much settled the issue: OSS could not operate in the Southwest Pacific.

MacArthur was astute enough to realize that he would need an organization like the OSS at his disposal. After all, it was still necessary to conduct clandestine intelligence collection operations behind the lines, support guerrilla campaigns, and send trained saboteurs into enemy-controlled areas to wreak havoc. And MacArthur was the first to see that he would need an organization to control all of this activity. He also believed that propaganda was "a crucial ingredient in modern warfare," one that could help raise the morale of friendly troops and populations, and lower the enemy's. He decided that this was a job for his G-2, Major General Charles A. Willoughby. Willoughby established an oversight staff for the organization that included both American and Australian officers. On July 6, 1942, MacArthur approved the formation of the Allied Intelligence Bureau (AIB).

Two of the three examples of the special operations that follow were not conducted by American units, but were directed and supported by the AIB, which was subordinate to MacArthur's command. The examples selected are in the area of intelligence gathering, sabotage, and support to guerrilla operations.

OPERATION FERDINAND

At least two years before the attack on Pearl Harbor, Australian intelligence had created the Coastwatcher Organization, which maintained a series of outposts on islands throughout the Pacific. These outposts were manned by Australian civilians, who were specifically recruited for the operation. Their job was to report, via radio, on the movement of Japanese air and sea assets and ground military operations. Soon after the AIB was created, it assumed the responsibility of supervising the Coastwatchers. The Coastwatchers located themselves on remote parts of islands to avoid detection. They were usually supported by local natives. Many of the Coastwatchers had lived and worked on the islands where they were stationed prior to the war.

The principal means of communications was by small durable "teleradios." These specially developed radios were resistant to rot or mildew, heat, and rough handling. Although each station had several radios, the individual items were fairly easy to transport. However, they had the same vulnerability that all radios have - they can be located by means of direction finding techniques. The Coastwatchers had no illusions about what would happen to them if they were captured. Since they were civilians, they could be treated as spies by the Japanese. For this reason, AIB gave the Coastwatchers military rank but the Japanese did not always honor it. Many of those who were caught were brutally interrogated and killed.

The intelligence and early warning information gathered by the Coastwatchers was of invaluable assistance in planning air and naval operations and amphibious assaults.

OPERATIONS JAYWICK AND RIMAU

Major Ivan Lyon, a British Army officer, had escaped from Singapore before the Japanese had conquered the peninsula in February 1942. After several months at sea, he reached Australia, where he learned that his wife and son had been taken prisoner by the Japanese and were on a prison ship that had been sunk. He swore vengeance against the Japanese and devised a plan to strike at his hated enemy. He explained his plan to the Service Reconnaissance Department of AIB and they liked it. AIB authorized Lyon to begin recruiting and training a team to carry out the mission.

Lyon's plan was to return to Singapore harbor aboard a sailing vessel disguised as a local fishing boat. The boat was complete with Japanese flag and skin-darkened special operators. Short of the target, teams in Folbot canoes (two-man rigid rubber kayaks) would paddle into the harbor at night and attach limpet mines to Japanese ships, then depart. AIB called it a "boom-and-bang raid." Lyon spent months putting his team through intensive training, without telling them where they were going. In the meantime, a 70-foot fishing boat, *Krait*, was found and outfitted for the operation. The 14-man crew departed Australia on 2 September 1943. It was not until they were at sea that Lyon told them where they were bound. On the 25th, Lyon and five others, in three Folbots, paddled about their target area, mining ships. Eventually six ships were sunk and the raiders escaped to their pick-up point.

The following year, Lyon was back in the same area with another team and a different idea. This time a submarine had brought his team in. They would be moving to and around the harbor using small, two-man mini-subs. But something went wrong. No one knows for certain what happened, but before they could launch their attack, the Japanese caught and executed all the raiders.

5217TH RECONNAISSANCE BATTALION

In October 1943, the Army activated the 5217th Reconnaissance Battalion in Brisbane, Australia. At nearby Fraser Island, the 5217th, commanded by Lieutenant Colonel Lewis Brown, set up a commando school to train soldiers for service in the Philippines. There, they would further train and coordinate the activities of guerrilla units on the various islands. The three-month training course included jungle operations, small boat and submarine landings, cryptography, and Japanese language lessons. Radio and Morse code were the primary means of communications and the men of the 5217th spent a lot of training time learning these techniques. Of course, physical training was also stressed. The training staff used the physical training to weed out those not qualified.

By October 1944, 20 teams of varying sizes had been sent in to various islands in the Philippine chain. In November, after the invasion at Leyte, the unit designation was changed to 1st Reconnaissance Battalion, but operations continued as before. Within two months, U.S. forces in strength had landed on Luzon, but the Japanese continued to fight hard and offer heavy resistance. Many of the teams began to report back in person. Eventually, a headquarters element coordinated all guerrilla activities. On 5 July, the Philippines were declared liberated. The 5217th deserves its share of the credit for the work done by the guerrillas and in fighting the Japanese.

1ST SPECIAL SERVICE FORCE

"The Black Devils are all around us . . ." read a diary found on the body of dead German officer at Anzio. "We never hear them!" The entry, an enemy's fearful tribute to the blackened-faced warriors of the 1st Special Service Force, attested to the unit's stealth and fierce fighting style. The hard-hitting men of the combined U.S./Canadian unit, armed with their distinctive Case V-42 stiletto and machine guns, earned such a reputation in combat that they were aptly nicknamed "The Devil's Brigade." As the unit's record attests, it was a moniker well deserved.

Activated on 9 July 1942, at Fort William Henry Harrison, Montana, under the command of Colonel Robert T. Frederick, the 1st Special Service Force was formed to conduct winter hit and run raids against Nazi forces occupying Norway, or Rumania. The series of raids, known as the "Plough Project," was the brainchild of Admiral Louis Mountbatten, the British commander of Combined Operations. The project called for the destruction of hydroelectric plants, power stations, and oil refineries. Frederick reviewed the proposal for this project while assigned to the War Department General Staff. He thought it was a bad idea and recommended against it. Consequently, the plan was eventually scrapped in September 1942, when it was determined that the raids would cause more harm to the civilian population than to the Germans. Rather than disband the Force, Chief of Staff General George Marshall opted to utilize it as a multi-purpose unit, one which could be used in combat or as a raiding force.

Due to the dangerous nature of the missions, Frederick wanted a special breed of volunteers. He looked for tough, rugged, independent men who were at home in the mountains and wilderness. To find such men he recruited hunters, lumberjacks, forest rangers, prospectors, northwoodsmen, game wardens, and explorers from U.S. Army units throughout the Southwest and Pacific seaboard. But many of the men were more spirited than Frederick expected. Malcontents, ne'er-do-wells, and criminals were often "volunteered" by commanders just to get them out of their unit. Of the original volunteers, about half were American and half Canadian. On the whole, the Canadians were better behaved but, in the final analysis, no better soldiers than their American counterparts.

The Force was formed into three integrated regiments, two commanded by Americans officers and one by a Canadian officer. To insure fairness and balance, each regimental executive officer was the national counterpart of the regimental commander.

Also known as "Forcemen," the 173 officers and 2194 enlisted men of the 1st Special Service Force were among the most highly trained and highly rated soldiers of any army during the Second World War. Upon arrival, volunteers received an accelerated parachute course, and were trained in hand-to-hand combat, demolitions, and mountaineering. Sergeant Jack O'Neil of the Canadian Army devised and taught a method of hand-to-hand fighting that the U.S. Army continued to use for more than 20 years. During winter months, trainees learned to operate tracked snow vehicles, such as the Weasel, and received ski training in the Rocky Mountains and along the Continental Divide. Later, in the spring of 1943, the Forcemen received amphibious training in Norfolk, Virginia, in preparation for the 15 August invasion of Kiska, in the Aleutians.

The Forcemen were disappointed at Kiska and would have to wait for some real action. The Japanese forces on Kiska had anticipated an Allied landing and had slipped off the island under cover of heavy fog. The invasion force was so close to catching the enemy on the island that American troops discovered food still simmering in cooking pots when they arrived. Elements of the Force also landed on Segula Island, but it too was deserted. Another Force element was prepared to conduct a parachute assault if needed, but the jump was cancelled.

The Forcemen returned to the United States for a brief rest and additional training at their new camp at Fort Ethan Allen,

1st Special Service Force, Ft. William Harrison, Montana, 1943. DOD Photo.

Vermont, then embarked for the Mediterranean Theater on 27 October. After arriving at Casablanca, and traveling across North Africa, the Forcemen were champing at the bit to get into action. The unit landed at Naples, Italy, on 19 November; and on 3 December, the men of the 1st Special Service Force finally got the chance to show their stuff.

The 3,000-foot Monte de Difensa, and its twin peak Monte La Remetanea, were key components of the German Winter Line guarding the approach to the Liri Valley. Allied planners thought it would take at least three days to secure them. Rather than assault the mountain fortress from the front, Frederick decided to go in the back door. Despite battling a steep 200-foot cliff and bitter cold, 600 Forcemen scaled the mountain and launched a savage attack against the rear of the German defenses. After two hours of fierce combat, the Forcemen accomplished their mission. Three days later they seized Monte La Remetanea, which effectively cracked the Winter Line and paved the way for an Allied advance to Cassino.

The Forcemen didn't stop there. On Christmas Day they took Mt. Summucro, and for the next two weeks engaged in heavy combat at Radicose, Monte Majo, and Monte Vischiataro. Decimated from the bitter fighting, the unit was finally pulled from the line on 17 January 1944.

After a brief rest and refitting with some 250 Rangers, the Forcemen were sent to Anzio, on 2 February. Their mission was to help shore up an eight-mile stretch on the extreme right flank of the beachhead. Operating primarily at night in small groups, the Forcemen raided German outposts, radioed in artillery targets, and made life miserable for the nervous defenders; all of which contributed much to their reputation and to the Forcemen's proud sobriquet.

On 9 May, after nearly 100 days on the front lines, the Forcemen withdrew and prepared for the drive to Rome. Beginning on 23 May, the Forcemen participated in the breakout from the Anzio beach-head and engaged the Germans at Monte Arrestine, Rocca Massima, and Colle Ferro. On 4 June they entered the Eternal City and securing the bridges spanning the Tiber River.

Following several weeks of rest and refitting, the Forcemen participated in assault landings in Southern France, on 14 August. These landings were part of Operation Anvil, the combined amphibious-airborne-glider invasion that kicked off the so-called "Champagne Campaign." Landing by rubber boat on Ile D'Hyeres, a series of three rocky land formations located on the left flank of the invasion beach, the Forcemen quickly seized German artillery batteries. Within two days the "Devil's Brigade" had secured the isles. The unit then joined the 1st Airborne Task Force on the mainland and fought eight minor battles in three weeks, cutting off enemy escape routes and occupying cities.

But the price of success was high. After fighting its way north, the Forcemen settled in along the French and Italian border, where they spent the next three months. By late fall, the Forcemen had suffered terrible casualties, totaling some 2,300 men. The unit was then relieved in late November by elements of the 442nd Regimental Combat Team. On 5 December, the 1st Special Service Force was disbanded at the city of Menton. On 6 January 1945, the Forcemen were officially inactivated.

The bulk of American Forcemen joined the 99th Infantry Battalion to form the 474th Regimental Combat Team, while others joined the 82nd and 101st Airborne Divisions. Likewise, Canadian Force members were absorbed into Canadian infantry and airborne units. "The First Special Service Force made no distinctions when it went into battle," said President Ronald Reagan, in 1981, marking the 39th anniversary of its formation. "Its men had the common cause of freedom at their side and the common denominator of courage in their hearts. They were neither Canadian nor American. They were, in General Eisenhower's term, liberators."

NAVY SCOUTS & RAIDERS

Shortly before the United States entered World War II the Navy recognized the need for an amphibious reconnaissance unit which could slip behind enemy lines, reconnoiter beaches for suitable invasion sites, and later guide the invasion forces to the beaches. The Navy Scouts & Raiders were the first in line of elite units formed to do just that—to lead the way.

At the heart of the Scouts & Raiders was Phil H. Bucklew, a six-foot-two-inch, 235-pound former professional football player for the Cleveland Rams, and later the first commanding officer of the Naval Operations Support Group. Before becoming one of the ten original Scouts & Raiders, Bucklew served briefly with former World Heavyweight Boxing Champion Gene Tunney's "Tunney Fish," which provided physical education training for Navy personnel. But the program didn't offer the kind of action Bucklew was looking for.

Answering a call for volunteers for "amphibious commandos," Bucklew and other outstanding men from "Tunney's Fish," including all-pro tackle John Tripson and others, were accepted for training into the fledgling Scouts & Raiders, then housed at Norfolk, Virginia. All were outstanding physical specimens; tall, muscular, and highly motivated.

Physical requirements to get into the Scouts & Raiders were stringent. Candidates were generally from 20-28 years old, did not wear glasses, and had to swim 400 yards. Physical training was extensive. The rigorous eight-week course featured the Navy's first organized physical training program. It included distance swimming, running, speed marches in deep sand, and log exercises, in which the teams worked together performing numerous calisthenics with a 400 pound log. The program also included extensive training in hand-to-hand combat, boat handling, radio operations, engineering, signaling, scouting and patrolling, and hydrographic and topographic measurements.

But the institution the Scouts & Raiders are most known for is "Hell Week." During the final phase of training, candidates were pushed to the edge of their physical and mental limits. Not allowed more than a few hours sleep for five days and nights, the trainees were put under enormous pressure to determine if they would "crack" when the going got tough.

In May 1942 the volunteers moved to an amphibious training site near Patuxent Naval Air Station, Maryland, where 90 additional volunteers were accepted. After more training, the top 30 candidates went to Little Creek, Virginia. In September they were commissioned into the Scouts & Raiders. The following January the Scouts & Raiders relocated to Fort Pierce, Florida, which became the largest amphibious training base on the east coast and the permanent home of the unit.

Formed into seven-man teams, the Scouts & Raiders and the Naval Combat Demolition Units (NCDUs), a unit formed to conduct similar missions, got their first taste of action during Operation Torch, the invasion of North Africa. The Scouts & Raiders' mission was to cut antishipping nets spanning the Wadi Sebou stream near Port Lyautey, French Morocco. After a near disastrous first attempt due to violent weather, the Scouts tried again and were successful.

Their next operations were in the invasion of Sicily where Bucklew and the Scouts, along with British scouting parties, were dropped off aboard two-man kayaks near the coast. The parties paddled ashore and checked beach gradients and located obstacles in preparation for the invasion. After completing the reconnaissance, Bucklew and his team guided Lieutenant General George S. Patton's Seventh Army ashore on the southern coast under heavy fire. Working from a small motor boat under a quarter moon, Bucklew sped from one end of the landing beach to the other placing his men, who carried flashlights to signal the perimeters of the landing beach, in position. Bucklew then centered himself between his men and led the invasion force in under the glare of German spotlights. In their first real test the Scouts & Raiders performed brilliantly, earning eight Navy Crosses. Two months later, Bucklew was at it again, this time on the beaches of Salerno, on the Italian mainland.

But it was on the beaches of Normandy that the Scouts & Raiders were at their best. Six months before the June 1944 invasion, Bucklew and his four-man team landed quietly on the French coast and took soundings of water depth along Omaha Beach. The daring Scouts even crawled ashore and gathered a bucket of sand to take back to headquarters to determine if it was suitable for supporting tanks and heavy vehicles. Despite being discovered, the small team eluded the Germans and made their way out to sea under the cover of dense fog, only to run into an enemy convoy. After laying "dead in the water" while the ships passed by, the Scouts were recovered and towed to one of their training bases on the Isle of Wight. Later, on D-Day, Bucklew guided invasion troops ashore and even captured a German pillbox containing a dozen Germans. A few months after the invasion Bucklew was sent to China to gather intelligence on possible invasion sites. While in the Far East, Bucklew began work on plans to bring 150 Scouts & Raiders to China to train "Amphibious Group Roger," a unit of waterborne saboteurs, but the plan never materialized.

Meanwhile, in the Southwest Pacific Theater, Rear Admiral Daniel E. Barbey established an Amphibious Training Command at Port Stephens, Australia, on 1 March 1943, to train units for similar scouting functions. Although known as Amphibious Scouts, the S & R cousins performed the same function as their counterparts in the European Theater. Officially known as the 7th Amphibious Force Special Unit #1, the Amphibious Scouts were a joint Army-Navy-Marine-Australian unit under Commander William B. Coultas.

The unit successfully reconnoitered the landing beaches prior to the landings at Lae, Finschaven, at Gasmata on Western New Britain. Later, the unit reconnoitered Cape Gloucester. In early 1944, the Amphibious Scouts became an all-Navy unit. Those Scouts from other services and the Australians returned to their parent units.

In July 1944, a joint team composed of ex-members of the Amphibious Scouts, Air Corps, and a team of Sixth Army's Alamo Scouts, performed a daring reconnaissance of Sansapor, the "bird's head" area of New Guinea. The reconnaissance netted vital terrain information for the construction of Allied airfields. The Amphibious Scouts later helped the 6th Ranger Battalion secure Dinagat and Homonhon Islands by setting up navigation lights to guide the invasion forces bound for Leyte through the straits.

With the inception of the NCDUs and the Underwater Demolition Teams (UDTs), the Scouts & Raiders for the most part faded away. The men were absorbed by the demolition units and utilized as Scout Intelligence Officers, Beachmasters, and Control Officers. The unit was deactivated when the training base at Little Creek was decommissioned in February 1946.

NAVAL GROUP CHINA

Naval Group China was one of the strangest units organized during World War II or any other war for that matter. Formed in September 1942 by Captain (later Admiral) Milton E. Miles, an experienced naval officer who had spent much of his professional career in China, Naval Group China's primary responsibility was to train and equip indigenous Chinese guerrillas and to establish coastwatcher, radio, and weather stations.

As if a Navy unit composed of Army, Navy, and Marine advisors training Chinese ground troops wasn't odd enough, Miles and his "Tigers" performed a mixed bag of operations. They fielded a camel corps in Turkistan, horse-mounted cavalry and weathermen in Mongolia, a Chinese naval carrier pigeon unit, and served as counter espionage trainers for Lieutenant General Tai Li's Chinese Secret Police.

Naval Group China was allied with the cunning and ruthless Li under the one-sided SACO Agreement (Sino-American Cooperative Organization). This effectively placed the U.S. military under Chinese command and gave it the "honor" of supplying, arming, and training Chinese troops in return for Sino promises that they would generously furnish all the manpower for transporting and storing equipment. Miles and Naval Group China established an extensive intelligence network from Shanghai 800 miles south to Hong Kong, and helped train and equip the 15,000-man Loyal Patriotic Army, which was the core of the Chinese guerrilla force.

Miles established his headquarters in late 1942 at Happy Valley near K'un-ming. In April 1943, the first of ten training facilities was established near Weichow. Subsequent camps were erected at Loyang, Sian, Amoy, Foochow, Wenchow, in Mongolia, near the southern border of Indochina, and other places. Since the Chinese were naturally distrustful of foreigners, Miles directed his men to blend in with them and to adopt their customs and mannerisms. His men carried out his instructions with vigor and enthusiasm. Military discipline became almost non-existent. Saluting was forbidden and officers, enlisted men, and Chinese mixed openly.

The advisors, who numbered only one officer and six enlisted men in 1942, grew to nearly 1,300 at the end of the war. Most of the advisors had no specialized training in guerrilla warfare, but adapted their particular skills, such as demolition, radio operations, and others, to fit the needs of the Chinese.

The role that Navy Group China played in unconventional warfare in China wasn't easy. Miles, called "Winter Plum Blossom" by the Chinese, lacked a clearly defined mission. He constantly battled a difficult language barrier, shortages of supplies, interservice rivalries with the OSS and the Army, and the general lack of priority given to China by American military leadership. The greatest obstacle facing Naval Group China was the intense inter-Chinese rivalry between Nationalist and Communist factions. Miles tried to keep both sides satisfied, which became a constant balancing act.

Rarely did the Chinese guerrilla leaders allow SACO advisors to accompany them on missions. Of the 1,000 reported engagements (which appears highly exaggerated) conducted by Chinese guerrillas, only 80 were observed by the advisors. This

SACO advisors train Chinese troops in use of communications equipment. 1945. U.S. Navy Photo.

did much to hamper SACO's evaluation of the guerrillas capabilities and performance. Caught in the middle of murderous inter-Chinese rivalry, the advisors were often stonewalled by Chinese commanders. Guerrilla reports, especially of operations that had no accompanying advisors, were often grossly exaggerated and many of them were outright lies, concocted to bolster the prestige of guerrilla leaders who would need it to jockey for post-war political power. In effect, the guerrillas did little more than harass the Japanese.

According to inflated official reports, SACO-trained guerrillas killed over 25,000 enemy troops, wounded 11,642, captured 508 prisoners of war, destroyed 209 bridges, 82 locomotives, 193 ships and river craft, and aided in the rescue of 76 Allied pilots and crewmen. Astonishingly, no advisors were killed—either by the enemy or the Chinese.

Despite the questionable value of the guerrillas, Naval Group China/SACO had its share of legitimate success. The most effective SACO trained unit was the "Yangtze River Raiders" under Navy Lieutenant Joseph Champe. In December

1944, the first class of "Yangtze River Raiders," graduated from training. Composed of a group of some 36, including American advisors and Chinese, the elusive Raiders struck often and successfully at Japanese supply lines within northern Kiangsi, southern Hupei, and western Human Provinces. These provinces contained the country's two major transportation routes, the Yangtze River and the Peking-Hankow-Canton Railroad. The daring Raiders reportedly killed nearly 1,000 enemy troops and wounded 200, while only losing 14 of their own.

About the same time the Yangtze Raiders were graduating, Naval Group China began assembling 150 experienced Naval Scouts & Raiders, many of whom had seen action in Europe, for the task of forming "Amphibious Group Roger." The Scouts & Raiders would be responsible for training Chinese waterborne saboteurs to harass enemy shipping in coastal waters, lakes and rivers, and to conduct clandestine scouting and coastwatching duties. Amphibious Group Roger was also to be one of the units spearheading the proposed invasion of Kyushu, the first phase of the invasion of Japan. But most of the Scouts & Raiders never set foot in China. They fell prey to joint American/Chinese administrative bureaucracy which left them stranded in Calcutta, India, until the summer of 1945.

Naval Group China's greatest contribution was not churning out trained guerrillas or elite commando-type teams. It was providing the 14th Army Air Force, known as the Flying Tigers, and numerous other Allied commands, with vital aerological data. Since many weather systems originated in Mongolia and moved eastward towards Japan and into the Pacific Ocean, timely and accurate weather reports were of utmost importance in planning tactical operations. By war's end the unit had trained some 100 Chinese weathermen and established 45 weather stations throughout China and in nearby countries. Clearly, without their meteorological efforts, thousands of Allied troops might have died.

OSS OPERATIONAL GROUPS

Operational Groups (OGs) were created in late 1942 by the Office of Strategic Services to collect intelligence and conduct sabotage in German-occupied countries. The OGs were organized by "target countries," such as Italy, Greece, France, Yugoslavia, and Norway. Later in the war OG members organized teams to be used against the Japanese in China. Each OG consisted of approximately four officers and 30 men. But most groups deployed as 15-man teams and operated in three-man liaison groups.

Volunteers for the OGs were selected from airborne personnel at Fort Bragg, North Carolina; Fort Benning, Georgia; and from Camp Forrest, Tennessee. All volunteers underwent a rigorous selection and training process. Each uniformed member was airborne qualified, fluent in a foreign language, and extensively trained in sabotage, demolitions, hand-to-hand combat, Allied and enemy weapons, and guerrilla operations. Operational Group candidates underwent much the same training as other OSS groups, such as the Jedburghs, but more emphasis was placed on weapons and communications training, rather than on clandestine fieldcraft.

The order establishing the OGs was issued in 1942, but it wasn't until April 1943, following four months of training at a number of camps throughout the United States and Great Britain, that the first OG was deployed.

Dropped by parachute or infiltrated by sea, the OGs were substantially larger than the Jedburgh Teams, and were akin to a conventional military unit operating behind the lines. The OGs set up or worked with established resistance groups and organized partisan activities. Although the OGs were large enough to perform independent raids and acts of sabotage, their primary function was to train, arm, and supply indigenous guerrillas.

Once established in occupied territory, the OGs developed extensive intelligence networks and occasionally led guerrilla attacks against the enemy's rear. These attacks not only tied

OSS Operational Group (NORSO) in Norway, 1945. DOD Photo.

down thousands of troops needed to guard the rear areas, they also prevented enemy forces from deploying their troops and resources to the front.

As with any unit attempting to go behind enemy lines, there was inherent danger. In late March 1944, OG "Ginny II" infiltrated into Northern Italy, and was captured. Following interrogation by the Germans, all members were executed as spies under Hitler's infamous and illegal Commando Order, even though they wore military uniforms. Despite the perilous nature of their mission and the scope of their operations, OGs suffered relatively few casualties.

During the summer of 1944, 21 French-speaking OGs, and one Norwegian group, parachuted into France from bases in London and Algiers, in support of the Normandy invasion. Working in concert with OSS Jedburgh Teams, French partisans, or independently, the OGs engaged the enemy, blew up bridges and rail lines, disrupted enemy lines of communication, and relayed intelligence to Allied Headquarters in London. All told, the combined OSS effort supplied and organized some 300,000 French partisans. The Norwegian OG eventually went to Norway where it conducted several successful sabotage operations against railroad targets and various supply areas. Known as "NORSO," this OG was led by Major William E.

Colby, who years later became Director of the Central Intelligence Agency.

Earlier, in the Mediterranean Theater, the first of at least 11 OGs had infiltrated into Yugoslavia and Greece, and established ties with partisan groups. Following the German capture of all the Dalmatian Islands, except Vis, in December 1943, the 3rd Contingent Operational Group, later known as Company C of the 2671st Special Reconnaissance Battalion, along with a mixed band of Tito's Yugoslav Partisans and commandos from the British Raiding Support Regiment joined forces and conducted a number of successful raids against German installations along the Dalmatian coast. The OGs also helped Tito's Partisans construct a 600-foot airstrip from which some 400 downed Allied airmen were safely returned.

In Greece, OGs and OSS agents supplied partisans with arms and equipment and helped sabotage bridges, railroads, and harass the enemy. During one operation, OSS men and partisans ambushed 14 trains, demolished 15 bridges, and destroyed over 60 German cargo trucks. The OGs also established a mobile field hospital, transported by 134 mules, which went from village to village treating partisans and civilians.

In August 1944, all OGs, consisting of some 1,100 men, were redesignated as the 2761st Special Reconnaissance Battalion, Separate (Provisional). Company A, along with an attached German-speaking OG, operated in the Italian Theater. Company B was assigned to France, and Company C to Yugoslavia, Albania, and Greece.

As the war in Europe drew to a close in the spring of 1945, approximately 400 veterans from several of the OGs, including two companies from the 2671st Special Reconnaissance Battalion, traveled to Kunming, China, and established an OSS jump school. The OGs trained the fledgling Chinese Commando units in parachute and commando tactics. Although the OGs suffered from lack of equipment and were supplied with poorly conditioned Chinese troops, they were instrumental in training China's commando units into a highly effective force by war's end.

The Operational Groups were officially disbanded on 20 September 1945, when President Harry S. Truman deactivated the Office of Strategic Services. The experience of the Operational Groups of World War II, along with their Jedburgh cousins, later led to the development of the modern Special Forces "A Team" concept.

NAVAL COMBAT DEMOLITION UNITS

On 11 November 1942, on the eve of the Allied invasion of North Africa, a team of 17 Army and Navy demolition men boarded a small wooden-hulled Higgins boat filled with explosives. They quietly paddled up the Wadi Sebou River leading to Port Lyautey, French Morocco. Their mission was to cut the antishipping net spanning the river and clear the way for Allied troop transports assigned to capture the city and its vital military airfield. Unlike the previous night when the group was detected and had to abort the mission, the demolitioneers set their charges and accomplished their goal. Suddenly, Vichy French machine guns erupted. The men fought frantically to reach the mouth of the river. When they did, they were met by monstrous waves which nearly capsized their craft. Fortunately, the haggard soldiers and sailors made their way safely out to sea and were recovered by waiting transports.

So went the first underwater demolition mission performed by the U.S. military. Called a "Combat Demolition Unit," the first group proved the value of employing trained demolitioneers who could clear obstacles for invasion craft and troops. Nine months later, a resilient and determined Navy Commander, Draper Kauffman, graduated the first 11 Naval Combat Demolition Units (NCDUs). Less than a year later, the NCDUs would play an integral role in the reconquest of Europe. Eventually, 126 NCDU teams saw action in the Atlantic, Mediterranean, and Pacific Theaters.

In 1933, Kauffman graduated from the U.S. Naval Academy. Because he was "blind as a bat" he was denied a commission. Not to be discouraged, Kauffman became a merchant seaman and was in Europe when the war broke out. He immediately enlisted in the American Volunteers Ambulance Corps in France. After heroic service which earned him the Croix de Guerre for bravery, Kauffman was captured by the Germans, but was released as a noncombatant in August 1940. The following month Kauffman talked the British into accepting him into the Royal Navy Volunteer Reserve. The newly-commissioned sublieutenant never saw water. Instead, Kauffman volunteered for service in a bomb disposal unit. After a near disaster on his first attempt, Kauffman successfully disarmed several bombs and was commended by King George VI for heroism.

Word of Kauffman's exploits quickly reached the U.S. Navy. He was welcomed back into the fold, commissioned, and charged with the task of putting together the Navy's new bomb-disposal unit. With the invasion of Sicily not far off, the Navy redirected Kauffman to begin training his unit for beach demolition and reconnaissance. The heavily defended beaches of Sicily and France were rife with man-made obstacles that had to be destroyed before the landing forces arrived. Kauffman first found a suitable training site and then the right kind of men to conduct the dangerous mission.

Fort Pierce, Florida, was the ideal place, but finding enough quality men was difficult. Just as in the Scouts & Raiders, candidates for the NCDUs had to be highly intelligent and have the ability to adapt quickly to changing situations. With the top men being snatched away by higher ranking commanders for similar units. He eventually found enough suitable candidates and began the difficult task of putting together small, highly-trained teams that could land on enemy shores under the cover of darkness and gather information on beach defenses. The teams, consisting of one officer and five enlisted men, were launched from submarines aboard seven-man rubber boats. The unoccupied space aboard the boat would be used to carry extra explosives.

Following the Sicily landings, where the NCDUs performed extensive hydrographic reconnaissance on the landing beaches, they began training for Operation OVERLORD, the invasion of Europe. Several NCDUs were slated to be used in the invasion. The first team arrived in England in November 1943, but it wasn't until April of the following year that a single team

Men of a Navy Combat Demolition Unit on board a LCV boat while blasting open a channel at Morotai, 15 Sept. 1944. They are (L-R) W.R. Hilker, E.A. Waddell, B.G. Byron, T.J. Sulenta, C.C. Bowersa and T.R. Lehmann. (National Archives)

was included in the planning of the invasion. To make matters worse, the Navy was undecided about what to do with the NCDUs. Despite the confusion, NCDUs eventually found a training site near Falmouth, and later at Appledore.

For the next six months the NCDUs, along with a number of Scouts & Raiders, trained in beach-obstacle demolition. With its myriad of man-made obstacles and heavy defenses, the beaches of Normandy provided a formidable challenge to NCDUs, particularly the large "Belgian Gates" with attached Teller mines.

One inventive demolitioneer, Lieutenant (jg) Carl P. Hagensen, constructed a pack filled with C-2 explosive and a primacord fuse which could be attached to the obstacle with hooks. The charge, known as the Hagensen Pack, was later adopted by the Navy as standard demolition issue.

As the invasion date neared and the Germans installed more beach obstacles, the NCDUs were placed into larger Gap Assault Teams. These teams consisted of five NCDUs, three

SeaBees, and five Army combat engineers. A 26-man team of Army engineers was also assigned to each team. The joint teams were responsible for clearing 50-yard gaps along Omaha and Utah beaches.

Despite rough weather and murderous enemy fire, all NCDU teams arrived at Omaha Beach at 0633 on 6 June. Without the planned effect of support fire, which failed miserably, the determined NCDUs still blew eight complete gaps and two partial gaps through the beach defenses. But the death toll was horrendous. The NCDUs suffered a staggering 52 percent casualties. Of the 175 NCDUs assigned to Omaha Beach, 31 were killed and 60 wounded.

Meanwhile, at Utah Beach the NCDUs fared much better. Due to lighter enemy fire, fewer obstacles, and more cooperative weather conditions, the NCDUs cleared 1,600 yards of beach by day's end, resulting in only six killed and 11 wounded.

After the bloodletting on Omaha Beach, serious questions were raised concerning the value of NCDUs. Given the vast number of obstacles, it was apparent that the teams were too small and that more demolitioneers had to be employed in future invasions. Following one last operation in Southern France in August 1944, the NCDUs in the Atlantic Theater were all but through. Many transferred to the Pacific Theater and were absorbed into larger Underwater Demolition Teams in preparation for the Allied drive toward Japan.

Clearly, the Naval Combat Demolition Units of World War II hold a solid place among America's elite fighting units. Although the unit's mission was not to engage the enemy, rather to destroy what it built, their expertise, training, and courage certainly qualify it as one of the best of the best.

JEDBURGHS

"We are going to need very badly the support of the Resistance groups in France," wrote General Eisenhower, Supreme Commander of the Allied Forces, in a secret cable just two months before the Allied invasion of Normandy. To ensure a

A Jedburgh with his full operational equipment. National Archives.

successful operation, Eisenhower needed special teams of French-speaking agents who could parachute behind German lines on the eve of the invasion, establish communications with Allied Headquarters, and organize and supply the several ill-equipped bands of Maquis (Resistance) operating in Brittany. Once organized, the Maquis were to tie down as many German troops as possible in the region, while Allied armies secured a foothold on the beaches. But the OSS and British SOE, which were responsible for inserting agents into Nazi-occupied territory and organizing partisan activity, were already at work.

Volunteers for the three-man Jedburgh teams, composed usually of a British or American officer, a French officer, and an enlisted radio operator, were drawn from various Allied units. Beginning in August 1943, the OSS began recruiting about 100 of its best men from American units based in the European and Mediterranean Theaters, and at installations throughout the United States. The British drew many of their volunteers from the Special Air Service, while French recruits were obtained from former French military units.

On 3 January 1944, the first class of recruits, which included a colorful mix of professional soldiers, thrill-seekers, and intellectuals, was taken to a secret commando training camp in the Scottish Highlands to begin the first phase of their training. One account states that it was from the location of the camp, situated on a 12th century royal burgh on the Jed River, that the "Jedburghs" took their name, but most accounts indicate that the name was chosen at random in July 1942, from a list of "pre-approved codenames." The group was originally to be called "Jumpers," but the SOE Chief of Security didn't like it.

Each man was carefully handpicked and had to meet exceedingly rigid selection criteria. Volunteers had to speak French, possess high intelligence, and be in outstanding physical condition. Candidates had to display courage, leadership ability, strong bearing, tolerance, fairness, and sound judgment. It was also helpful if they had some experience in guerrilla operations. Since capture meant certain torture and most likely death, each man underwent three days of strenuous psychological and physical testing. Those who passed attended a rigorous hands-on training course and received classes on agent fieldcraft, Morse Code, enemy weapons, silent movement, raiding tactics, and various forms of unarmed combat. Silent killing and hand-to-hand combat was taught by former members of the Shanghai Police, who had learned their deadly craft under the ruthless Tongs in China. One of the most important skills taught at the camp was demolitions. The Jeds spent hours setting charges and blowing up old railroad lines, bridges, and buildings.

Those who passed the first phase were sent to Ringway, England, for an abbreviated three-day parachute course, and then on to Milton Hall, for advanced training. It was there, at the transformed country estate of an aristocratic English family, that the agents formed their own teams based on friendship, trust, and ability. Each team was normally designated by either a male or female first name, such as TEAM ANDY or TEAM HILLARY. At Milton Hall, the teams refined their craft, learning sabotage, evasion, and a host of other skills. They even learned lockpicking and safecracking from one of Britain's top burglars.

By late April, the first teams of Jedburghs had completed training. On the eve of the Allied invasion, after nearly two months of waiting, the Jeds were ready to jump into France.

Between 6 June and 16 September 1944, 99 Jedburgh teams, consisting of 276 men, parachuted into France, Belgium, and the Netherlands. In support of the Normandy invasion in June, the landing in Southern France (Operation Dragoon) in August, and the airborne invasion of occupied Holland in September, the Jedburghs organized, equipped, and trained rag-tag bands of partisans into a highly-effective force and passed valuable information back to London. The Jedburgh teams, French partisans, and OSS Operational Groups often worked hand-in-hand. For nearly four hectic months, the Jeds and partisans successfully protected the flanks of advancing Allied units, radioed vital information to headquarters, rescued downed pilots, ambushed German convoys, destroyed rail lines and bridges, cut telegraph wires, liberated towns, and tied down thousands of enemy troops.

On 13 October 1944, all American and British Jedburgh teams were ordered to return to Great Britain where the teams were disbanded and the project closed. Many American Jedburgh members then joined Operational Groups. Others were sent to the China-Burma-India Theater or to Indochina, where they trained, equipped, and organized partisans in their struggle against occupying Japanese forces.

Later, in 1952, the U.S. Army Special Forces was formed by a former Jed, based largely on the training and operations of the World War II Jedburghs.

AIR COMMANDO GROUPS

On 13 September 1943, General Arnold, the farsighted chief of the United States Army Air Force, approved the formation of PROJECT NINE. The top secret plan provided for the creation of a "self-reliant composite fighting force" to support Brigadier General Orde C. Wingate and his "Chindits" in their long-range penetration into Japanese-occupied Burma.

The concept of PROJECT NINE intrigued Arnold. As an aviation pioneer, Arnold was the 29th pilot licensed in the United States, and the first, in 1911, to deliver mail by air. He was also one of the earliest and strongest advocates of airborne warfare. Arnold recognized the value of an air unit which could act independently from a larger organization, provide tactical support, and coordinate missions with ground units. In effect, he authorized the first Air-Ground Task Force.

Although designated PROJECT NINE to maintain secrecy, the unit was later called the 5318th Provisional Unit (Air). In March 1944, the unit was redesignated the 1st Air Commando Group (1 ACG) in honor of Lord Louis Mountbatten, the British leader of the Southeast Asia Command.

In a unique arrangement, Arnold selected two lieutenant colonels Philip G. Cochran and John R. Alison to co-command the unit. Each was an experienced fighter pilot and had earned a reputation as an improviser. Cochran had seen extensive combat in North Africa while Alison had served with Claire Chennault's Flying Tigers in China and as the Assistant Air Attache at the American Embassy in Moscow. Cochran was the stereotype fighter pilot, young, handsome and audacious. Alison, on the other hand, was shy and introverted, and preferred to work behind the scenes. Despite the difference in their personalities, both men were mavericks. In combat they each used unorthodox methods and were highly successful. This impressed Arnold. Upon meeting Cochran, Arnold proclaimed frankly, "Let's transform the Wingate show into an air show!" That's just what they did.

Wingate, considered by many to be a military genius for his innovative use of deep penetration tactics, was desperate for small utility aircraft to help resupply his troops and evacuate the wounded. During his first Chindit expedition into Burma in 1943, Wingate was forced to leave several wounded men behind because the Allies were unable to get them out of the jungle. Naturally, morale among his troops plummeted. Any help that Wingate could get from the Air Corps would be a plus. What he got far exceeded his expectations.

With Arnold's weighty support, Cochran and Alison requested and received approximately 300 aircraft of all kinds.

This included approximately 100 CG-4A (WACO) gliders, 20 C-47 and 20 UC-64 transports, 100 L-1 and L-5 light utility craft, 30 P-51 Mustang fighters, 20 B-25 Mitchell medium bombers, and six of the newly-built R-4 Sikorsky helicopters.

Not only did the unit get the latest aircraft, it also got the finest men and equipment available. The 600 volunteers of 1st Air Commando Group were the only U.S. airmen trained in jungle ground tactics. They were outfitted with paratrooper uniforms and Marine Corps jungle boots, and armed with folding stock carbines, .45 caliber pistols, and two knives.

In January 1944, the 1st Air Commando Group and Wingate began testing innovative ways to use their gliders. They experimented with troop insertion, extraction, and with recovery of glider craft. Recovery was accomplished by mounting specially-designed snatch mechanisms on the nose of the glider, which enabled troop transports to pull them out. Since Wingate believed that pack mules were the most reliable cargo carrier on earth, Cochran and Alison also staged the first successful glider transport of pack mules. To add to their firepower, Cochran mounted multiple .5 inch machine guns in the nose of the Mitchell bombers. "We were the first air outfit to do a rocket-firing job" said Cochran. "We had to make the rocket equipment ourselves . . ." By February 1944, 1st Air Commando Group was ready for action.

Cochran led five P-51 Mustangs on the unit's first combat mission on 3 February. The next day, the Air Commando Group conducted a treetop supply mission to the encircled British at the battle of Admin Box, and flew the first of 54 fighter and bomber missions against Japanese lines of communications in northern Burma. Within a week 1st Air Commando flew the first B-25 bomber mission in Burma. It was during March and April 1944 that the Air Commandos left an indelible mark in the history of special operations.

"Nothing you've ever done, nothing you're ever going to do counts now, only the next few hours," said Cochran to the glider pilots of 1st Air Commando just moments before they took off from Lalaghat, India, to spearhead the first all-airborne invasion in history. "Tonight you are going to find your souls."

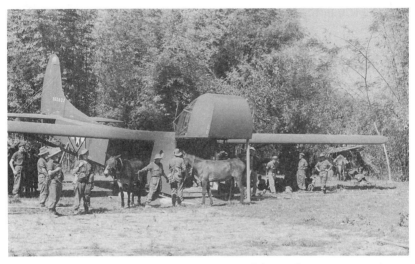

1st Air Commando Grp. loads mules on gliders prior to an operation in Burma, 1944. Courtesy Nat. Air & Space Museum.

Pilots and crew of YR4B helicopter used in Burma, 1944, to rescue downed airmen. Part of 1st Air Commandos. Nat. Air & Space Museum.

Within a few hours, 46 gliders laden with Chindits, landed by surprise deep behind Japanese lines south of Myitkyina, in the Koukkwee Valley. Despite a rough landing and several casualties, "Operation THURSDAY" was a success. Wingate's men quickly secured the area, nicknamed "Broadway," and began constructing a 4800-foot airstrip and supply center from which the Chindits could be resupplied. The next day the 1st Air Commando Group conducted a second all-airborne invasion at Chowringhee, 50 miles to the south.

Less than a day later, Cochran launched 92 C-47 cargo planes and resupplied the Chindits behind enemy lines. For the remainder of the month Air Commando Group planes harassed enemy aircraft and troops on the ground and provided close air support for the Chindits. During March, the 1st Air Commando Group accounted for one-fifth of the Japanese Air Force planes destroyed in Burma. Meanwhile, pilots resupplied and evacuated wounded Chindits, which boosted their morale.

The 1st Air Commando Group also blazed the trail in the art of medical evacuation. On 21 April 1944, First Lieutenant Carter Harman, a light plane pilot who was grounded because of asthma, flew the first helicopter combat mission into Burma and rescued a downed pilot. Harman went on to fly 22 more rescue missions. By the end of the campaign in Burma, the 1st Air Commando Group had evacuated more than 2,000 wounded.

It was also in April that Alison returned to the United States to form the 2nd and 3rd Air Commando Groups based on the model established by the 1st ACG. On 27 April the 2nd and 3rd Air Commando Groups were activated and sent to India. Because of the approaching monsoon season, the units didn't get the chance to work in Burma, but they did transport combat troops into China.

By 1 May 1944, the 1st Air Commando Group was exhausted and the Air Corps decided to disband the group, effective that day. Before the unit left the theater, they got in one parting shot at the Japanese. On 19 May, seven Mustangs engaged a convoy of Japanese bombers over Burma. Within minutes one bomber and two fighter escorts were in flames.

What seemed like the final, illustrious chapter in the history of the Air Commandos, was actually the beginning. The tactics developed by Cochran and Alison are still used by today's Air Force Special Operations Command.

MERRILL'S MARAUDERS

Code named GALAHAD, the 3,000-man 5307th Composite Unit (Provisional) was formed on 3 October 1943, to perform long-range penetration missions behind Japanese lines in the hot, steamy jungles and rugged mountains of northern Burma. Organized into three battalions, the 5307th was originally commanded by Colonel Charles N. Hunter, and modeled after Orde Wingate's Chindits. The Chindits, a mixed brigade of British, Indian, Gurkha, and Burmese troops, had been assembled to disrupt Japanese lines of communications in northern Burma.

Volunteers for the 5307th received extensive training near Deolali, India, where they underwent a grueling physical conditioning regimen and learned advanced deep penetration tactics under Wingate's watchful eye. The unit then moved to Deogarh, in central India, where it trained in scouting and patrolling, demolitions, air resupply drops, medical evacuation, and assorted survival skills. They also spent two weeks in the jungle training alongside the Chindits, where they learned the "finer points" of jungle warfare.

Although the Marauders were formed to conduct deep penetration reconnaissance, they were rarely used that way. Instead, General Joseph W. "Vinegar Joe" Stilwell, the American theater commander, used the Marauders as a flanking force in concert with two Chinese divisions in an attempt to clear northern Burma, and reopen an overland supply route into China. Since Stilwell was reluctant to place American combat forces under foreign command, he selected Brigadier General Frank D. Merrill of his staff to lead the unit. Shortly after Merrill took command in early 1944, *Time-Life* correspondent James Shelby dubbed the rough and tumble men of the 5307th as "Merrill's Marauders." It was Hunter, however, not Merrill, who usually led the Marauders into combat. To Merrill's great frustration, he suffered from a heart condition which often prevented him from remaining with his troops throughout an entire operation.

Beginning in late February 1944, the Marauders marched 140 miles from their staging area at Ledo, India, to Shingbwiyang, Burma. From there they fought their way through 500 miles of hellish jungles and mountains and engaged Japanese forces at Walawbum, Jambu Bum, and Shaduzup. They conducted a series of sweeps to the east, getting behind Japanese lines and establishing roadblocks to ambush unsuspecting Japanese units. At Nhpum Ga one battalion was encircled and nearly wiped out. Merrill was evacuated just prior to this action, having suffered a massive heart attack. Hunter and Merrill were both told by Stilwell that this would be the last mission for GALAHAD.

But following victories in the Hukawng and Mogaung valleys, Stilwell and Allied planners turned their eyes to Myitkyina, the lone enemy stronghold in the area. Situated along the Irrawaddy River, Myitkyina contained the only all-weather airstrip in northern Burma and was a vital link in Japanese communication and supply efforts in northern Burma. Control of Myitkyina and the nearby airstrip would deny the Japanese a fighter base from which to attack Allied transports delivering supplies to China.

Due to the shortage of American replacements in the China-Burma-India (CBI) Theater, Stilwell had no choice but to use the Marauders. They were now almost completely exhausted and in no condition to mount a major attack. The Marauders had already spent almost three grueling months in the field and had lost over 700 men. To shore up the unit, Stilwell reinforced the Marauders with Kachin tribesmen and Chinese troops, which raised the unit's combined strength to 7,000 men. The combined force was designated the Myitkyina Strike Force and consisted of three columns. Hunter was the leader of H Force, which was charged with capturing the airfield. The other two columns, M Force and K Force, named for their leaders, were to provide flank security for Hunter while a force of Kachin Rangers screened the Marauder's movement to the east.

On 28 April, the Marauders began the arduous 65-mile trek over the unforgiving 6000-foot Kumon Mountain Range toward Myitkyina. For three weeks the Marauders, along with 700

An element of GALAHAD crosses the Tanai Hka on 18 March 1944 on its way to set up a roadblock at Inkangantawng. National Archives.

Brig. Gen. Frank D. Merrill and two of his twin brother aides, Lts. Elbert & Albert Higgins. Burma, 1944. DOD Photo.

equally tired pack mules and horses, slogged their way over the steep, muddy trails toward their objective. Blinding monsoons, stifling heat, and the constant effects of dysentery, typhus, and other tropical diseases, added to the rigors.

On 17 May the Marauders reached the outskirts of the town and launched a surprise attack. They quickly seized the airfield and a nearby ferry site on the Irawaddy river, but were unable to capture Myitkyina. Merrill arrived at the airfield that afternoon but suffered another heart attack. He was evacuated on the same plane that brought him in. After a few days, Japanese reinforcements arrived and mounted several vicious counterattacks.

For the next two weeks the beleaguered Marauders held on by their fingernails. Hunter was now in command of the entire force but grew increasingly irritated by headquarters' apparent lack of concern about his men and its cancellation of a preplanned supply drop. Despite sinking morale, fanatic Japanese attacks, high casualties, deplorable sanitary conditions, disease, and the overwhelming stench of rotting pack mules, the Marauders held on. Finally, on 1 June, reinforcements arrived.

By that time nearly 50 men a day were being evacuated due to disease and malnutrition. The combined unit had dwindled to an effective strength of less than 700. Of the 1,300 men of the 5307th who fought at Myitkyina, only 200 remained to witness the town fall to Allied troops on 3 August. That same day, Hunter was relieved of command. One week later, "Merrill's Marauders" was inactivated.

Those Marauders who were left after Myitkyina, and replacements, who were called NEW GALAHAD, were reorganized into the newly-formed 475th Infantry Regiment. The unit then combined with the 124th Cavalry Regiment, a Texas National Guard unit, and other units to form Mars Task Force, a similar deep-penetration unit commanded by General John P. Willey. From August 1944 to March 1945, Mars Task Force and Kachin tribesmen harassed Japanese supply lines from Myitkyina, south to Lashio, along the all-important Burma Road.

On 7 March, the Japanese pulled out of Lashio. This enabled the Allies to link a road from Ledo, India, to the Burma Road and to reopen the route to China.

In retrospect, Merrill's Marauders were never given a chance to do what they were trained for. This elite unit was wasted on operations that were more suited to conventional line infantry units, rather than to a highly-mobile, hit-and-run type unit. Despite being regarded as "unwanted stepchildren" of Stilwell's command, Merrill's Marauders value in taking Myitkyina cannot be underrated. In combat only six months, the 5307th Composite Unit fought five major and 30 minor engagements with Japanese forces.

CARPETBAGGERS

"Flying on instruments over the fog-shrouded English Channel—in total silence, in a small capsule high above the earth—produced a silent, helpless terror," wrote author Joseph E. Persico. He was describing the atmosphere aboard a specially modified B-24 Liberator on its clandestine flight to drop Allied agents, supplies, and propaganda leaflets into occupied Europe. Under the direction of the OSS and SOE, the top secret drops, known as the "Carpetbagger Project," were conducted by two squadrons of the United States 8th Air Force 801st Bombardment Group (Heavy), later redesignated as the 492nd Bombardment Group.

Nicknamed "Carpetbaggers," the 801st/492nd Bombardment Group operated under tight security from Harrington Air Field, outside London. Since Carpetbagger flights were flown at night over enemy territory, the pilots and crew were specially trained in low level, night flying. The normal ten-man crew was reduced to eight for extra cargo space. The fleet of special-purpose B-24's was modified for optimum stealth. To cut down on the reflection of German search beams, each plane was painted glossy or matte black. The plexiglass ball-turret on the belly of the aircraft was removed and covered with a retractable plywood door. During agent drops, the crew removed the door and

A Carpetbagger crew in front of its black B-24 Liberator. National Archives.

the agent dropped through the hole. As an additional precaution, each plane was fitted with flame dampeners which helped conceal the glow of the exhaust. Special flash suppressors were also attached to the muzzles of the tail guns.

To increase space inside the plane, all unnecessary armament and equipment was removed. This allowed the planes to carry up to eight agents and their supplies. Since Carpetbagger drops were conducted at altitudes as low as 500 feet over mountainous terrain, the oxygen system was removed and special radar navigation aids installed. Because of the sophisticated radar, the planes also contained detonators. If the planes crash-landed in enemy territory, the crew ensured that the plane, its cargo, and its equipment were completely destroyed.

To insure secrecy, the crews were not even allowed to talk to the agents they were dropping. In fact, the drops were so sensitive that the pilots and crews signed non-disclosure statements and were not allowed to speak to other Carpetbagger crews about their missions.

The first operational mission was flown on 4 January 1944. Two months later, on 2 March, the Carpetbaggers conducted their first drop of an OSS agent, or "Joe" drop. From March through September 1944, the Carpetbaggers dropped hundreds of OSS Jedburgh, Operational Group, and SOE agents into occupied France in support of the Allied invasion. The Carpetbaggers also supplied the agents and the French resistance with weapons, food, communications equipment, and whatever else they needed.

On 16 September, with most of France liberated, the Carpetbagger missions were complete. The Carpetbaggers then turned their attention to resupply, rescue, psychological warfare, and strategic bombing. During the last week of September, the Carpetbaggers began flying C-47 "Dakota" planes and helped resupply the Allies' fast-moving armored divisions with nearly one million gallons of fuel. They also flew into Switzerland and repatriated several Allied flyers who had escaped from enemy territory.

In November 1944, one squadron was attached to the 406th Night Leaflet Squadron and helped drop millions of propaganda leaflets into Nazi Germany. In late December, the Carpetbaggers began conducting night bombing raids on light industrial installations and coastal batteries.

The Carpetbaggers resumed their mission of dropping Allied agents and supplies into occupied territory on 1 January 1945, while continuing to bomb German targets. On 23 March, the Carpetbaggers, who were now largely operating from an airfield in Dijon, France, dropped their first agent into the Bavarian Alps. At the same time, the Carpetbaggers intensified their efforts in Norway and Denmark. During the last three weeks of April, the Carpetbaggers flew over 160 missions into the Low Countries.

On 7 May, the war in Europe was over. By mid-August the entire unit was back in the United States and was redesignated as the 492nd Bombardment Group (Very Heavy). One month later the 45 officers and 1,200 men were reassigned. On 17 October 1945, the 801st/492nd Bombardment Group was officially inactivated at Kirtland Field in Albuquerque, New Mexico.

ALAMO SCOUTS

"To heck with this. I'll form my own intelligence unit!" screamed Lieutenant General Walter Krueger in October 1943. Krueger, the commanding general of Sixth Army, was furious with what he perceived as the Navy's lack of cooperation during the recent joint Army/Navy Gasmata Operation. This was merely the straw that broke the camel's back. Krueger had been reluctant to place his intelligence assets under the command of General Sir Thomas A. Blamey, the Australian commander of all Allied ground troops. He had also been alarmed by the Army's recent bungling of the Kiska operation in the Aleutians. Poor intelligence resulted in a massive bombardment and subsequent assault of the enemy-deserted island causing numerous friendly fire casualties. All of this prompted Krueger to form the Sixth Army Special Reconnaissance Unit, known as the Alamo Scouts.

By creating his own intelligence unit and formulating a general outline of training garnered from the best training programs from the 1st Special Service Force, Darby's Rangers, the Naval Combat Demolition Units, and the Navy's Scouts & Raiders, Krueger was determined to have a first-rate unit "at his disposal," and took every step to insure that there would be no "Kiska" in his area of responsibility.

The Alamo Scouts were formed as an *ad hoc* unit on 28 November 1943 to conduct long-range reconnaissance, intelligence collection, and raider operations in the jungles and on the beaches of the Southwest Pacific Area. Members of the Alamo Scouts were selected from among Sixth Army's finest volunteers.

Candidates underwent a grueling six-week training course developed by Krueger and his staff at various Alamo Scouts Training Centers which were established on New Guinea and in the Philippines throughout the war. Each time Sixth Army moved forward, it re-established the training center. As each camp was set up, the previous camp was closed. Candidates received intensive instruction in all facets of rubber boat oper-

Alamo Scout in jungle, New Guinea, 1944.

ations, scouting and patrolling, survival, navigation, conditioning, language, communications, weapons, and intelligence collection. Top graduates were retained and formed into small,
highly-trained six-to-seven-man teams. The remaining graduates returned to their previous units and performed similar
reconnaissance operations.

Of the 400 graduates of the Alamo Scouts Training Centers,
only 117 enlisted men and 21 officers were retained. Throughout World War II, 19 teams were formed, with a peak strength
of 12. The teams were normally led by a lieutenant and assumed
the last name of the team leader. The remainder of the team
was composed of five or six noncommissioned officers and
enlisted men. Contrary to belief, the Alamo Scouts were not an
all-airborne qualified unit. Only two teams of Alamo Scouts
were airborne qualified, having been recruited from the 11th
Airborne Division and the 503rd Parachute Infantry Regiment.

The Alamo Scouts conducted 106 known missions behind
Japanese lines throughout World War II. Operating within their
teams, the Scouts normally landed on hostile territory by rubber
boat, submarine, PBY flying plane, or PT boat. After completing

their mission, Scout teams exfiltrated by rubber boat and were picked up by a contact team of trained Scouts waiting aboard a PT boat.

The Scouts conducted their first mission on 27-28 February 1944 on Los Negros, the second-largest of the Admiralty Islands. Two days prior to the Allied landing a crack team of Alamo Scouts infiltrated by rubber boat and radioed vital information on enemy troop strength to a support team flying overhead in a B-25.

"This place is lousy with Japs!" exclaimed team leader Lieutenant John R.C. McGowen, as he reported his findings. As a result of the Scouts information, the reconnaissance-in-force element, commanded by Brigadier General William C. Chase, became an invasion force and successfully landed on Los Negros. This secured access to the Bismarck Sea and established a staging base for operations against the Japanese along the northern coast of New Guinea.

During the Bismarck Archipelago and New Guinea Campaigns the Scouts performed 35 pre-invasion reconnaissance and intelligence missions and one extraordinary prison camp raid. Two teams of Scouts liberated 66 Dutch and Javanese prisoners from a camp near Cape Oransbari and killed 18 Japanese guards in only four minutes. At that point the Scouts typical mission lasted about three days and covered approximately 40 miles. As the Scouts advanced into the Philippines, their mission changed. While working on Leyte and the surrounding smaller islands, the Scouts conducted 13 missions and assumed a greater role in intelligence collection by organizing extensive guerrilla networks and setting up road-watch stations.

It was on Luzon that the Scouts did their most outstanding work. From 9 January to early August 1945, the Alamo Scouts conducted 55 successful missions, many lasting more than 45 days. The most notable mission was the combined Alamo Scouts/6th Ranger operation in which the units conducted a daring night raid on Cabanatuan Prison Camp. In less than 30 minutes the Scouts and Rangers liberated 513 Allied prisoners of war, many of whom had been captured on Bataan and on Corregidor.

The Scouts worked very closely with various guerrilla groups on Luzon, providing them with supplies, equipment, weapons, and even leadership. A special section of Sixth Army G-2 supported the effort. The Scouts final two missions were in support of Sixth Army occupational landings in Japan. The most impressive feat is that the Alamo Scouts performed 106 missions behind enemy lines and never lost a man killed or captured.

Not only did the Alamo Scouts conduct reconnaissance and intelligence missions which supported conventional combat units, they also traveled with Krueger as his personal escort and bodyguard. The duty provided the Scouts with a little rest and relaxation, but it also had an unpleasant side. "We had orders to kill the General if his capture was imminent," recalled one Scout. "He simply knew too much."

After traveling to Japan with Krueger, the Alamo Scouts were administratively attached to the 6th Ranger Battalion and were unceremoniously disbanded in Kyoto in late November 1945.

"I wouldn't take the whole Jap Army for one Alamo Scout!" declared Krueger, speaking of his beloved Alamo Scouts. "This little unit has never failed the U.S. Army."

The Alamo Scouts are considered to be the Army's first Long-Range Reconnaissance Patrol and Long-Range Surveillance Unit. In 1988 the Alamo Scouts were awarded the Special Forces Tab by the John F. Kennedy Special Warfare Center & School at Fort Bragg, recognizing them as a forerunner of the modern Special Forces.

UNDERWATER DEMOLITION TEAMS

"The most effective method of destroying beach mines and obstacles is to send men in to perform individual demolitions in advance of landing," lamented Admiral Richmond Kelly Turner, following the bloodletting on the beaches of Tarawa. Scores of U.S. Marines were slaughtered due to inadequate reconnaissance of the barrier reef surrounding the island. Determined not to repeat the disaster on future landings, Turner recommended to Admiral Ernest King on 26 December 1943, that nine Underwater Demolitions Teams (UDTs) be formed to remove natural and man-made obstacles, scout enemy beaches, and guide invasion forces ashore. Turner also called for an "Experimental and Tactical Underwater Demolition Station" to be established in Hawaii. Plans for such units, however, were already in motion. Within little more than a month, the first two UDTs graduated from the Waimanalo Amphibious Training Base, on Oahu. In February 1944, the Naval Combat Demolition Training and Experimental Base was established on Maui. The Navy "Frogmen" were born.

Although the Navy had been using Scouts & Raiders to conduct beach and inland reconnaissance, and NCDUs to help clear beaches and guide invasion troops, neither unit was capable of handling the large-scale clearing operations that would be needed on the countless islands of the Pacific. Consisting of 13 officers and 87 men, mostly drawn from the NCDUs, the newly-formed UDTs were just right for the job.

The hallmark of the UDTs was training. Each UDT candidate underwent a grueling, highly-disciplined, six-week course in which he familiarized himself with numerous types of explosives and underwater obstacles. The course also emphasized long distance swimming. Unlike the NCDUs at Fort Pierce, which trained in heavy combat gear and helmets, the men of the UDTs took a different approach. Men trained only in swim trunks, tennis shoes, and a mask, and were not allowed to wear a life belt. Each man had to swim two miles in open water, float with 25 pounds of gear, dive several feet below the surface, measure water depth, identify coral formations and sand composition, and set explosive charges.

As if the course wasn't demanding enough, during the final days candidates were put through "Hell Week," a ruthless physical and psychological weeding out process instituted by the Navy's Scouts & Raiders. Those who survived Hell Week and graduated, were placed on a team and began preparing for the perilous duty ahead—the slow, bloody drive toward Japan.

The World War II UDTs resume is long and distinguished: Kwajalein, Eniwetok, Roi-Namur, Tinian, Guam, Peleliu, Yap, Anguar, Ulithi, Leyte, Luzon, Iwo Jima, Okinawa, Balikpapan,

Tokyo Bay, and countless other tiny islands. But it was on Saipan, in mid-June 1944, where the UDTs cemented their place among America's elite forces.

SAIPAN

Saipan marked the first large-scale operation in which the Frogmen conducted their surveys in broad daylight. Clad only in swim trunks, tennis shoes, knee pads, and ringed with black grease paint every 12 inches to measure water depth, the "Naked Warriors" of UDT 5, now commanded by ex-Scout & Raider commander Draper Kauffman, and UDT 7 also carried a plexiglass tablet around their necks to record their findings. The Frogmen of World War II rarely used SCUBA equipment (it had not yet been perfected).

Although the swimmers normally swam no more than 600 yards to their destination, Saipan was different. On the morning of 14 June, under heavy mortar and artillery fire from 20,000 Japanese defenders, and under the constant threat of their own naval covering fire, the men were dropped off in pairs at 50-yard intervals. They zigzagged their way over a mile of open water. While one man of the pair marked mines and obstacles with balsa wood floats, the other measured the distance between the reef and given points using a reel and fishing line that was knotted every 25 yards. After surveying the reef, the frogmen continued into the lagoon coming as close as 30 yards from the shore where Japanese troops tried in vain to pick them off with small arms fire.

Despite the intense fire, the UDTs coolly performed their mission and made their way back to sea. They were picked up and taken aboard ships to map out the approach routes for the Marine landing forces. Miraculously, of the 200 men of UDTs 5 and 7, only three were killed and 15 wounded.

The next day Marines successfully assaulted the beaches of Saipan with lighter than expected casualties. Later, on 9 July, Saipan was secured. There was no repeat of Tarawa. The Allies now had a base from which their B-29 bombers could reach the Japanese home islands. The UDTs had done their job well.

There was still a lot of work to do, however. Following the success on Saipan, the UDTs increased the number of teams and were involved in nearly every major amphibious landing in the Pacific. On Guam, UDTs 3, 4, and 6 cleared 620 obstacles on Asan Beach. Members of UDT 4 even violated orders and went ashore on Agat Beach prior to the invasion and left the Marine landing force a sign reading:

Welcome, Marines
AGAT USO TWO Blocks
Courtesy UDT 4

OKINAWA

The largest UDT operation of the war was performed on Okinawa in April 1945. Ten teams, consisting of 1,000 men, thoroughly combed the waters of the island and the nearby smaller islands of Kerama Retto, Keise Shima, and Ie Shima, in preparation for the landing on one of the most bitterly contested pieces of ground in the Pacific. Months later, on 4 July, the UDTs performed their final combat mission of the war at Balikpapan in Borneo. All told during the war, 31 teams were formed, numbering almost 3,500 men.

Had the invasion of Japan been necessary, at least 30 of these UDTs would have been needed. The UDTs got their chance to work in Japanese waters anyway, clearing obstacles and mines in Tokyo Bay, demilitarizing ships, destroying suicide boats and torpedoes, and disarming coastal batteries. For a month after the Japanese surrender, the UDTs performed unsung service in Japan, China, and Korea.

"The results achieved by these UDTs are far above anything one might imagine," said Turner, "...when one watches them perform under the gunfire of the enemy, one cannot fail to be impressed by their boundless courage. The nation's future is safe when defended by such men." By November 1945, the 31 UDTs were back in the United States and their fate was sealed. Peace meant drastic cuts in manpower and equipment. The UDTs would never again reach their World War II size, but five years later, they would be called on again, this time in the frigid waters of Korea.

KOREAN WAR

UDT operations during the Korean war were accomplished with mixed results. Following the Allied landing at Inch'on in

September 1950, UDTs successfully cleared the harbor of mines and obstacles. Additionally, the UDTs were increasingly used as onshore raiding parties. In early August 1950, a UDT landed on North Korean shores and attempted to sabotage a railroad tunnel, but the mission was unsuccessful. The UDTs then joined forces with a Marine reconnaissance force and formed a joint Special Operations Groups. Later that month the joint UDT/Marine force blew up three bridges and a number of railroad tunnels without suffering any casualties. Despite its success, the unit was disbanded and the UDTs were back in the hydrographic surveying and mine clearing business.

By the spring of 1951, the UDTs primary role changed again. The UDTs were once more employed as raiding forces along the North Korean coast. They were also formed into special "Salamander" teams that delivered and supplied Korean guerrilla units operating on several small islands off the west coast. Over the next year, the Salamander teams, which worked in conjunction with the CIA and the Eighth Army Miscellaneous Division, infiltrated hundreds of agents into North Korea.

In the summer of 1952, UDTs 3 and 5 participated in Operation FISHNET, in which they attempted to damage North Korea's commercial fishing industry. Although the teams damaged a number of nets and sank some sampans, the operation had little effect on the enemy's food supply.

Despite the ambiguous nature and arguable value of UDT operations in Korea, the UDTs laid much of the groundwork for the creation of modern naval special warfare units, especially the Navy SEALs. Following the truce in the Korean War, most UDTs returned to the United States. Some teams settled in at Coronado, California and others at Little Creek, Virginia. Each location conducted qualification training, known as UDT Basic or UDT Replacement. Following formation of the SEAL teams in 1962, the remaining UDTs' days were numbered.

PART VII

POST WORLD WAR II PERIOD

INTRODUCTION

Shortly after the end of World War II nearly all U.S. elite units were disbanded. As mentioned, only a token force of Navy UDT personnel remained on active duty. In 1950, the cold war that raged between democratic and communist philosophies for the past five years, turned hot. Communist North Korean forces exploded across the 38th Parallel and invaded South Korea. The United States was again propelled into war.

Unlike the last war, with its clearly defined objectives, Korea was deemed a "police action," and the traditional aim of "winning" became secondary to stabilization. The unforgiving terrain, extreme elements, ferocity of combat, and the static nature of the war, again forced the conventional U.S. military to adapt its forces. A small number of elite units was formed to conduct raids and wage unconventional war. Navy UDTs, with advances in SCUBA technology, not only performed their standard role of obstacle and beach clearing, they also conducted sabotage and commando raids behind the lines. The Marines and Air Force got involved in unconventional warfare. Marine Force Recon units were created to perform deep, long-range ground reconnaissance, while Air Force units performed air rescue missions and dropped and resupplied partisans and CIA agents into North Korea.

The Army formed the 8240th Army Unit to train and coordinate partisan resistance groups. It also brought back the Ranger concept in the form of airborne companies. It was at Fort Bragg, North Carolina in 1952, in response to the expected Soviet invasion of western Europe and the largely unsuccessful efforts at unconventional warfare in Korea, that it established the Special Forces, a permanent unconventional warfare unit. Special Forces groups did not participate in the Korean War on a large scale, but they developed and refined the art of unconventional warfare throughout the 1950s.

In the early 1960s, as U.S. involvement in Southeast Asia escalated and the cold war in Europe intensified, President John F. Kennedy ordered the military to increase its unconventional warfare capability. This resulted in the formation of elite Navy SEALs and the expansion of the existing Army Special Forces. During the Viet Nam War, Special Forces, SEALs, and UDTs conducted "their own brand of war." Special Forces advisors spearheaded early efforts in Viet Nam by training indigenous troops and attempting to win the hearts and minds of the Vietnamese people. Later, as the war grew, Special Forces and SEAL teams were increasingly used in direct action missions and clandestine intelligence operations. Air Force Special Operations Forces enjoyed a resurgence, as did Marine Force Recon, and Army Ranger and Long Range Reconnaissance Patrol units (LRRPs).

In 1970, elite Army and Air Force units combined forces and raided a North Vietnamese POW camp at Son Tay, deep inside North Viet Nam. The raid was conducted with precision, but no American POWs were found due to outdated intelligence. The near textbook operation proved that highly-trained, elite forces working in unison, could achieve extraordinary results. The raid was led by Colonel Arthur "Bull" Simons, who was a member of the 6th Ranger Battalion in World War II.

The humiliating withdrawal of U.S. forces from Viet Nam in 1975 nearly destroyed the reputation and effectiveness of the military. The strength and quality of elite units, such as the SEALs and Special Forces dwindled considerably. The condition worsened in 1980, when several operators from Delta Force, the Army's newly-formed counterterrorism unit, died in a fiery accident on a desert runway in Iran while preparing to rescue American hostages held by Iranian fundamentalists. This worsened condition was not a result of the caliber of men in the units, but by the style of the "management of forces" from the top leadership.

Following the tragic events in Iran, U.S. special operations forces re-evaluated themselves. The interservice rivalry and oversecrecy suffered by World War II units had reappeared. As a result, the Army formed its own air support units, while the SEALs absorbed existing UDTs to streamline Navy operations. Additionally, the Navy formed SEAL Team Six to conduct missions similar to the Army's Delta Force. The Air Force, in turn, consolidated and transferred its Special Operations Forces under one command. Moreover, newly-elected President Ronald Reagan committed his administration to rebuilding the military.

In 1983, U.S. special operations forces combined during the invasion of Grenada, with mixed results. Four years later, the U.S. Special Operations Command (USSOCOM) was established at MacDill Air Force Base, which served as a unified command responsible for coordinating special operations. Even Congress got into the act. It required the Department of Defense to establish an Assistant Secretary to oversee planning and policy of special operations and low intensity conflict. During the invasion of Panama in late 1989, special operations forces again worked together. Despite the overall success of Operation JUST CAUSE, special operations forces endured another setback. Although they were under a unified command which was responsible for employing special operations forces with an appropriate mission, the elite SEALs were misused. Just as many elite units of World War II had been, the SEALs were committed to an operation that would have been better suited to a larger conventional unit. As a result, eight SEALs were killed while attempting to capture an airfield, typically a mission performed by Army Rangers or even "straight leg" infantry.

After ten long years U.S. special operations forces redeemed themselves. During Operations DESERT SHIELD and DESERT STORM, elite Army, Navy, Air Force, and Marine units achieved outstanding results. Armed with the latest space-age technology, the elite units performed a gamut of missions, including deep reconnaissance, air rescue, direct action, intelligence, psychological warfare, demolition, mine clearing, and numerous clandestine operations.

Like their World War II predecessors, the men and women of the modern elite units are selected for their unique abilities, professionalism, and physical and mental toughness, and are among the most highly-trained and motivated troops in the world.

AIRBORNE RANGER COMPANIES

On 25 June 1950, 90,000 communist North Korean troops slashed across the 38th parallel into South Korea, starting the Korean War. The massive North Korean Army quickly rolled over United Nations forces and plunged deep into South Korea. Meanwhile, scores of communist agents infiltrated South Korean cities and wreaked havoc. As an ally of South Korea, the United States was suddenly and violently thrust into a war it neither wanted nor was prepared to fight.

In early August 1950, in response to the widespread infiltration of communist agents and the brutal nature of the conflict, Army Chief of Staff General J. Lawton Collins called for the creation of an elite, airborne, raiding force. He wanted a force that could "infiltrate through enemy lines and attack command posts, artillery, tank parks, and key communications centers or facilities."

Lieutenant Colonel John H. McGee, a veteran of guerrilla operations in the Philippines during World War II and brother of one of the battalion commanders of Merrill's Marauders, sprang into action and began assembling such a unit. The ghosts of the U.S. Army Rangers who had fought and died in North Africa, Europe, and in the Philippines, during World War II, were given new life—this time in the Land of the Morning Calm.

On 24 August 1950, the Eighth Army Ranger Company, with a strength of three officers and 73 men obtained from Eighth Army infantry units, was formed at Camp Drake, Japan. Following a brief weeding out process, the men sailed for Pusan, Korea, to begin seven weeks of training at the newly-established Eighth Army Ranger Training Center. The unit was later redesignated the Eighth Army Ranger Company, 8213th Army Unit.

A short time later, on 29 September, the 1st through 4th Ranger Companies were formed, and a Ranger Training Center established at the Army's Infantry School, Fort Benning, Georgia. Top volunteers for the Ranger units were selected from the 11th and 82nd Airborne Divisions, and from men who had served with the World War II Ranger Battalions. Others were drawn from former members of the 1st Special Service Force and Merrill's Marauders. The new Ranger Companies were modeled after their World War II counterparts, and contained approximately five officers and 107 enlisted men. Between September 1950 and September 1951, 18 Ranger Companies were formed. Seventeen were airborne. Only eight companies saw combat in Korea while the remainder served throughout the United States and Europe.

Realistic and tough training was the hallmark of the Ranger Companies. The training, which began with calisthenics followed by a five-mile run in the thick, red, Georgia clay, weeded out all but the strongest men. Candidates trained 60 hours a week and learned Allied and foreign weapons, small unit tactics, demolitions, sabotage, communications, patrolling, and land navigation. To enhance training, the Rangers were given field problems under real combat conditions and allowed little sleep. This was in addition to the frequent twenty-mile speed marches which Darby's Rangers had instituted as a Ranger tradition in 1942.

The most unique of all the Ranger Companies was the 4th Ranger Company. This all-black unit was the only such company of Rangers ever formed. For some unexplained reason, on 9 October 1950, the 4th and 2nd Ranger Companies swapped designations. The 2nd Ranger Company later distinguished itself in bitter combat against Chinese Communist Forces at Tanyang, Sang Kwiryang, and on several other battlefields in Korea.

The 2nd and 4th Ranger Companies, along with the 2nd and 3rd Battalions of the 187th Regimental Combat Team, also had the distinction of performing the first Airborne Ranger drop in history. On 23 March 1951, the combined force parachuted into battle at Munsan-ni, in support of Operation TOMAHAWK, the planned airborne envelopment of North Korean forces retreating north from Seoul. The Rangers quickly reached their objective and captured the first enemy soldiers taken in the operation. Later, in April 1951, the 4th Ranger Company crossed the Pukhan River aboard rubber boats and assaulted enemy positions on the high ground above the Hwachon Dam,

2nd Airborne Rangers Co. Korea. DOD Photo.

M.Sgt. George Rankins, 2nd Ranger Co, being awarded Silver Star by Maj. Gen. Ferenbaugh for heroism in action. Korea, 7 Jul 1951. DOD Photo.

preventing retreating Chinese Communist Forces from blowing the dam.

Meanwhile, the 1st, 3rd, 5th, and 8th Ranger Companies were also busy assaulting enemy strongholds, capturing prisoners, and patrolling behind enemy lines. In a bitter struggle on "Bloody Nose Ridge," a hill near the village of Kantongyon, the 3rd Ranger Company attacked Chinese forces with fixed bayonets. After reaching the top of the hill, the Rangers fought a savage hand-to-hand struggle and captured the objective. For this action the company became known as the "Cold Steel

Third." Other Ranger Companies' actions were similar to those at "Bloody Nose Ridge," with Rangers assaulting enemy-held high ground.

The bulk of Ranger operations in Korea was far less exciting. According to the original concept of Ranger operations in Korea, which called for one company of Rangers to be attached to each infantry division to conduct raids, mount combat patrols, and set up ambushes, the Rangers were grossly misused. As with elite World War II units, such as the 1st and 3rd Ranger Battalions at Anzio, or Merrill's Marauders at Myitkyina, the highly-aggressive Airborne Ranger Companies were often thrown into conventional battles against superior forces. This usually resulted in appalling casualties, evidenced by the high Ranger death toll, which numbered 146 killed. Roughly one out of nine Rangers who served in Korea was killed in action.

One explanation for the high casualty rate is that conventional military commanders were unsure how to use the Rangers. Many leaders resented the Rangers' "elite" moniker and relegated them to minor roles as guards and as ordinary replacements for their line units. It was also a burden on the commanders to supply, arm, and equip the Rangers.

On 10 July 1951, with the demarcation line more-or-less stable, the Army ordered the deactivation of all Ranger Companies. The official reason was that "racial differences" existed "between the Oriental and Caucasian soldiers" which made it difficult to utilize such a force. But the true reason the Rangers were disbanded is probably a combination of resentment of the Rangers among conventional military commanders, coupled with the ongoing efforts by U.N. forces to obtain a truce. Since the war became more static in the summer of 1951, both sides probably realized that it would eventually end in a stalemate. Neither side wanted to upset the status quo by appearing "too successful." Since the new brand of warfare was unsuited to the Rangers, who were adept at conducting deep nocturnal raids behind enemy lines, they were simply deactivated.

On 1 August 1951, the remaining six companies of Rangers in Korea, were inactivated, and the men transferred to the 187th Airborne Regimental Combat Team in Japan. By the third week of September 1951, all Ranger Companies had been deactivated. Just as they had been at the end of World War II, the Airborne Ranger Companies of the Korean War were put on a shelf. It wasn't until well into the Viet Nam War that they would be called on again. The Ranger legacy, however, did not disappear when the Airborne Rangers were disbanded. The highly successful Ranger Course became a regular part of the Infantry School. Ranger training was available to any officer or noncommissioned officer who applied and could pass the entrance requirements. Just as with graduates of the Alamo Scouts Training Center, students who were awarded the coveted Ranger Tab returned to their units to pass on the training and techniques that they had learned.

AIR FORCE SPECIAL OPERATIONS FORCES

The genesis of the modern United States Air Force Special Operations Forces (AFSOF) can be traced back to the 1st Air Commando Group in Burma during World War II, but it was during the Korean War that the seed of today's sophisticated air warriors took root. Since 1950, AFSOF have performed a diverse array of overt and clandestine missions, including tactical and strategic bombing, air combat, rescue, resupply, psychological operations, troop insertion and extraction, reconnaissance and surveillance, and a host of others. The number of past and present units that qualify under the AFSOF umbrella is so large that it is beyond the scope of this work to detail each one.

KOREA

Three of the first AFSOF were Detachment 2 of the 21st Troop Carrier Squadron, the 581st Air Resupply & Communications Wing, and the 2157th Air Rescue Service. Detachment 2, a highly-classified unit consisting of approximately eight C-47s, flew covert missions for the Central Intelligence Agency and a variety of military commands. The detachment had two basic, but complex missions, psychological warfare and agent insertion.

Beginning in 1951, the detachment, commanded by Captain Harry Aderholt, launched a psychological warfare campaign against the North Korean and Chinese forces. From their C-47s, some of which were fitted with loudspeakers, the detachment dropped millions of propaganda leaflets and broadcast messages urging enemy troops "to surrender or face inevitable death."

Inserting agents behind enemy lines was the unit's true forte. Working in conjunction with the Combined Command for Reconnaissance Activities, Korea, Detachment 2 infiltrated Korean partisan units and Allied intelligence agents deep into North Korea. The partisans, most of whom were trained and handled by the 8240th Army Unit, gathered intelligence and conducted small hit-and-run raids against communist forces along the western coast of Korea, north to the Manchurian border.

Reminiscent of the 801st/492nd Bombardment Group's "Carpetbaggers," the 581st Air Resupply & Communication Wing performed much the same mission as their World War II counterparts. Like the B-24 Liberators used by the "Carpetbaggers," the 581st, which operated under the control of the Far East Command Liaison Detachment used modified B-29 Superfortresses for their propaganda missions. The underside and tails of the planes were painted black for stealth and modified for low-level flying. For inserting and resupplying various numbers of agents, the unit employed an array of aircraft, including SA-16 Amphibians, C-118, C-119, C-47, and C-54 cargo and transport planes. The 581st also used the versatile H-19A helicopter for clandestine missions and in support of the 2157th Air Rescue Service (ARS). The ARS, which employed approximately 12 H-19A's, was based at an airfield near Seoul, South Korea, and specialized in recovering downed pilots and air crews from enemy territory.

Throughout the 1950s, numerous AFSOF units supported anti-communist and U.S. special operations forces in Indochina, Tibet, Iran, and countless other places. As the United States' commitment to battling communism throughout the world escalated, so did its need for a unified air effort. It was in April 1961, at Hurlburt Field, Florida, that it all began to come together. In response to the growing AFSOF need, the 4400th Combat Crew Training Squadron (CCTS) was formed. Nick-

Psycop. leaflet drop in Korea during War (AFSOF), DOD Photo.

named "Jungle Jim," the unit originally consisted of 16 C-47s, eight B-26s, and eight T-28 aircraft. Within six months, a detachment of the 4400th, consisting of some 150 men, would be in Viet Nam.

VIET NAM

In March 1962, the CCTS was redesignated the First Commando Group. With a simple stroke of a pen, the modern "Air Commandos" were born. According to their original mission, the Air Commando pilots and ground crews, who were extensively trained in escape and evasion, survival, foreign language, parachute operations, and other skills, were to be sent to train South Vietnamese Air Force pilots. But they soon found themselves supporting increasing numbers of Army Special Forces teams in clandestine and direct action missions, and training Thai and Laotian forces in counterinsurgency warfare. Over the course of the next two years, the Air Commandos flew over 100,000 sorties.

The original Air Commandos reached a strength of six squadrons. As American involvement in Viet Nam escalated, other special operations forces were formed. At peak strength in 1966, the combined AFSOF maintained 19 squadrons and 6,000 personnel. Their expanded arsenal included an array of newly-obtained aircraft, including A-1 "Skyraiders," UH-1 "Huey" and CH-3 "Jolly Green Giant" helicopters, and others. Among the most effective combat aircraft were the AC-119

"Stinger" gunship and the AC-47 gunship, nicknamed "Puff the Magic Dragon."

Accordingly, AFSOF operations also expanded to include interdiction, reconnaissance, defoliation, air rescue, and psychological warfare. Soon, the air war grew too large for AFSOF to handle alone. The bulk of the air missions in Viet Nam was gradually absorbed by larger Army, Air Force, Marine, and Navy air units. Meanwhile, other Air Commando units deployed to Greece, Panama, Saudi Arabia, Ethiopia, Thailand, Germany, Iran, the Congo Republic, and other places. In August 1968, all Air Commando units were officially redesignated Air Force Special Operations Forces (AFSOF).

In 1970, a Green Beret force carried by heavily armed AFSOF Huey and Jolly Green Giants, attempted to rescue American POWs from a prison camp at Son Tay, 23 miles outside Hanoi. Intelligence indicated that approximately 70 prisoners were being held at the camp but when the raiding force arrived they discovered that the prisoners had been relocated to another camp. Although the rescue was unsuccessful, the well-executed operation validated the use of special air and ground operations forces.

POST VIET NAM

Following the Viet Nam War, AFSOF, like the rest of the U.S. military, began downsizing and underwent several organizational changes. In 1974, the AFSOF was redesignated the 834th Tactical Composite Wing. A year later it was renamed the 1st Special Operations Wing.

In 1980, following the disastrous attempt to rescue American hostages during the Iran Hostage Crisis, AFSOF got a shakeup. In late 1982, Air Force special operations was transferred from the Tactical Air Command to the Military Airlift Command. In March 1983, the 23rd Air Force was activated at Scott Air Force Base, Illinois, and assumed the lion's share of the Air Force's special operations missions worldwide. Later, in August 1988, the 23rd Air Force moved to Hurlburt Field, the original home of the "Air Commandos."

Throughout the 1980s, AFSOF supported a variety of military operations around the world. Air Force special operations forces assisted U.S. law enforcement agencies in their war on drugs by monitoring the illegal flow of narcotics into the country by air and by performing direct interdiction. During operations in Grenada, AFSOF units provided transport aircraft and logistical support. In Panama, during Operation JUST CAUSE, AFSOF dropped Airborne Ranger units at key airfields, and supported Army Special Forces, Delta Force, and Navy SEAL units in the search for Manuel Noreiga. They also assisted in psychological operations and provided combat controllers and medics to ground combat units.

In May 1990, the 23rd Air Force was redesignated as Air Force Special Operations Command (AFSOC), consisting of the 1st, 39th, and 353rd Special Operations Wings. AFSOC also included the 1720th Special Tactics Group, the Air Force Special Operations School, the Special Missions Operational Test and Evaluation Center, and an Air Force Reserve and Air National Guard group.

Two years later, AFSOF were deployed in strength during Operations DESERT SHIELD and DESERT STORM. AFSOF brought with them a formidable arsenal, including the MC-130 Talon, the AC-130H Spectre gunship, and the EC-130 Volant Solo II, but the workhorses of the AFSOF effort were the MH-60G Pave Hawk and MH-53J Pave Low III helicopters. The Pave Low, with a speed of 165 miles per hour, night capability, and a sophisticated radar and navigation system, is a modified version of the HH-53 Super Jolly Green Giant helicopter. It is the most technologically advanced helicopter in the world. During the Gulf War the Pave Low infiltrated, supplied, and exfiltrated special operations teams throughout Kuwait and Iraq. The Pave Low was also used for combat search and rescue missions, special reconnaissance, and numerous clandestine activities.

Following the war, AFSOF operated in the Balkans and in Northern Iraq, where they supplied Kurdish refugees during Operation Provide Comfort. In December 1992, AFSOF participated in Operation RESTORE HOPE in Somalia. That same year AFSOF again reorganized. The 1720th Special Tactics Group was redesignated the 720th Special Tactics Group.

The following year the 1st Special Operations Wing became the 16th Special Operations Wing, a designation it holds as of 1996.

Despite the mind-numbing redesignations, United States Air Force Special Operations Forces have played an important role in U.S. military endeavors for nearly 50 years. Whether called "Air Commandos" or by any other name, the men and women of AFSOF displayed courage, professionalism, and expertise in virtually every U.S. military venture since 1945. True to their motto, AFSOF have been ready "Any Time, Any Place."

8240TH ARMY UNIT

Following the United Nations retreat from the Yalu River in late 1950, "thousands of partisans [Korean], armed with Japanese and Russian weapons, were battling communist forces and falling back to offshore islands on the Western coast" of North Korea. The U.S. Eighth Army realized that the partisans could play a key role in future UN offensives and quickly set out to organize the largely unarmed and untrained guerrillas into an effective fighting force. On 15 January 1951, the Attrition Warfare Section, Eighth Army G3 Miscellaneous Division, was created for the job. Four months later it became the 8086th Army Unit, and in December 1951, it was redesignated the Far East Command Liaison Detachment Korea (FEC-LD(K)), 8240th Army Unit.

Unfortunately, the unit's task was as complicated and confusing as its name. Colonel John H. McGee, an experienced guerrilla fighter who had escaped the Japanese at Mindanao during World War II, and one of the driving forces behind the formation of the Army Airborne Ranger Companies, was charged with sorting it all out.

To better organize the partisans, McGee divided them into three separate Guerrilla Organizations according to geographic region. Each organization was controlled by a small detachment of advisors from Eighth Army. On 15 February 1951, Task Force WILLIAM ABLE (later LEOPARD), established headquarters on Paengyong Island seven miles off the west coast of

Korea. The unit later moved its headquarters to Cho Island, some 60 miles north of the 38th Parallel off the west coast of North Korea. There, it organized all west coast partisan groups operating from the 38th Parallel north to the Yalu River bordering China. The groups operated under the name "Donkey Units." Partisans along the south coast of Hwanghae Province, were commanded by Task Force WOLFPACK; Task Force KIRKLAND (later SCANNON), controlled partisans on Korea's east coast.

Later, in December 1952, LEOPARD, WOLFPACK, and SCANNON were redesignated as Partisan Infantry Regiments (PIR), and placed under the newly-designated United Nations Partisan Forces, Korea (UNPFK). This designation was eventually changed to United Nations Partisan Infantry, Korea (UNPIK).

At peak strength the partisan groups fielded seven organized regiments and numbered 21,000 strong. In June 1953, the partisans operated from 18 bases, nine of which were located on the mainland behind North Korean lines. Rather than oppose communist forces in open combat, the partisans harassed the enemy rear, disrupted supply lines, sabotaged railroads, gathered intelligence, performed reconnaissance, and supplied military targets to United Nations air force and naval units. Partisan groups reportedly killed 69,000 communist troops, captured 950 POWs, and blew up over 80 bridges. The partisans also disrupted North Korean food production by destroying rice crops and killing some 2,400 farm animals. Their most tangible contribution was assisting in the rescue of downed UN pilots and airmen along the Yellow Sea coast.

The partisan groups were mostly made up of North Korean refugees, former POWs, and Chinese deserters. One hand-picked group, code named "RABBITS," consisted of airborne trained personnel. Of the 1,000 "RABBITS" dropped behind enemy lines between September 1950 and June 1951, one remarkable group consisted of 16 beautiful and capable female agents recruited for service by Madame Rhee, wife of the South Korean President Syngman Rhee. The women, many of whom were actresses, parachuted into communist-held territory and sought out to "become friendly" with ranking North Korean officers. After attaching themselves as companions, the agents used whatever means available to collect intelligence. With their mission complete, the agents escaped to friendly lines and surrendered themselves.

The partisans were supported by BAKER, an airborne special missions unit established by Lieutenant Colonel Jay D. Vanderpool. Vanderpool assumed command of the 8240th in late 1951, when McGee returned to the United States. From its base at Pusan, BAKER established an airborne training school and a special airborne operations section. In December 1951, BAKER's training section was renamed the 1st Partisan Airborne Infantry Regiment (PAIR). Its operational section moved to Seoul, and was renamed the "Airborne Special Missions Platoon."

During the war, BAKER, along with two top-secret Air Force units, Detachment 2 of the 21st Troop Carrier Squadron, and the 581st Air Resupply & Communications Wing, dropped CIA agents, special operations teams, and Korean partisans behind enemy lines. These agents performed direct action missions, sabotaged tunnels and railways, and collected intelligence. The units also resupplied the agents and partisans in the field, providing them with ammunition, food, uniforms, and replacements.

One of the strangest airborne operations occurred in late 1952, when BAKER dropped 200 partisans, clad in surplus World War II Nazi paratrooper uniforms, near the Yalu River on the Manchurian border. In a daring night raid, the airborne commandos disabled several communist radar sites along the east bank of the river. Although the raid was successful, none of the commandos made it out of North Korea during the war.

Throughout the Korean War, 40 teams, consisting of 389 partisans, conducted 12 airborne operations behind communist lines. These airborne units suffered terrible casualties. During 1951-52, few of the units successfully exfiltrated from North Korea.

The military impact of the 8240th Army Unit and its partisans was minimal. Although they tied down some 75,000 communist troops, the partisan groups lacked effective leadership and were difficult to control. Once out of the 8240th's reach, the partisans were unable to mount a coordinated effort against the enemy. The static nature of the war itself also hampered the unit's advisory effort and the partisan's effectiveness. Despite the 8240th's mixed success, it preceded by at least a year the formation of Army Special Forces. This unit was created to wage the same kind of unconventional warfare that the 8240th had attempted. The experiences of the 8240th were passed on to the Special Forces, and contributed to the Special Forces' later success.

ARMY SPECIAL FORCES (GREEN BERETS)

"De Oppresso Liber," literally "Freedom from Oppression," is the motto of United States Army Special Forces, more commonly known as the "Green Berets." Established on 20 June 1952, at Fort Bragg the 10th Special Forces Group (Airborne) was created to train and mobilize indigenous forces to wage an unconventional guerrilla war of sabotage and subversion against communist forces in the event of a Soviet Bloc invasion of western Europe.

With the exception of the World War II OSS Jedburgh teams, Operational Groups, Detachment 101, and American-led Philippine guerrilla units, the U.S. military had no established unit experienced in unconventional warfare, and, for the most part, it didn't want one. But a small group of men on the staff of Brigadier General Robert A. McClure's Office of the Chief of Psychological Warfare, were not so short-sighted. Colonels Russell Volckmann and Aaron Bank, recognized the need and value of a permanent unconventional warfare unit and thrust their energies into convincing the Department of the Army to see it their way.

Both men had extensive experience in unconventional warfare and guerrilla operations during World War II. They applied the best training and operational methods from what they learned, along with that from 1st Special Service Force, the Army Rangers, the 5307th Composite unit (Provisional), the

Alamo Scouts, and Navy, Marine Corps, and elite British units, to form the basis of Special Forces training and doctrine.

Volckmann and Bank had each earned a reputation as a master of unconventional warfare. Following the surrender of U.S. forces in the Philippines, in May 1942, Volckmann escaped to the mountains of northern Luzon and organized a 12,000-man Filipino guerrilla force which terrorized the Japanese Army for the remainder of the war.

It was Bank's extensive experience with the OSS, however, which earned him the honor of becoming the first commander of Army Special Forces. In the summer of 1944, Bank was part of OSS Jedburgh team "PACKARD" that organized resistance groups in southern France.

In early 1945, he formed a team of some 100 German POWs, each a professed communist, into an elite German mountain infantry unit (*Gebirgjager*). This highly-trained unit was formed with the sole purpose of capturing or killing top Nazi leaders, including Adolph Hitler, Hermann Goring, and Joseph Goebbels, but the operation, codenamed IRON CROSS, was cancelled. Later that summer, Bank traveled to China, with the OSS and then on to southern Laos, where he attempted to locate Allied POWs. Following the war, Bank served with the Counterintelligence Corps in Europe, and later commanded the 187th Airborne Regimental Combat Team during the Korean War.

SELECTION AND TRAINING

When the call went out requesting volunteers for the fledgling Special Forces in early 1952, former OSS agents, escapees from Eastern Europe, active duty paratroopers, and adventurous veterans from elite World War II units were the first to apply. Throughout the 45-years of its existence the Special Forces selection process and concept of training became more sophisticated. The advent of technology and expanded mission requirements compelled the Special Forces to adapt to change, but the basic quality of men has remained unchanged. Volunteers for Special Forces must be airborne qualified and have at least three years military experience.

The greatest attribute a candidate needed was intelligence. Candidates had to possess knowledge, and more importantly, have the ability to teach what they knew. Special Forces looked for men who could endure long periods of isolation and adapt to other cultures.

To ensure the quality of a soldier, Special Forces developed a demanding selection process and one of the most difficult training programs in the world. Originally, officers and enlisted men trained separately, but in 1982 the training was combined. Special Forces training consists of two phases.

The first phase, assessment and selection, lasts three weeks and is designed to determine if the soldier has the potential to pass Special Forces qualification training. During the assessment phase, trainees are evaluated on their individual performance. Candidates are put through physically and mentally demanding tasks, including airborne refresher courses, long marches, and physical conditioning. Basic soldiering skills, such as map reading, land navigation, and weapons are also stressed. The most demanding part of the assessment phase is survival or SERE training. Candidates are inserted into North Carolina's unforgiving Uwharrie National Forest with only the clothes on their backs and a knife, and are required to live off the land. The difficulty is compounded by an escape and evasion course which requires the candidates to elude their would-be captors. Those who get caught, fail. Of those who enter the assessment phase, 70 percent wash out.

Those who pass the assessment phase are accepted into the Qualification Course or "Q Course." The Q Course consists of common training in special operations techniques, including training of indigenous personnel in military techniques and MOS or Military Occupational Specialty training. It is in this last area that the Special Forces candidate becomes an expert in one of five areas: weapons, demolitions, medicine, intelligence, and communications. The training for each area varies in length. Weapons experts undergo a two-month course, while demolitions, intelligence, and communications trainees are required to complete a four-month course. Medical trainees receive the most extensive training, lasting approximately ten months. By the time candidates graduate from medical training they are highly-skilled in field surgery, preventative medicine, and combat medicine.

After graduation, the men are formed into a Special Forces Operational Detachment A or "A Team." The A Team, which originally contained 15 men, was modeled after the OSS Operational Groups but was reduced to 12 men, including one captain, one lieutenant, and 10 experienced noncommissioned officers. Within the A Team, the men form into a highly-cohesive, self-sufficient unit. As a team the men continue to train for all contingencies in all types of environments. This includes jungle, mountain, and arctic survival training. The men continue to learn and refine skills, such as high-altitude low opening (HALO) and high altitude high-opening (HAHO) parachuting, seaborne infiltration, sniping, SCUBA operations, and others. As an A Team member, each man must be trained in at least one foreign language.

SOUTHEAST ASIA

The Special Forces' earliest significant operations began in Southeast Asia in 1957. Under the guise of the 8251st and 8231st Army Units, Special Forces Mobile Training Teams (MTT) organized, trained anti-communist troops in Taiwan, Thailand, and in South Viet Nam. It wasn't until 1961, however, that the Special Forces truly came of age. Invigorated by President John F. Kennedy's "Freedom Doctrine," which enhanced America's unconventional warfare capability to meet the growing communist threat and to assist fledgling democracies win "wars of national liberation," the Special Forces stepped up their operations in Southeast Asia, particularly in Laos and Viet Nam. It was there that the Special Forces were thrust headlong into a ruthless, protracted struggle.

From 1957 to 1973, Special Forces soldiers ran the gamut of operations, from "winning hearts and minds" through civil assistance to performing joint covert special operations missions with the CIA. Special Forces conducted three types of missions: special unit, clandestine, and paramilitary. The Special Forces' most successful program was conducted in the Central Highlands of Viet Nam. In July 1963, Special Forces teams began organizing, training, and equipping the various Montagnard tribesmen into a highly effective guerrilla force known as the

Civilian Irregular Defense Group (CIDG). The force later reached 27,000. In 1965, Special Forces began employing "Mike Forces," consisting of highly mobile guerrilla units. Under Project Delta, 7,000 guerrillas defended strategic Vietnamese hamlets from attack by Viet Cong forces and performed deep reconnaissance and sabotage operations against the enemy. In 1966, Special Forces teams opened the Military Assistance Command, Viet Nam (MACV) Recondo School to train Allied personnel in deep reconnaissance techniques. At its peak in 1969, 11 Special Forces detachments consisting of over 11,000 men, operated in Viet Nam.

SON TAY RAID

The most spectacular Special Forces operation during Viet Nam War was the near flawless raid on a suspected POW camp at Son Tay, 23 miles outside the North Vietnamese capitol of Hanoi. At 2:18 a.m. on 21 November 1970, an assault force of 56 heavily armed Green Berets aboard attack helicopters swooped down on the unsuspecting compound, which reportedly held some 70 American POWs. A lead gunship quickly cut down the guard towers. Within seconds, a HH-3 helicopter containing the main 14-man assault force crash landed inside the compound. Part of the force laid down supporting fire while the remainder rushed through the cellblocks looking for American prisoners. At the same time, a second gunship containing a security force of 20 men landed outside the prison and burst through the gates to join in the attack.

Meanwhile, a quarter mile to the south, the command and security force of 22 men errantly landed outside a military barracks housing several Chinese advisors. The force, under the command of Colonel Arthur "Bull" Simons, quickly killed 150 advisors. The force was then airlifted to Son Tay prison where it assisted in the attempted liberation.

But there were no American POWs at the camp. Despite months of planning and rehearsal, intelligence had not detected that the POWs had been moved. Despite this poor intelligence, the Son Tay Raid was a textbook operation. In less than 30 minutes, the Special Forces task force had performed one of the most daring and sophisticated rescue operations in U.S. military

Special Forces troops following Son Tay raid, 1970. DOD Photo.

Special Forces troop train ARVN in motar use. Viet Nam. DOD Photo.

history, without losing a man. The raid, although a great disappointment to the men involved, was a highlight of the war.

The Viet Nam War was a bittersweet experience for the Special Forces. Although it enjoyed great success in unconventional warfare operations, Special Forces were frequently embroiled in heavy combat and suffered terrible losses. However, personal sacrifice and heroism were two things that never suffered. The 5th Special Forces Group emerged from the war as America's most decorated unit, winning 17 Congressional Medals of Honor, 90 Distinguished Service Crosses, 814 Silver Stars, 13,234 Bronze Stars, and 2,658 Purple Hearts.

Viet Nam was not the only place Special Forces soldiers were operating during the 1960s. Special Forces Mobile Training Teams were deployed to Laos, El Salvador, Guatemala, and

Panama in 1962, and to the Dominican Republic, following the military crisis there in 1965. In 1967, Special Forces teams trained Bolivian recruits to fight a counterinsurgency war against Che Guevara, the communist guerrilla leader. The Bolivian troops later captured and killed Guevara, which quelled the communist movement and reestablished stability in Latin America. At the same time, hundreds of other teams were fighting the Cold War in scores of other nations throughout the world.

The quality of the Special Forces soldier in Viet Nam prior to 1965, was outstanding. As casualties mounted and the size of the Army grew, sub-par replacements arrived. Military strategy on how to best fight the war became confused and many Special Forces soldiers became disillusioned and left the Army. Following the withdrawal of the 5th Special Forces Group from Viet Nam, in March 1971, the survival of Special Forces was in doubt. In 1974 the 1st Special Forces Group was inactivated. Throughout the remainder of the decade the quality and quantity of not only the Special Forces but the entire United States military suffered. By 1980, Special Forces numbered barely 3,000 men.

With the election of President Ronald Reagan in 1980, Army Special Forces and other special operations forces got a shot in the arm. The cold war grew hotter and tensions between the United States and the Soviet Union escalated throughout the world. In the Far East, communist guerrillas were increasing their military activity, particularly in the Philippines, where there was a strong U.S. presence. In the Middle East, Soviet forces were firmly entrenched in an expansionist war in Afghanistan, and anti-U.S. terrorism was on the rise. In Africa, the communist threat continued to grow. In Europe, NATO and Warsaw Pact forces hardened their stance. The already delicate situation was exacerbated by the rising communist threat in Central America, including civil war in El Salvador between communist and democratic factions. Of course, there was the ever present threat of Fidel Castro's Soviet-backed communist regime, situated at the United States' back door.

Since the reputation of the Special Forces and the military as a whole, had been tarnished by Viet Nam and by the ill-fated attempted rescue of American hostages during the Iran Hostage Crisis in 1980, the United States military adopted the doctrine of Foreign Internal Defense (FID). This called for minimized direct military involvement with maximum results. The new doctrine emphasized training and support of indigenous forces. The new doctrine, although much like one used in Viet Nam, was tailor-made for the Green Berets.

Beginning in the early 1980s Special Forces drastically increased operations throughout the world and continued to advise, train, assist, and in some cases, lead indigenous forces in their own struggles. It was the exact type of mission that the Green Berets were trained for. In 1989, the "Quiet Professionals" were back on the battlefield.

PANAMA INVASION

By late December 1989, Panamanian dictator General Manuel Noriega had gone too far. For years, Noriega and his regime, which had ties to Cuba, had increasingly supported the communist regime in Nicaragua, which, in turn was funneling arms and money to communist guerrillas in El Salvador and Honduras. Noriega was also implicated in money laundering and drug trafficking. As a result, the United States levied an economic embargo and supported a coup to remove Noriega. Both the embargo and the coup failed. Despite the failure, the U.S. made life uncomfortable for Noriega, whose popularity at home was dwindling. Noriega's Panamanian Defence Forces (PDF) responded and became increasingly hostile to U.S. citizens, killing one serviceman and beating another. Frustrated by U.S. attempts to remove him from power, Noriega declared war on the United States. Operation JUST CAUSE was underway.

At 1 a.m. on 20 December 1989, an Army Special Forces team assaulted the television tower at Cerro Azul, and prevented communications between Noriega and some of his military forces. Five minutes later, Army Rangers and paratroopers from the 82nd Airborne Division dropped from the sky commencing the invasion. As the Rangers battled PDF forces at Rio Hato, Special Forces teams pinned down PDF forces at a number of key locations, including Tinajitas, and at the Pacora River bridge. These actions prevented the PDF from reinforcing Rio Hato. As the operation progressed, additional teams moved throughout the country gathering and relaying vital intelligence

7th Special Forces Group (Airborne) soldiers patrol in Panama during Operation JUST CAUSE, Dec. 1989. DOD Photo.

Special Forces troops during DESERT STORM war. DOD Photo.

on PDF troop movements and pinpointing targets for conventional forces. On 3 January 1990, Noriega surrendered and the brief operation was over.

GULF WAR

Following the 2 August 1990 occupation of Kuwait by Iraqi forces, the United States mounted its largest military operation since Viet Nam. At the forefront of General Norman Schwarzkopf's Coalition forces were Green Berets. Within a month of the invasion, the entire 5th Special Forces Group was deployed to Saudi Arabia, in support of Operation DESERT SHIELD.

During the pre-war buildup, Special Forces teams assessed and trained numerous Arab Coalition troops in urban and desert warfare. The Green Berets set up communications between all Coalition Forces and Central Command (CENTCOM), and provided real-time intelligence to the command on the location of Allied units. Special Forces soldiers were attached to each of the Coalition Force units to act as translators. This resulted in virtually no communications breakdowns based on lack of understanding. The Green Berets, along with other special operations forces, manned surveillance outposts on the Saudi border, conducted special reconnaissance missions inside occupied Kuwait, and provided intelligence on Iraqi troops movements. Special Forces teams also located and rescued a downed F-16 pilot inside Iraq. It was in Operation DESERT STORM that the Special Forces truly redeemed themselves and forever buried the ghosts of Viet Nam.

In the early morning hours of 17 January 1991, prior to the start of the air war against Iraq, several teams of Green Berets dropped onto the desert floor on the border of western Iraq. The teams quickly set up signaling beacons. Within an hour, Apache and Pave-Low attack aircraft, guided by the beacons, struck enemy radar sites inside Iraq. For the next month Allied aircraft flew unimpeded through the corridor on their way to Baghdad.

On 24 February, as Coalition Forces stormed across the Iraq border initiating the ground war, special Green Beret reconnaissance teams infiltrated deep into Iraq along the Euphrates River. From their concealed positions the teams reported on enemy troop movement from Baghdad to Kuwait.

Fortunately, Saddam Hussein's army crumbled under the sheer firepower of the Coalition Forces and soon capitulated. During the brief 100-hour ground war, Special Forces fared well. Special Forces teams conducted numerous direct action, intelligence, support, and clandestine missions.

A soldier from Iragi Army waves a leaflet as he surrenders to U.S. Forces during DESERT STORM, 1991. DOD Photo.

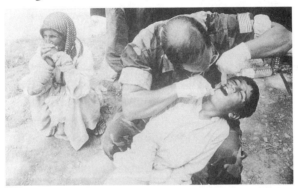

A Special Services medical staff member provides health care to a local boy during "Op PROVIDE COMFORT." DOD Photo.

POST GULF WAR OPERATIONS

As is typical in any army, Special Forces' outstanding showing in the Gulf War led to more work. Special Forces teams remained in the Middle East and performed a number of postwar duties. In Kuwait, Special Forces helped rebuild the country's military and establish order in war-torn Kuwait City. From March to May 1991, Special Forces teams and other special operations forces participated in Operation PROVIDE COMFORT, where they helped organize refugee camps and provided medical care to Kurdish refugees suffering in Northern Iraq.

Within a year, Special Forces would be deeply embroiled in Operations PROVIDE RELIEF and UNOSOM II, as part of a United Nations effort to neutralize bitter clan conflicts and restore political stability to the starving people of Somalia. In September 1994, Special Forces and conventional troops were deployed to Haiti (Operation UPHOLD DEMOCRACY), to reinstate pro-democratic President Jean-Bertand Aristide, who had been ousted from power by a military junta. The invasion was ultimately cancelled when the junta agreed to peacefully return control to Aristide and to allow the U.S. military to oversee the transfer of power. During the operation, Special Forces teams seized arms and military vehicles from the Haitian military, and conducted civil assistance programs.

Although the Green Berets have undergone tremendous growing pains during their 45-year existence, they have come full circle. Today, the Army Special Forces are a critical asset to the United States' conventional military and can be found any place the military goes, including the deployment to Bosnia as part of the U.N. peace-keeping effort in the 1990's. Whether in a direct combat or advisory role, the Special Forces continue to operate throughout the world, training and advising armies of other nations to better defend themselves, the mission for which they were originally created.

NAVY SEALS

As the world's most elite, well trained, and versatile military unit, the Navy SEALs are the culmination of more than 50 years of unconventional naval warfare experience. Formed in 1962 at Little Creek, Virginia, the SEALs (SEa-Air-Land) are America's premier unconventional warriors, capable of performing missions at sea, in the air, or on land. They combine the ferocity, expertise, and intelligence of Army Rangers, Navy combat swimmers, and the Green Berets.

The SEALS are configured (1996) into two Naval Special Warfare Groups (NAVSPECWARGRP). Each contains four SEAL Teams, one Seal Delivery Vehicle (SDV) Team, and supporting boat units. Special Warfare Group One (NAVSPECWARGRP 1) is based at Coronado, California, and consists of SEAL Teams 1,3,5 and 7. Special Warfare Group Two is located at Little Creek and contains teams 2,4,6 and 8. Each team consists of approximately 1,700 men and is supported by Special Boat Units. The teams of 30 officers and 180 men are broken down into eight platoons. During operations however, SEALs normally operate in small, highly-cohesive units of the seven-man boat crew.

TRAINING

The Basic Underwater Demolitions/SEAL (BUD/S) training course at the Naval Amphibious School at Coronado is one of the toughest in the world. This is evidenced by the seven-week pre-conditioning and indoctrination course that candidates have to undergo just to get into shape prior to the BUD/s course begins!

The BUD/S course is divided into three phases. The first phase lasts nine weeks and is the most difficult. Over half the candidates quit or are eliminated because of injury during this phase. The emphasis is on physical conditioning and rubber boat handling. Long runs in deep sand followed by two-mile swims are the norm. It is the sixth week of the first phase that separates the best from the good. During Hell Week, which lasts five-and-a- half days, candidates are pushed to their physical and emotional limits. Candidates are allowed roughly 45 minutes of sleep per night, most of which is spent in a mud hole or in water. When they are not sleeping they are constantly running, paddling rubber boats, or swimming. Doctors are on duty around the clock to monitor the candidates' physical condition. Those who survive Hell Week are given a couple days to heal and rest before completing the final three weeks, which is spent taking beach soundings, contour levels, and learning other basic hydrographic reconnaissance skills.

The second phase lasts seven weeks and stresses diving and SCUBA operations. Candidates learn to use various types of SCUBA gear in covert infiltration and exfiltration by submarine, underwater navigation, destruction of enemy harbor and port facilities, rescue and recovery of pilots and astronauts, and many other skills. Candidates also learn how to operate the several sophisticated underwater delivery vehicles, such as the Mark VII Seal Delivery Vehicle, which holds up to eight men and can be launched from a submarine.

The third phase of SEAL training is the Demolitions/Reconnaissance/Land Warfare phase. This also lasts nine weeks. Trainees spend long hours on ranges firing a myriad of Allied and foreign weapons ranging from high-tech sniper rifles to Chinese assault guns. Trainees learn to construct and set different charges using C-4 and other explosives. They also train in basic infantry skills, including survival, land navigation, patrolling, reconnaissance, and small unit combat. During the final five weeks candidates move to nearby San Clemente Island and perfect their skills in several live-fire and simulated combat exercises.

Following completion of the third phase, SEAL candidates attend the three-week Army airborne training course at Fort Benning, Georgia. Once airborne training is completed, candidates are placed on a SEAL Team and complete six months of on the job training. Upon completion of probation, candidates are evaluated. Those who pass are certified as SEALs and awarded the coveted gold trident insignia, called "Budweiser" by SEALs because of its resemblance to that beer's logo.

Training doesn't stop after candidates are certified as SEALs. Teams continue to train with the latest technology and broaden their experience by working with other elite units, such as the Army Special Forces, Delta Force, and selected foreign units. Many complete additional airborne training and become certified in HALO and HAHO operations. During HALO training, SEAL team members learn to parachute from aircraft as high as 36,000 feet wearing oxygen masks and special warm clothing. SEALs also receive jungle and arctic training.

Until the SEALs and UDTs merged, they had distinct and separate missions. The UDTs continued their traditional mission of conducting hydrographic surveys, beach reconnaissance, demolition of beach and navigation obstacles, and even explosive ordnance disposal. The operational boundary on UDT operations was the high water mark. On the other hand, SEAL missions "began" at the high water mark and moved *inland*, although this did not limit where they were inserted. SEAL missions were unconventional in nature. They included ambushes, harassing supply routes, prisoner snatches, and training indigenous naval forces in these techniques. Sailors moved back and forth between SEAL teams and UDTs on various assignments. The procedure usually was from UDT to SEAL team, rarely the reverse. Occasionally, the two organizations operated together. Eventually, in 1983, the UDTs were disbanded and the various SEAL teams absorbed their missions.

SEAL MISSIONS

One of the earliest SEAL/UDT missions was performed in October 1962. As the world teetered on the brink of nuclear war over the presence of nuclear missiles sites in Cuba, SEAL Team 2 and UDT 22 teamed up and performed a daring reconnaissance of the Havana Harbor. Fortunately, a war was averted; but in 1963, the first SEALs arrived in Viet Nam. Over the next eight years the SEALs conducted their own brand of "muddy-water" warfare and earned a reputation as one of the most feared combat units in the world.

Referred to as "the men in green faces" by the North Vietnamese, because of their green camouflage paint, the SEALs/UDTs performed a gamut of operations during the War. Early in the war, the SEALs spent most of their time training South Vietnamese frogmen and working with the Central Intelligence Agency on clandestine operations. But as the war escalated their mission changed.

Beginning in 1965, the SEALS began performing more combat missions. Operating between the Mekong Delta and the area southeast of Saigon known as the Rung Sat Special Zone, the SEALs conducted numerous combat patrols, ambushes, and raids on enemy supply routes. The SEALs conducted clandestine intelligence gathering missions in Cambodia, Laos, and in North Viet Nam. They also trained many of the highly-effective Vietnamese Provincial Reconnaissance Units (PRUs) and participated in the CIA's PHOENIX Program. One of their most successful missions was also one of their most unheralded. On 6 October 1968, the SEALs liberated 26 South Vietnamese POWs from a prison camp on Dung Island. Since the prisoners were not American, the release received little attention. All told, the SEALs accounted for 580 confirmed and some 300 probable kills during the Viet Nam War. Both SEAL Team 1 and 2 were highly decorated and received the Presidential Unit Citation for extraordinary heroism.

The Viet Nam War, however, wasn't the only thing that the SEALs and UDTs were involved in during the 1960s. Throughout the decade, the teams recovered Gemini and Apollo astronauts and their craft at sea following their return from space. The SEALs/UDTs also performed numerous underwater tests which supplied researchers and physicians with valuable data on the effects that exposure to extreme weather conditions and water depth cause to the human body.

Following Viet Nam, the SEALs, like other special operations forces, fell prey to military cutbacks and downsizing. Interest in elite units was piqued during and after the Iran Hostage Crisis of 1979-80. In the wake of the crisis SEAL Team Six was formed as the Navy's counterterrorism organization. Nicknamed the "Jedi," after the intergalactic warriors in the movie *Star Wars*, SEAL Team Six recruited top SEALs from existing teams and trained for the opportunity to showcase their talents.

GRENADA

During the 1983 invasion of Grenada, the Jedi got their chance, but they didn't fare well. Four SEALs drowned during a parachute drop into the ocean. The remainder struggled ashore and attempted to rescue the Governor-General at his residence. Before they reached the residence the SEALs were detected and pinned down, only to be rescued by the Marines. Despite capturing Radio Grenada and performing several reconnaissance missions, the overall SEAL effort was seen as an embarrassment.

OPERATION JUST CAUSE

Six years later it got worse. During Operation JUST CAUSE, a 13-man squad of SEALs was ambushed by Panamanian guards at Paitilla airfield while attempting to disable Manuel Noriega's jet. In the ensuing firefight, four SEALs were killed and eight wounded. Again, the SEALs' accomplishments, such as the destruction of Panamanian patrol boats in Balboa Harbor, were overshadowed by disaster. Questions were raised about the effectiveness of the SEALs. Were they truly of value?

Could they actually be used with conventional troops? Less than a year later, those questions and more were answered in the Gulf War.

GULF WAR

On 11 August 1990, a contingent of SEALs was the first American ground force to arrive in Saudi Arabia. Throughout Operation DESERT SHIELD to the beginning of the ground war in February 1991, SEAL teams from Naval Special Warfare Group One worked independently and in unison with Delta Force and Army Special Forces teams. The SEALs conducted surveillance of the Kuwait border and performed ground and air reconnaissance missions into occupied Kuwait. The SEALs also hunted for mines in the Gulf, monitored the blockade of Iraq, assaulted Iraqi oil platforms, and rescued downed Allied pilots.

One of their most successful and important missions was tricking the Iraqis into believing that U.S. Marines were launching an invasion south of Kuwait City. At various times prior to the start of the ground war SEALs sneaked ashore near the city and deliberately left evidence of their reconnaissance. At 1 a.m. on 24 February 1991, a platoon of SEALs silently slipped ashore right under the noses of the Iraqi defenders and set a series of explosive charges along a 200-yard stretch of beach. After returning to their recovery craft, the SEALs opened up on the defenders with machine gun fire. Allied fighters joined in on the deception and blasted the shoreline. Two divisions of Iraqi armor moved to the coast to meet the expected invasion. Within hours, Coalition ground forces were on the move through western Iraq. One hundred hours later the ground war was over. The SEALs had helped pull off one of the most successful deceptions in U.S. military history.

During DESERT SHIELD and DESERT STORM the SEALs performed over 270 successful missions without losing a man. The SEALs performed virtually every type of mission they were trained for, including direct action, ground, air and seaborne reconnaissance, sabotage, rescue, and intelligence gathering. They also captured 23 POWs. For the first time in their history, the SEALs were utilized correctly in support of conventional forces, not in place of them.

Two SEALS participate in a training exercise. April 1985. U.S. Navy Photo.

A member of the SEALS in scuba gear holds his carbine during a traning exercise, 1993. U.S. Navy Photo.

Members of SEAL Team 5, take up positions on beach during training exercises. Photo DOD.

75TH RANGERS

In 1969, almost 300 years after the first provisional Ranger unit was formed in America, the Army established the 75th Infantry Regiment (Ranger), its first permanent Ranger unit. The regiment took its designation from the 75th Regimental Combat Team, which had originally been formed in Burma in August 1945 from the remnants of the 5307th—Merrill's Marauders. The Marauders were reactivated as the 475th Infantry Regiment at Myitkyina and combined with the 124th Cavalry Regiment (a Texas National Guard unit) to form Mars Task Force.

Although the Army had formed Airborne Ranger companies at the beginning of the Korean War, they were disbanded about a year later. However, the Army permanently established the Ranger Department at Fort Benning in October 1951 to keep Ranger training on an individual basis for the Army. In November 1954, the 75th Regimental Combat Team was reactivated on Okinawa. Its new life was short as it was deactivated in March 1956. The designation, however, had been allocated to the Regular Army.

LRRPs

In 1958, soon after the 75th RCT was deactivated in the Far East, the Army formed a small, experimental Long Range Reconnaissance Patrol (LRRP) detachment for duty in Europe. It wasn't until 1961, however, that the first two authorized LRRP units were formed. They were organized under two different Tables of Distribution, the 3779th and 3780th Companies, and were assigned to V and VII Corps, respectively. In 1965, these two companies were reorganized, based on a common organization, and designated as companies in regular infantry regiments.

In early 1966, General William C. Westmoreland, Commander, MACV, ordered all divisions and separate brigades assigned to Viet Nam to form LRRP units. Westmoreland's decision was a field expedient action that did not need, or seek, Army approval. Eventually, I and II Field Forces also formed LRRP units. Later, in September, the 5th Special Forces Group (Airborne) established the MACV Recondo School in Nha Trang to train LRRPs in country. During the three-week course, the students learned advanced reconnaissance techniques, particularly how to navigate and operate in the jungles and mountains. The LRRP's primary mission included intelligence collection, target acquisition, security, small ambushes, and battle and bomb damage assessment.

In late 1967, the Army authorized activation of LRRP units. These companies, often composed of many Ranger-qualified soldiers, acted independently but were attached to each infantry division. In addition to performing the gamut of reconnaissance missions, the LRRPs, who normally worked in small teams of four-to-six men, conducted ambushes and hit-and-run raids. Thirteen of the 15 LRRP companies activated were redesignated as Airborne Ranger companies and placed under the newly reactivated 75th Infantry Regiment.

As Army combat units departed Viet Nam between 1969 and 1972, their attached Ranger companies went with them. A company of "Arctic Rangers," however, was formed at Fort

Richardson, Alaska in 1970, to rescue downed airmen and to serve as a quick reaction force.

Since Rangers were historically a flexible, light infantry force available to commanders, the Army, guided by the influence of General Creighton Abrams, Army Chief of Staff, activated two battalions of Rangers in 1974 to give them some added special operations punch. The 1st Ranger Battalion was activated on 31 January at Fort Benning but soon moved to Fort Stewart, Georgia. Ten months later the 2nd Ranger Battalion was activated at Fort Lewis, Washington, giving the Army an active Ranger unit on each coast.

URGENT FURY

On 25 October 1983, the 1st and 2nd Ranger Battalions saw their first action during Operation URGENT FURY in Grenada. The Rangers, who had hoped to land with little opposition at Point Salines airfield on the southern tip of the island, were forced to parachute in at daybreak. The Rangers were met by several hundred well-armed Cuban "construction workers" who were remodeling the airfield. The Cubans were dug in and put up heavy resistance. Following a two-hour fire fight, the Rangers secured the airfield and moved to True Blue campus to rescue the American medical students held there. To the Rangers' surprise, most of the students were located at the Grand Anse hotel two miles away.

The next afternoon, the Rangers were flown to the Grand Anse, transported by Marine Helicopters. Within 30 minutes the Rangers released the remaining 224 students. The following afternoon, the Rangers were to assault a landing zone to mount an attack on Calivigny barracks, a suspected Cuban-run terrorist training site. Tragically, two helicopters collided on the landing zone and eight Rangers were killed and several were wounded. The barracks was deserted. Despite the tragedy, the Rangers had performed well.

In July 1984, the 3rd Ranger Battalion was activated at Fort Benning. At the same time, all three battalions were incorporated into the 75th Ranger Regiment, also located at Fort Benning. The Regiment was given the additional mission of running the Ranger training course at The Infantry School. In 1986, the lineage and honors of the six World War II Ranger

Rangers on patrol in Panama during Operation JUST CAUSE, 1989. DOD Photo.

battalions, the honors of the 16 Airborne Ranger Companies of the Korean War, and the 15 LRRP companies from the Viet Nam era were transferred to the 75th Ranger Regiment.

PANAMA

The Rangers next action occurred during Operation JUST CAUSE in Panama. Shortly before 12:45 a.m. on 20 December 1989, the 1st and 3rd Ranger Battalions (Task Force Red) commenced the invasion. Parachuting from less than 500 feet, the 1st Ranger Battalion descended on the runway of the airport at Rio Hato in western Panama, and engaged the Sixth and Seventh Infantry Companies of the PDF. After a brief but fierce battle, the Rangers captured the airfield, a nearby armory, and took 250 prisoners. The Rangers, joined by elements of a brigade from the 82nd Airborne Division and supported by AC-130 "Specter" gunships, then blocked the movement of a key PDF battalion that was attempting to reinforce PDF troops in Panama City.

Meanwhile, in the eastern outskirts of Panama City, the 3rd Rangers parachuted from 500 feet onto the runways of Torrijos-Tocumen International Airport. Within hours the Rangers had secured the airport.

When Saddam Hussein's forces invaded Kuwait in August 1990, most of the Rangers remained at home. Only Company B, 1st Battalion deployed to the Gulf, where they served as General Schwarzkopf's personal strike force and bodyguard. In October 1993, the Rangers were in action again. Serving as part of a U.N. effort to curb inter-tribal violence in Somalia, the 3rd Ranger Battalion was called on to prevent war lord General Mohammed Farrah Aidid's loyalists from escalating the bloodshed inside Mogadishu, the capitol city. On 3 October, the Rangers left Mogadishu airport aboard helicopters, but Aidid's forces were waiting. In the ensuing 18-hour battle 18 Rangers were killed and 75 wounded. This mission was conducted in conjunction with the Army's Delta Force, whose mission that day was to capture key lieutenants of Aidid.

As with Darby's Rangers of World War II, the modern Rangers are among the finest troops in the military. The Ranger Training Course, which is open to all soldiers regardless of branch, lasts approximately two months. It stresses small unit leadership, weapons, and tactics. The training is realistic, physically grueling, mentally demanding, and dangerous. During the course candidates are allowed little food and sleep. Many candidates lose 30 pounds or more during the training.

The dangerous nature of Ranger Training was recently brought to light in February 1995, when four Ranger students died of hypothermia during the swamp phase of training in Florida.

As with Army Special Forces and Navy SEAL training, Ranger trainees must also attend a pre-training course to insure that they are in shape and are capable of passing the course. Candidates must pass a three-week Ranger Indoctrination Course or "RIP" course before acceptance into the Ranger Course. All candidates must also be airborne qualified.

Since Rangers are called upon to operate in all climates, they train in three distinct environments. Candidates receive desert training at Fort Bliss, Texas, swamp and water training at Eglin Air Force Base, Florida, and mountain training at Camp Merrill, Georgia. Ranger reconnaissance teams also train in rubber boat tactics, SCUBA operations, and receive HALO training. Those completing the course are awarded the coveted

"Ranger Tab," but are not obligated to serve in a Ranger unit. Those who go on to serve in a Ranger Battalion are also authorized to wear a black beret. As with other elite units, training intensifies once the soldier joins an active Ranger unit.

DELTA FORCE AND THE JEDI

"You guys kept Israel out of the war!" exclaimed a grateful General Schwarzkopf, in a letter to Delta Force following its outstanding performance in Operation DESERT STORM. On the last day of the ground war, Delta sniper teams located 26 SCUD missiles in western Iraq, each aimed at Israel. Armed with high-powered .50-caliber sniper rifles from as far as 3,000 yards, Delta squadrons punctured the missiles' fuel tanks and killed their crews. Had the SCUDs been launched, Saddam Hussein's last-gasp attempt at luring Israel into the conflict might have been successful. With Israel in the fight, the delicate Arab coalition opposing Hussein could have unraveled. But it didn't.

Although much of Delta's training, organization, and operations are classified, it is clear that the unit played a key role in the victory in the Gulf War. Delta, in conjunction with the 160th Special Operations Aviation Regiment (SOAR), Navy SEALS, Army Special Forces, and other coalition special operations forces, conducted numerous clandestine and conventional military operations. Outfitted with the most sophisticated equipment and weaponry, Delta combed the deserts of western Iraq pinpointing SCUDs for Allied aircraft, performing special reconnaissance, searching for downed Allied airmen, gathering intelligence, and conducting "black" or classified missions. Delta also served as Schwarzkopf's personal bodyguard.

Delta Force was formed in June 1977, under Colonel Charles "Chargin Charlie" Beckwith, a pugnacious Special Forces veteran of Viet Nam, and former commander of the Special Forces School at Fort Bragg. In response to the rise in world terrorism, Delta Force was created to quietly combat terrorism inside the United States and abroad. This included recovery of stolen nuclear devices, operations against terrorists using them, and hostage recovery operations. During war time, Delta would be used to release POWs and conduct reconnaissance in "denied or hostile areas."

OPERATION RICEBOWL

The American Embassy in Tehran, Iran, was one such place. In November 1979, Ayatollah Khomeini's radical fundamentalists overran the U.S. Embassy and took 66 American hostages. About that time Delta Force became fully operational under Beckwith and began planning a rescue. Operation RICEBOWL, consisting of 93 Delta Force operators, a 13-man Special Forces Team, and supporting Ranger, Navy, and Marine personnel, was set for 24 April 1980. Unfortunately, the military leadership's insistence on "jointness" in this operation doomed it from the start. Two of the support helicopters got lost in a dust storm and failed to arrive at Dasht-e Kavir airstrip (Desert One) in Iran, the preliminary staging area. A third helicopter arrived but was unable to continue. Beckwith's plan required a minimum of six helicopters. When the third, of eight, failed to arrive the mission was canceled. The raiding force then reloaded aboard available aircraft. The rotor of one of the helicopters then struck a C-130 transport carrying fuel and a team of Delta Force operators. The helicopter burst into flames. Five Delta Force operators aboard the helicopter and three aboard the C-130 were killed, as well as several badly burned. Delta was off to inauspicious beginning.

SEAL TEAM SIX

Less than four months later, the Navy directed Commander Richard Marcinko to put together and lead a SEAL team. This team's mission was to parallel that of Delta's, with emphasis on naval applications. Marcinko, a highly-decorated combat veteran and former commander of SEAL Team Two, hit the ground running. He designated his new command as SEAL Team Six, an operations security measure designed to confuse a potential enemy on the actual number of SEAL teams, and began recruiting from both East and West Coast SEAL teams. He chose SEALs he knew personally and with whom he had served or fought. He had an almost limitless training budget and used it to condition his counter-terrorists in various potential assaults they might encounter, from moving ships to oil rigs.

SEAL Team Six practiced all of the usual entry and shooting techniques, under severe weather conditions. Marcinko's training and operation philosophy was, "You don't have to like it, you just have to do it!" He also conducted training operations with Delta, the FBI's Hostage Rescue Unit, and several foreign counter-terrorist organizations, including Germany's vaunted GSG-9.

DELTA FORCE TRAINING

The original 70 volunteers for Delta Force were obtained primarily from existing Army Special Forces units at Fort Bragg. Delta's first headquarters was the Bragg stockade, a relatively up-to-date detention center. Later, volunteers from the active reserves, Regular Army, and National Guard were accepted. Like their British SAS and German GSG-9 counterparts, Delta volunteers have to pass an assessment phase before being allowed to attend the selection course.

During the assessment phase at Camp Dawson, West Virginia, volunteers are put through rigid physical examinations. Candidates must be at least 22 years of age with four years military service, have above average intelligence, hold a secret security clearance, have a clean record, and be airborne qualified or willing to become so. Enlisted candidates must hold the rank of sergeant, staff sergeant, or sergeant first class, while officers are required to be college graduates, hold the rank of captain or major, and have at least one year of command experience at the company level.

After initial assessments are made, candidates are culled out through a rigorous selection process, and must complete a series of timed physical tests. One of the most difficult is a 45-mile march through mountainous terrain, which must be completed in under 20 hours. Those who pass the physical tests are then taken, without sleep, and put through an intense psychological examination by several senior officers and psychologists. The examination includes a written test on the candidates' interpretation of various books, such as Machiavelli's *The Prince*. Candidates must read the book and then describe what they learned. They are also assessed on their willingness to kill, and on their moral and emotional fitness. For many, the examination, or "interrogation," is the toughest and most stressful part of the process.

Those who survive the assessment and selection phase are then evaluated by a selection board. The board examines the candidates' performance during training and their experience and special abilities. Once selected for Delta Force, candidates undergo a specialized 19-week course. During that time, operators learn antiterrorist techniques and fieldcraft, hostage management, advanced demolitions, Allied and foreign weapons, silent killing, maritime operations, communications, intelligence operations, hostage negotiation techniques, and a host of other skills, many of which are classified.

Upon completion of the course, candidates are assigned to an active Delta platoon for a period of three years. Since Delta operators need to blend in with the public and not appear so "military looking," they are allowed to grow their hair longer and wear casual civilian clothes, but their attitude is anything but casual.

Still reeling from the failure of Operation RICEBOWL, Delta redeemed itself somewhat in 1981. In conjunction with Thai commandos, Delta Force successfully stormed a hijacked airliner in Bangkok, killing four hijackers and capturing another. Three years later, Delta Force and Venezuelan commandos joined forces on the Netherlands Antilles island of Curacao, where they killed two hijackers and freed several hostages aboard a hijacked Venezuelan DC-9.

GRENADA

Despite their success in foiling hijack attempts, Delta's woes continued throughout the early 1980s. In October 1983, Grenada's Prime Minister Maurice Bishop, was killed by General Hudson Austin, head of the rival Revolutionary Military Council. The safety of 1,000 Americans, including 400 medical students, was suddenly in doubt. Delta Force was called in to capture Hudson's 16-man Revolutionary Council, seize the airport at Port Salines, and to storm Richmond Hill Prison. Although Delta was successful in capturing the Revolutionary Council, it was pinned down by heavy fire from Cuban and

Grenadian soldiers at the airfield and at the prison, resulting in six killed and 16 wounded.

SEAL Team Six had its problems in Grenada as well. Several of its operators were dropped in the wrong place at sea in high and very rough waves, and in daylight instead of the planned hours of darkness. Four of them drowned as a result. The remaining SEALs made it to shore several hours behind schedule and were unable to complete their mission.

SPECIAL OPERATIONS COMMAND

The recurring mistake of using elite forces in a conventional infantry role had reared its ugly head. Delta had suffered a second embarrassment. Although URGENT FURY was successful, it was seen as one of the most confused, unorganized, and reckless operations ever conducted by the U.S. military. As a result, Delta and other special operations forces came under intense scrutiny and were placed under the control of a Joint Special Operations Command (JSOC), and later the United States Special Operations Command (USSOCOM).

On 20 December 1989, Delta got another chance. During Operation JUST CAUSE, it was given the mission of releasing a CIA operative from Modelo Prison and capturing Panamanian dictator Manuel Noriega. Just prior to the invasion, Delta stormed the prison and liberated the agent, but after an extensive search of Panama City, Delta Force and the Navy SEALs were unable to locate the elusive Noreiga. Despite not locating the dictator, Delta had succeeded. For the first time in modern warfare, U.S. conventional and special operations forces had combined successfully. It was a marriage only improved during Operations DESERT SHIELD and DESERT STORM.

In October 1993, the valiant exploits of a team of Delta Force operators became known to the world. In an air and land assault against Somalian rebels during Operation RESTORE HOPE, two Delta Force snipers unselfishly sacrificed their lives to rescue four downed airmen near Mogadishu. Master Sergeant Gary Gordon and Sergeant First Class Randall Shughart volunteered to be inserted near a helicopter crash site to perform the rescue. While under heavy fire, the two men extracted the seriously wounded airmen from the wreckage and covered their evacuation. Both men were killed and later awarded the Congressional Medal of Honor posthumously.

Today, Delta Force and SEAL Team Six continue to operate in the shadows. As the threat of terrorism grows both overseas and in within the borders of the United States, Delta Force and SEAL Team Six are critical assets, capable of acting independently, or in conjunction with conventional military forces. Unfortunately, most of their operations will never be known to the public.

NIGHT STALKERS

Following the disastrous attempt to rescue American hostages from Iran in 1980, the Army needed an elite, top-secret, aviation unit, one that was ready, willing, and able to support special operations forces around the clock, but especially at night. It wanted cool, daring, and capable helicopter pilots and crews who put the success of the mission above all else. It got more than it was seeking. It got the "Night Stalkers."

Originally formed as "Task Force 158," in 1980, the unit started with 40 men and aircraft from the 158th Aviation Battalion of the 101st Airborne Division at Fort Campbell, Kentucky. The following year it was redesignated Task Force 160. In 1989, the unit was renamed the 160th Special Operations Aviation Group and in 1990, it became the 160th Special Operations Aviation Regiment (SOAR).

As with most new units, the "Night Stalkers" endured growing pains. During its first two years in operation the unit suffered a series of fatal crashes while testing the limits of new cutting-edge aircraft and equipment. Since it would be supporting clandestine special operations forces, which operated primarily at night in high-risk areas, the unit would have to be proficient in the use of the latest high-tech aircraft and night vision devices. It was a risk that the "Night Stalkers" were willing to take.

Like other elite units, the 1,400 men and women of the 160th are volunteers. Pilot candidates must have clocked at least 1,500 hours of flight time, be in excellent physical condition, and pass a written aviation test. Upon selection by a special board, they attend an 18-week course learning the particulars of special operations. Enlisted volunteers, consisting of crew members and trained support personnel, are evaluated and selected on their record. Before assignment to the unit, they undergo at least one month of additional training in their field of expertise. Once assigned, members of the unit travel throughout the world and train hand-in-hand with other special operations forces.

At the heart of the 160th SOAR are specially modified MH-60 Black Hawk and MH-47 Chinook helicopters. The Black Hawk serves as the unit's primary attack, assault, and utility aircraft, while the bigger twin-rotor Chinook handles larger infiltration and exfiltration operations, cargo drops, and humanitarian relief efforts. Nearly 40 of the small, highly-mobile AH-6/MH-6 "Little Bird" scout helicopters are available for specialized high-risk missions. All told, the 160th SOAR consists of three battalions. The 1st and 2nd Battalions are stationed at Fort Campbell, and the 3rd operates from Hunter Army Airfield near Fort Stewart where it supports the 1st Ranger Battalion.

The Night Stalkers had their first taste of action in Grenada, where they supported Delta Force and Army Special Forces. During the Panama invasion, the 160th flew similar support missions in search of Manuel Noriega. The 3rd Battalion was among the first units to arrive in Saudi Arabia, and performed countless special operations missions during Operations DESERT SHIELD and DESERT STORM.

In the dead of night, the pilots and crews of the 160th SOAR flew deep into Iraq and delivered Delta Force, Green Beret, and Navy SEAL reconnaissance teams into the enemy's backyard to search for SCUD missiles, gather intelligence, and recover downed airmen. Among the hundreds of missions performed during DESERT SHIELD and DESERT STORM, the 160th SOAR conducted four successful rescue missions, including the first night rescue. The Night Stalkers also attacked their share of enemy radar installations, troop convoys, and other targets. Their motto, "Death Waits in the Dark," was rightly earned.

MI-25 HIND Soviet helicopter obtained by 160th SOAR Group June 1988. DOD Photo.

Unfortunately, many of the clandestine missions conducted in support of special operations forces remain classified. But one such mission was so successful it could not remain a secret.

In June 1988, the unit received orders to airlift an "abandoned" Soviet-made MI-25 HIND attack helicopter from "a remote location in Africa" to an undisclosed airfield for transport to the United States. Recovery of the helicopter intact would be a valuable prize, since the aircraft was one of the mainstays of the Soviet air arsenal. Two specially modified MH-47 Chinooks were charged with the mission. The pilots, wearing night vision devices, flew 500 miles through a blinding sandstorm without navigational aids and arrived safely at the extraction site. The crews quickly rigged the Soviet HIND and the Chinooks were on their way. Despite the storm, which reached 3,000 feet in the air, the pilots successfully delivered the HIND to its destination. Sixty-seven hours after arriving in Africa, the Night Stalkers were gone without a trace.

PART VIII

CONCLUSION

The tragic end of the first Iran hostage rescue attempt at Desert One was a low point in the long, disconnected history of U.S. special operations forces, for it publicly exposed the humiliating defeat of a secret unit and the utter failure of a clandestine operation. It also exposed a weakness in planning, namely that it suffered from the same oversecrecy and lack of interservice cooperation that plagued earlier elite forces, particularly those active during World War II. Even more glaring was that the planning for this special operation was conducted using an *ad hoc* philosophy, which tends to be more reactive than proactive.

This review of the history of elite warriors shows that for over 300 years special operations forces have repeatedly re-invented the wheel and learned little from their predecessors, with the exception of some training techniques. It has also shown that there is little direct connection or lineage of special operations forces as there is with conventional regiments, divisions, or corps.

Virtually *every* elite unit was created to respond to an immediate military requirement, that is, *ad hoc*. Once that requirement was filled, or the war was over, most elite units were disbanded or put away for another time. In hindsight it would have been more sensible to keep elite forces available, trained, and ready to strike, than to create them on short notice, plan and train in a hurry, and then hope all goes well. Clearly, for three centuries there was no long-range planning when it came to maintaining elite forces.

Desert One changed all that. The Department of Defense conducted after action studies to find out why the operation failed. The roots of the problem were in the lack of long range planning and the absence of a permanent central command and control element for special operations forces. Both Congress and the Department of Defense took steps to correct these problems. Over time, two military commands took charge of America's elite warriors—the Joint Special Operations Command, at Fort Bragg and the United States Special Operations Command, located at MacDill Air Force Base. To facilitate these commands, Congress established by law, the organization of the Assistant Secretary of Defense for Special Operations and Low-Intensity Conflict to operate within the Under Secretary of Defense (Policy).

These organizations changed the face of modern special forces. By 1996 special operations forces were self-contained, relying on their own command and control and operational capabilities. Special operations forces no longer have to beg, borrow, and steal from the tail end of the force food chain to meet their needs. Special operations are planned more in advance and contingencies are trained for before they occur, not afterwards. Moreover, special operations commanders are more aware of their capabilities and how to best employ them. Through unprecedented interservice cooperation and joint training, commanders of conventional forces also know and understand the limitations and abilities of special operations forces and what kind of missions these forces should and should not be conducting.

What remains is for planners to remember that there will always be a need for special operations forces, those composed of well-trained and highly-motivated men and women with special abilities and skills who are better suited to unconventional missions. Whether future wars will be fought from a computer keyboard, in rice paddies, under the seas, or in the final frontier of space, there will always be a place for elite warriors.

APPENDIX I

Major Robert Rogers' Rules of Discipline

These volunteers I formed into a company by themselves, and took the more immediate command and management of them to myself; and for their benefit and instruction reduced into writing the following rules or plan or discipline, which, on various occasions, I had found by experience to be necessary and advantageous, viz.

I. All Rangers are to be subject to the rules and articles of wars to appear at roll-call every evening on their own parade, equipped each with a firelock, sixty rounds of powder and ball, and a hatchet, at which time an officer from each company is to inspect the same, to see they are in order, so as to be ready on any emergency to march at a minute's warning; and before they are dismissed the necessary guards are to be drafted, and scouts for the next day appointed.

II. Whenever you are ordered out to the enemy's forts or frontiers for discoveries, if your number is small, march in a single file, keeping at such a distance from each other to prevent one shot from killing two men, sending one man, or more, forward, and the like on each side, at the distance of twenty yards from the main body, if the ground you march over will admit of it, to give the signal to the officer of the approach of an enemy, and of their number etc.

III. If you march over marshes or soft ground, change your position, and march abreast of each other, to prevent the enemy from tracking you (as they would do if you marched in a single file) till you get over such ground, and then resume your former order, and march until it is quite dark before you encamp, which do, if possible on a piece of ground that may afford your sentries the advantage of seeing or hearing the enemy at some considerable distance, keeping one half of your whole party awake alternately through the night.

IV. Some time before you come to the place you would reconnoiter, make a stand, and send one or two men in whom you can confide, to look out the best ground for making your observations.

V. If you have the good fortune to take any prisoners, keep them separate till they are examined, and in your return take a different route from that in which you went out, that you may the better discover any party in your rear, and have an opportunity, if their strength be superior to yours, to alter your course, or disperse, as circumstances may require.

VI. If you march in a large body of three or four hundred, with a design to attack the enemy, divide your party into three columns, each headed by a proper officer, and let these columns march in single files, the columns to the right and left keeping at twenty yards distance or more from that of the center, if the ground will admit, and let proper guards be kept in the front and rear, and suitable flanking parties at a due distance as before directed, with orders to halt on all eminences, to take a view of the surrounding ground, to prevent your being ambushed, and to notify the approach or retreat of the enemy, that proper dispositions may be made for attacking, defending, etc. And if the enemy approach in your front on level ground, form a front of your three columns or main body with the advanced guard, keeping out your flanking parties as if you were marching under the command of trusty officers, to prevent the enemy from pressing hard on either of your wings, or surrounding you, which is the usual method of the savages, if their number will admit of it, and be careful likewise to support and strengthen your rear guard.

VII. If you are obliged to receive the enemy's fire, fall, or squat down, til it is over, then rise and discharge at them. If their main body is equal to yours, extend yourselves occasionally; but if superior, be careful to support and strengthen your flanking parties, to make them equal with theirs, that if possible you may repulse them to their main body, in which case push upon them with the greatest resolution, with equal force in each flank and in the center, observing to keep at a due distance from each other, and advance from tree to tree, with one half of the party before the other ten or twelve yards, if the enemy push upon you, let your front fire and fall down, and then let your rear advance thro' them and do the like, by which time those who before were in front will be ready to discharge again, and repeat the same alternately, as occasion shall require; by this means you will keep up such a constant fire, that the enemy wil not be able easily to break your order, or gain your ground.

VIII. If you oblige the enemy to retreat, be careful, in your pursuit of them, to keep out your flanking parties, and prevent them from gaining eminences, or rising grounds, in which case they would perhaps be able to rally and repulse in their turn.

IX. If you are obliged to retreat, let the front of your whole party fire and fall back, till the rear has done the same, making for the best ground you can; by this means you will oblige the enemy to pursue you, if they do it at all, in the face of a constant fire.

X. If the enemy is so superior that you are in danger of being surrounded by them, let the whole body disperse, and everyone take a different road to the place of rendezvous appointed for that evening, which must every morning be altered and fixed for the evening ensuing, in order to bring the whole party, or as many of them as possible, together, after any separation that may happen in the day; but if you should happen to be actually surrounded, form yourselves into a square, or if in the woods, a circle is best, and, if possible, make a stand till the darkness of the night favours your escape.

XI. If your rear is attacked, the main body and flankers must face about to the right or left, as occasion shall require, and form themselves to oppose the enemy, as before directed, and the same method must be observed, if attacked in either of your flanks, by which means you will always make a rear of one of your flank-guards.

XII. If you determine to rally after a retreat, in order to make a fresh stand against the enemy, by all means endeavor to do it on the most rising ground you can come at, which will give you greatly the advantage in point of situation, and enable you to repulse superior numbers.

XIII. In general, when pushed upon by the enemy, reserve your fire till they approach very near, which will then put them into the greater surprise and consternation, and give you an opportunity of rushing upon them with your hatchets and cutlasses to the better advantage.

XIV. When you encamp at night, fix your sentries in such a manner as not to be relieved from the main body till morning, profound secrecy and silence being often of the last importance in these cases. Each sentry, therefore, should consist of six men, two of whom must be constantly alert, and when relieved by their fellows, it should be done without noise; and in case those on duty see or hear anything, which alarms them, they are not to speak, but one of them is silently to retreat, and acquaint the commanding officer thereof, that proper dispositions may be made and all occasional sentries should be fixed in like manner.

XV. At the first dawn of day, awaken your whole detachment; that being the time when the savages choose to fall upon their enemies, you should by all means be in readiness to receive them.

XVI. If the enemy should be discovered by your detachments in the morning and their numbers are superior to yours, and a victory doubtful, you should not attack them till the evening, as then they will not know your numbers, and if you are repulsed, your retreat will be favoured by the darkness of the night

XVII. Before you leave your encampment, send out small parties to scout round it, to see if there be an appearance or track of an enemy that might have been near you during the night.

XVIII. When you stop for refreshments, choose some spring or rivulet if you can, and dispose your party so as not to be surprised posting proper guards and sentries at a due distance, and let a small party waylay the path you came in, lest the enemy should be pursuing.

XIX. If, in your return, you have to cross rivers, avoid the usual fords as much as possible, lest the enemy should have discovered, and be there expecting you.

XX. If you have to pass by lakes, keep at some distance from the edge of the water, lest, in case of an ambuscade, or an attack from the enemy, when in that situation, your retreat should be cut off.

XXI. If the enemy pursue your rear, take a circle till you come to your own tracks, and there form an ambush to receive them, and give them the first fire.

XXII. When you return from a scout, and come near our forts, avoid the usual roads, and avenues thereto, lest the enemy should have headed you, and lay in ambush to receive you, when almost exhausted with fatigue.

XXIII. When pursue any party that has been near our forts or encampments, follow not directly in their tracks, lest you should be discovered by their rear guards, who, at such a time, would be most alert; but endeavor, by a different route, to head and meet them in some narrow pass or lay in ambush to receive them when and where they least expect it.

XXIV. If you are to embark in canoes, bateaux, or otherwise by water, choose the evening for the time of your embarkation, as you will then have the whole night before you, to pass undiscovered by any parties of the enemy, on hills, or other places, which command a prospect of the lake or river you are upon.

XXV. In paddling or rowing, give orders that the boat or canoe next the sternmost, wait for her, and the third for the second, and the fourth for the third, and so on, to prevent separation, and that you may be ready to assist each other on any emergency.

XXVI. Appoint one man in each boat to look out for fires, on the adjacent shores, from the numbers and size of which you may form some judgment of the number that kindled them, and whether you are able to attack them or not.

XXVII. If you find the enemy encamped near the banks of a river, or lake, which you imagine they will attempt to cross for their security upon being attacked, leave a detachment of your party on the opposite shore to receive them, while, with the remainder, you surprise them, having them between you and the lake or river.

XXVIII. If you cannot satisfy yourself as to the enemy's number and strength, from their fire, etc. conceal your boats at some distance, and ascertain their number by a reconnoitering party, when they embark, or march, in the morning, marking the course they steer, etc. when you may pursue, ambush, and attack them, or let them pass, as prudence shall direct you. In general, however, that you may not be discovered by the enemy on the lakes and rivers at a great distance, it is safest to lay by, with your boats and party concealed all day, without noise or show, and to pursue your intended route by night; and whether you go by land or water, give out parole and countersigns, in order to know one another in the dark, and likewise appoint a station for every man to repair to, in case of any accident that may separate you.

Journals of Major Robert Rogers

(New York: Corinth Books, 1961), pp. 43-51.

STANDING ORDERS

Rogers' Rangers, 1759

1. Don't forget nothing.

2. Have your musket clean as a whistle, hatchet scoured, sixty rounds powder and ball, and be ready to march at a minute's warning.

3. When you're on the march, act the way you would if you was sneaking up on a deer. See the enemy first.

4. Tell the truth about what you see and what you do. There is an Army depending on us for correct information. You can lie all you please when you tell other folks about the Rangers, but don't ever lie to a Ranger or officer.

5. Don't never take a chance you don't have to.

6. When you're on the march we march single file, far enough apart so one shot can't go through two men.

nMS/LEt

7. If we strike swamps, or soft ground, we spread out abreast, so it's hard to track us.

8. When we march, we keep moving till dark, so as to give the enemy the least possible chance at us.

9. When we camp, half the party stays awake while the other half sleeps.

10. If we take prisoners, we keep 'em separate till we have time to examine them, so they can't cook up a story between 'em.

11. Don't ever march home the same way. Take a different route so you won't be ambushed.

12. No matter whether we travel in big parties or little ones, each party has to keep a scout twenty yards on each flank and twenty yards in the rear, so the main body can't be surprised and wiped out.

13. Every night you'll be told where to meet if surrounded by a superior force.

14. Don't sit down to eat without posting sentries.

15. Don't sleep beyond dawn. Dawn's when the French and Indians attack.

16. Don't cross a river by a regular ford.

17. If somebody's trailing you, make a circle, come back onto your tracks, and ambush the folks that aim to ambush you.

18. Don't stand up when the enemy's coming against you. Kneel down, lie down, hide behind a tree.

19. Let the enemy come till he's almost close enough to touch. Then let him have it and jump out and finish him up with your hatchet.

Courtesy of U.S. Army Ranger School

Bibliography

Aaseng, Nathan. *Navajo Code Talkers*. NY: Walker, 1992.

Adams, James. *Secret Armies: Inside the American, Soviet, and European Special Forces*. NY: Atlantic Monthly Press, 1987.

Alexander, John H. *Mosby's Men*. NY: Neale Publishing, 1907. Reprinted by Olde Soldier Books, Gaithersburg.

Asprey, Robert B. *War in the Shadows: The Guerrilla in History*. Garden City, NY: 1975.

Axelrod, Alan. *Chronicle of the Indian Wars: From Colonial Times to Wounded Knee*. NY: Prentice Hall, 1993.

Bass, Robert D. *Swamp Fox: The Life and Campaigns of General Francis Marion*. Lexington, SC: The Sandlapper Store, 1959.

Beck, Steven. "The First Special Service Force." *Trading Post* (Jan-Mar 1993): 9-15.

Belleranti, Shirley W. "The Code That Couldn't Be Cracked." *The Retired Officer* (November 1984): 33-35.

Bidwell, Shelford. *The Chindit War: Stilwell, Wingate, and the Campaign in Burma, 1944*. NY: MacMillan Publishing Company, 1979.

Billias, George A. *General John Glover and his Marblehead Mariners*. NY: Henry Holt, 1960.

Bird, Harrison K. and Frederick T. Chapman; "Rogers' Rangers, 1756-1760." *Military Collector & Historian* (Spring 1955): 18-20.

Bixler, Margaret T. *Winds of Freedom: The Story of the Navajo Code Talkers of World War II*. Darien, CT: Two Bytes Publishing, 1992.

Black, Robert W. *Rangers in Korea*. NY: Ivy Books, 1989.

_____. *Rangers in World War II*. NY: Ivy Books, 1992.

Blassingame, Wyatt. *The U.S. Frogmen of World War II*. NY: Random House, 1964.

Boltz, Martha. "Cruel Death of Mosby Ranger Called Nathan Hale of the Confederacy." *Washington Times*, August 12, 1995.

Braisted, Todd W. "Georgia Rangers, 1773-1776." *Military Collector & Historian* (Spring 1993): 7-8.

Bray, George A. III. *Anglo-American Partisans of the French and Indian War*. Author's collection.

_____. *Major Scott's Provisional Light Infantry Battalion*. Author's collection.

Breuer, William B. *MacArthur's Undercover War: Saboteurs, Guerrillas, and Secret Missions.* NY: John Wiley & Sons, 1995.

Brown, Anthony Cave. *Bodyguard of Lies.* NY: Harper & Row, 1975.

Brown, Dee A. *Morgan's Raiders.* NY: Konecky & Konecky, 1959.

Burford, John. *LRRP Team Leader.* NY: Ivy Books, 1994.

Burhans, Robert D. *The First Special Service Force: A War History of the North Americans, 1942-1944.* Washington, D.C.: Infantry Journal Press, 1947.

Butler, Lorine L. *John Morgan and His Men.* Philadelphia: Dorance, 1960.

Callahan, North. *Daniel Morgan: Ranger of the Revolution.* NY: Holt, Rinehart and Winston, 1961.

Capistrano, Robert. "BAHALA NA: The 5217th/1st Reconnaissance Battalion and the Intelligence Penetration of the Philippines." *Trading Post* (Jan-Mar 1994): 2-9.

Cohen, Stan. *The Forgotten War.* Missoula, MT: Pictorial Histories Publishing Company, 1981.

Cuneo, John R. *Robert Rogers of the Rangers.* NY: Oxford University Press, 1959.

_____. "The Early Days of the Queen's Rangers: August 1776 to February 1777." *Military Affairs* (Summer 1958): 65-74.

_____. "Factors Behind the Raising of the 80th Foot in America." *Military Collector & Historian* (Winter 1959): 97-103.

Darragh, Shaun M. "Rangers and Special Forces: Two Edges of the Same Dagger." *Army* (December 1977): 14-19.

Davis, Burke. *The Cowpens-Guilford Courthouse Campaign.* Philadelphia: J.P. Lippincott, 1962.

Davis, William C. *Rebels and Yankees: Fighting Men of the Civil War.* N.Y.: Gallery Books, 1989.

Day, James Sanders. *Partisan Operations of the Korean War.* Master's Thesis. University of Georgia, 1989.

Delauter, Roger U., Jr. *McNeill's Rangers.* Lynchburg: H.E. Howard, 1986.

Department of the Army. Headquarters. *Doctrine for Army Special Operations Forces.* Field Manual 100-25. Washington, D.C.: GPO, 1991.

Dillan, Richard H. *North American Indian Wars.* NY: Facts on File, 1983.

Dilley, Michael F. *GALAHAD - A History of the 5307th Composite Unit (Provisional).* Bennington, VT: Merriam Press, 1996.

Duke, Basil W. *A History of Morgan's Cavalry.* Bloomington: Indiana University Press, 1960.

Dwyer, John B. *Scouts & Raiders: The Navy's First Special Warfare Commandos.* NY: Praeger, 1992.

Elting, John R. "Further Light on the Beginnings of Gorham's Rangers." *Military Collector & Historian* (Fall 1968): 74-77.

Epstein, Samuel and Beryl Epstein. *The Andrews Raid or the Great Locomotive Chase.* NY: Coward-McCann, 1956.

Erd, Darby and Fitzhugh McMaster. "The Third South Carolina Regiment (Rangers) 1775-1780." *Military Collector & Historian* (Summer 1980): 72-73.

Evanhoe, Ed. *Darkmoon: Eighth Army Special Operations in the Korean War.* Annapolis, MD: Naval Institute Press, 1995.

Fawcett, Bill (Ed.). *Hunters and Shooters: An Oral History of the U.S. Navy SEALs in Vietnam.* NY: William Morrow, 1995.

Fleming, Thomas J. *Downright Fighting: The Story of Cowpens.* Washington, DC: Department of the Interior, 1988.

Foote, William A. *The American Independent Companies of the British Army 1664-1764.* Doctoral Dissertation. University of California at Los Angeles, 1966.

Funk, Arville L. *The Morgan Raid in Indiana and Ohio (1863).* Mentone: Superior Printing, 1971.

Galvin, John R. *Air Assault: The Development of Airmobile Warfare.* NY: Hawthorn Books, 1969.

Gerson, Noel B. *Light Horse Harry.* NY: Ballantine Books, 1966.

_____. *The Swamp Fox, Francis Marion.* NY: Ballantine Books, 1967.

Goodhart, Briscoe. *History of the Independent Loudoun Virginia Rangers: U.S. Vol Cav (Scouts): 1862-65.* Washington: McGill & Wallace, 1896. Reprinted by Olde Soldier Books, Gaithersburg.

Gourley, Scott. "Special Weapons and Tactics of the Navy SEALs." *Popular Mechanics* (Nov 1995): 51-55.

Grant, Carl E. "Partisan Warfare, Model 1861-65." *Military Review* (Nov 1958): 42-56.

Gray, David R. *Black and Gold Warriors: U.S. Army Rangers During the Korean War*. Chap. 1. Doctoral Dissertation. Ohio State University, 1992.

Gutjahr, Robert G. *The Role of Jedburgh Teams in Operation Market Garden*. Master's Thesis, Command and General Staff College, 1990.

Haas, Michael E. *Air Commando! 1950-1975: Twenty-five years at the Tip of the Spear*. USAF, 1994.

Hafford, William E. "The Navajo Code Talkers." *Arizona Highways* (February 1989) : 37-45.

Haggerty, Jerome J. *A History of the Ranger Battalions in World War II*. Chap. 1. Doctoral dissertation. Fordham University, 1982.

Hardin, Stephen. *The Texas Rangers*. London: Osprey Publishing, 1991.

Heimark, Bruce H. *The OSS Norwegian Special Operations Group in World War II*. Westport, CT: Praeger, 1994.

Higginbotham, Don. *Daniel Morgan: Revolutionary Rifleman*. Chapel Hill: University of North Carolina Press, 1961.

Hogan, David W., Jr. *The Evolution of the Concept of the U.S. Army Rangers, 1942-1983*. Chap. 1. Doctoral Dissertation. Duke University, 1986.

_____. *Raiders or Elite Infantry? The Changing Role of the U.S. Army Rangers from Dieppe to Grenada*. Westport, CT: Greenwood Press, 1992.

_____. *U.S. Army Special Operations in World War II*. Washington: GPO, 1992.

Holbrook, Stewart H. *The Swamp Fox of the Revolution*. NY: Random House, 1959.

Holland, Cecil F. *Morgan and His Raiders: A Biography of the Confederate General*. NY: MacMillan, 1942.

Hoyt, Edwin P. *The Marine Raiders*. NY: Pocket Books, 1989.

HQ AFSOF/HO. *Heritage of the Quiet Professionals* [Brochure]. May 1994.

Hughes, Les. "Insignia of the OSS." *Trading Post* (Apr-Jun 1993): 8-15.

Hunter, Charles N. *GALAHAD*. San Antonio, TX: Naylor, 1963.

Hymoff, Edward. *The OSS in World War II*. NY: Ballantine Books, 1972.

Ind, Allison. *Allied Intelligence Bureau: Our Secret Weapon in the War Against Japan*. NY: Curtis Books, 1958.

Irwin, Wyman W. *A Special Force: Origin and Development of the Jedburgh Project in Support of Operation Overlord*. Master's Thesis, Command and General Staff College, 1991.

Ivers, Larry E. *The American Rangers: Their First Two Hundred Years*. Unpublished manuscript in author's collection (courtesy of the Infantry School Library, Fort Benning, GA), 1963.

_____. "Rangers in Florida, 1818." *Infantry* (Sep-Oct 1963): 37.

Jablonski, Edward. *America in the Air War*. Alexandria, VA: Time-Life Books, 1982.

Johnson, James M. *Militiamen, Rangers, and Redcoats: The Military in Georgia, 1754-1776*. Macon, GA: Mercer University Press, 1992.

Jones, Tom and John R. Elting. "Texas Rangers, 1823." *Military Collector & Historian*. (Fall 1977): 176-177.

Jones, Virgil C. *Gray Ghosts and Rebel Raiders*. NY: Ballantine Books, 1956.

_____. *Ranger Mosby*. Chapel Hill: University of North Carolina Press, 1994.

Jorgenson, Kregg P. "Long Range Recon Patrol: 1901." *Behind The Lines* (Nov-Dec 1992): 26, 32.

Kaufman, Dave. "Ranger Companies (Airborne) in the Korean War." *Trading Post* (Jan-Mar 1995): 2-10.

Keegan, John. *A History of Warfare*. NY: Alfred A. Knopf, 1994.

Keen, Hugh C. and Horace Mewborn. *43rd Battalion Virginia Cavalry, Mosby's Command*. Lynchburg: H.E. Howard, 1993.

Keller, Allan. *Morgan's Raid*. Indianapolis: Bobbs-Merrill, 1961.

Kelly, Orr. *Brave Men Dark Waters: The Untold Story of the Navy SEALs*. Novato, CA: Presidio Press, 1992.

_____. *Never Fight Fair: Navy SEAL's Stories of Combat and Adventure*. Novato, CA: Presidio Press, 1995.

Ketchum, Richard M. *The Winter Soldiers*. Garden City, NY: Anchor Books, 1975.

Kolb, Richard. "Somalia Service Provided its Share of Heroes." *VFW* (Aug 1994): 26-27.

Kufus, Marty. "Hearts and Minds: The U.S. Army Green Berets Today." *Command* (May-Jun 1993): 56-61.

Ladd, James. *Commandos and Rangers of World War II.* NY: St. Martin's Press, 1978.

Lanning, Michael L. *Inside the LRRPs: Rangers in Vietnam.* NY: Ivy Books, 1988.

_____ and Ray Stubbe. *Inside Force Recon.* NY: Ivy Books, 1989.

Landau, Alan M. and Frieda W. *Airborne Rangers.* Chap. 1. Osceola, WI: Motorbooks International, 1992.

Leach, Douglas E. *Flintlock and Tomahawk: New England in King Philip's War.* East Orleans, MA: Parnassus Imprints, 1958.

_____. *Arms for Empire: A Military History of the British Colonies in North America, 1607-1763.* NY: MacMillan, 1973.

Lee, Alex. *Force Recon Command: A Special Marine Unit in Vietnam, 1969-1970.* Annapolis, MD: Naval Institute Press, 1995.

Lewis, S.J. *Jedburgh Team Operations in Support of the 12th Army Group, August 1944.* Fort Leavenworth, KS: Combat Studies Institute, 1991.

Loescher, Burt G. *The History of Rogers Rangers.* Vols. 1-3. Privately published.

Marcinko, Richard and John Weisman. *Rogue Warrior.* NY: Pocket Books, 1992.

Majeska, Marilyn L. *A History of Naval Special Warfare: World War II to Panama.* Part 1 & 2. A Study Prepared for Office of the Deputy Assistant Secretary of Defense for Forces and Resources Office of the Assistant Secretary of Defense, Low Intensity Conflict. Washington, DC: 1992.

Manders, Eric I.; "Butler's Rangers, 1778-1784." *Military Collector & Historian* (Winter 1961): 117-118.

_____, Larry E. Ivers, and Tom Rodgers. "Georgia Provincial Companies, 1734-1747." *Military Collector & Historian* (Winter 1993): 176-177.

Marine Corps Educational Center. *History of Guerrilla Operations.* Quantico, VA, n.d.

Matloff, Maurice, ed. *American Military History.* Army Historical Series. Washington, D.C.: GPO, 1969.

May, Robin. *Wolfe's Army.* London: Osprey Publishing, 1974.

McBarron, H. Charles, Jr. "U.S. Mounted Ranger Battalion, 1832-1833." *Military Collector & Historian* (December 1949): 5-6.

_____ and John R. Elting. "Colonel Hays' Regiment of Texas Mounted Volunteers, 1847-1848." *Military Collector & Historian* (Fall 1970): 91, 93.

_____ and Rutledge F. Smith. "The Queen's Rangers (1st American Regiment), 1778-1783." *Military Collector & Historian* (Spring 1972): 20-22.

_____ and Frederick P. Todd. "Glover's Marblehead or Marine Regiment (14th Continental Infantry), 1775-1776." *Military Collector & Historian* (March 1953): 13-14.

Melson, Charles D., and Paul Hannon. *Marine Recon: 1940-90.* Osprey Elite Series. London: Osprey Publishing, 1994.

Miller, Allen C. II, Col, USA (Ret.). *Oral History of Indian Scouts.*

Miller, Kenn. "A Defense of Col. John Mosby: Rebel Cut-throat or Ranger Extraordinaire?" *Behind The Lines* (Jan-Feb 1993): 22-23.

Monteiro, Aristides. *War Reminiscences by the Surgeon of Mosby's Command.* Richmond, VA: 1890. Reprinted by Butternut Press, Gaithersburg.

Moon, Tom. *This Grim and Savage Game: OSS and the Beginning of U.S. Covert Operations in World War II.* Los Angeles: Burning Gate Press, 1991.

Morrison, Wilbur H. *Above and Beyond.* NY: St. Martin's Press, 1983.

Munson, John W. *Reminiscences of a Mosby Guerrilla.* Washington: Zenger Publishing, 1907.

Ogburn, Charlton, Jr. *The Marauders.* London: Quality Book Club, 1956.

O'Neal, Bill. *The Arizona Rangers.* Austin, TX: Eakin Press, 1987.

O'Neill, Charles. *Wild Train: The Story of the Andrews Raiders.* NY: Random House, 1956.

Parkman, Francis. *Montcalm and Wolfe: The French and Indian War.* NY: De Capo Press, n.d.

Parnell, Ben. *Carpetbaggers: America's Secret War in Europe.* Austin, TX: Eakin Press, 1987.

Peers, William R., and Dean Brelis. *Behind the Burma Road: The Story of America's Most Successful Guerrilla Force.* Boston: Little, Brown and Company, 1963.

Pittenger, William. *Daring and Suffering: A History of the Great Railroad Adventure*. Philadelphia: J.W. Daughaday, 1863. Reprinted by Time-Life Books.

Powell, Colin. *An American Journey*. NY: Random House, 1995.

Pugh, Harry. *Rangers: United States Army, 1756 to 1974*. Unpublished manuscript in author's collection.

Ramage, James A. *Rebel Raider: The Life of General John Hunt Morgan*. Lexington: University Press of Kentucky, 1986.

Rankin, Hugh F. *Greene and Cornwallis: The Campaign in the Carolinas*. North Carolina Division of Archives and History (North Carolina Bicentennial series), 1976.

Ray, Frederick and John R. Elting. "Gorham's Rangers." *Military Collector & Historian* (Spring 1960): 14-16.

Ray, Frederick E. Jr. and Frederick P. Todd. "60th British Foot (Royal American Regiment), 1756-1760." *Military Collector & Historian* (September 1953): 73-74.

Rearden, James. *Castner's Cutthroats: Saga of the Alaska Scouts*. Prescott, AZ: Wolfe Publishing Company, 1990.

Reid, Courtland T. *Guilford Courthouse*. Washington, DC: National Park Service, 1959.

Roberts, MacLennan. *The Great Locomotive Chase*. NY: Dell Books, 1956.

Roosevelt, Theodore. *The Rough Riders*. NY: Charles Scribner's Sons, 1924.

Rosner, Elliot J. *The Jedburghs: Combat Operations Conducted in the Finistere Region of Brittany, France from July-September 1944*. Master's Thesis, Command and General Staff College, 1991.

Rottman, Gordon L. *US Army Rangers & LRRP Units, 1942-87*. London: Osprey Publishing, 1987.

Russell, Charles W. (ed.). *Gray Ghost: The Memoirs of Colonel John S. Mosby*. NY: Bantam Books, 1992.

Schott, Joseph L. *Above and Beyond: The Story of the Congressional Medal of Honor*. NY: G.P. Putnam's Sons, 1963.

Schwarzkopf, Gen. Norman and Peter Petre. *It Doesn't Take A Hero*. NY: Bantam Books, 1992.

Schwartz, Seymour I. *The French and Indian War, 1754-1763: The Imperial Struggle for North America*. NY: Simon & Schuster, 1994.

Schultz, Duane. *The Doolittle Raid*. NY: St. Martin's Press, 1983.

Scott, John. *Partisan Life with Col. John S. Mosby*. NY: Harper & Harper Publishers, 1867. Reprinted by Olde Soldiers Books, Gaithersburg.

The Scouts. Alexandria, VA: Time Life Books, 1978.

Sexton, Martin J. *The Marine Raiders' Historical Handbook*. Richmond, VA: American Historical Foundation, 1987.

Siepel, Kevin H. *Rebel: The Life and Times of John Singleton Mosby*. NY: St. Martin's Press, 1983.

Simpson, Charles M. *Inside the Green Berets*. Novato, CA: Presidio Press, 1983.

Smith, Bradford. *Rogers' Rangers and the French and Indian War*. NY: Random House, 1956.

Smith, R. Harris. *OSS: The Secret History of America's First Central Intelligence Agency*. Berkeley, CA: University of California Press, 1972.

Smith, Richard W. *Shoulder Sleeve Insignia of the U.S. Armed Forces, 1941-1945*. n.p. 1981.

Stanton, Shelby L. *Green Berets at War: U.S. Army Special Forces in Southeast Asia, 1956-1975*. Novato, CA: Presidio Press, 1985.

_____. *World War II Order of Battle*. New York: Galahad Books, 1991.

Steffen, Randy. "Hays' Regiment, Texas Mounted Volunteers (Texas Rangers), 1847-1848." *Military Collector & Historian* (Winter 1959): 112-113.

_____. "Texas Rangers, 1884." *Military Collector & Historian* (Spring 1960): 13-15.

_____. "Texas Rangers, 1839." *Military Collector & Historian* (Fall 1958): 79-79-80.

Stratton, Roy. *The Army-Navy Game*. Falmouth, VA: Volta Company, 1977.

Sutherland, Ian. *Special Forces of the U.S. Army, 1952-1982*. San Jose, CA: R. James Bender Publishing, 1990.

Swiggert, Howard. *The Rebel Raider: A Life of John Hunt Morgan*. Indianapolis: Bobbs-Merrill, 1934.

Taylor, Blaine. "Before Invasions Commence." *Military History*. October 1987, 43-49.

Thomas, Edison H. *John Hunt Morgan and His Raiders*. Lexington: University Press of Kentucky, 1985.

Thomas, Lowell. *Back to Mandalay*. NY: Greystone Press, 1951.

Thompson, Leroy. "Son Tay." Chap. in *The Unique Units: The World's Crack Fighting Men*. Harrisburg, PA: The National Historical Society, 1989: 75-79.

_____. "War in the Hills." Chap. in *The Unique Units: The World's Crack Fighting Men*. Harrisburg, PA: The National Historical Society, 1989: 33-39.

Ugino, Richard. *Historical Outline: Ranger Units*. Unpublished paper in author's collection.

USSOC. *Memorial Plaza Dedication and USASOC Headquarters Ribbon-Cutting Ceremonies* [Brochure]. Fort Bragg, NC. December 1994.

Utley, Robert M., and Wilcomb E. Washburn. *Indian Wars*. Boston: Houghton Mifflin Company, 1977.

Walker, Greg. *At The Hurricane's Eye: U.S. Special Operations Forces from Vietnam to Desert Storm*. NY: Ivy Books, 1994.

Waller, Douglas C. *The Commandos: The Inside Story of America's Secret Soldiers*. NY: Dell Publishing, 1994.

Watson, Bruce. "Jaysho, Maosi, Dibeh, Ayeshi, Hasclishnih, Beshlo, Shush, Gini." *Smithsonian"* (Aug 1993): 34-43.

Webb, Walter P. *The Texas Rangers: A Century of Frontier Defense*. Austin: University of Texas Press, 1935.

Weigley, Russel F. *The Partisan War: The South Carolina Campaign of 1780-1782*. Columbia: University of South Carolina Press, 1970.

_____. *History of the United States Army*. London: B.T. Batsford, 1967.

Welhan, Michael. *Combat Frogmen: Military Diving from the Nineteenth Century to the Present Day*. Flagstaff, AZ: Best Publishing Company, 1989.

Weller, Jac. "Irregular but Effective: Partisan Weapons Tactics in the American Revolution, Southern Theater." *Military Affairs* (Fall 1957): 118-131.

_____. The Irregular War in the South." *Military Affairs* (Fall 1960): 124-136.

Wert, Jeffry D. *Mosby's Rangers*. NY: Simon and Schuster, 1990.

Wheeler, Richard. *Carlson's Raiders: The U.S. Marines and the Pacific War*. NY: Harper & Row, 1983.

Wilkins, Frederick. *The Highly Irregular Irregulars: Texas Rangers in the Mexican War*. Austin: Eakin Press, 1990.

Williamson, James J. *Mosby's Rangers*. NY: Ralph B. Kenyon, 1896. Reprinted by Time-Life Books.

Wilson, John B. *Campaign Streamers of the United States Army.* Arlington, VA: Association of the United States Army, 1995.

Zaboly, Gary. "The Battle on Snowshoes." *American History Illustrated.* December 1979, 12-24.

Zedric, Lance Q. *Silent Warriors: The Alamo Scouts Behind Japanese Lines.* Ventura, CA: Pathfinder Publishing, 1995.

Zich, Arthur, et al. *The Rising Sun.* Alexandria, VA: Time-Life Books, 1977.

INDEX

Irving, Washington, 82

J
Jackson, Andrew, 66, 72-76
Jenkins, 25
Jim, Sgt., 111
Johnson, William, 34
Johnston, Philip, 139, 140
Jones, "Grumble", 101
K
Kauffman, Draper, 171, 172, 194
Kawaguchi, Kiyotake, 125
Kearney, Philip, 66
Kearney, Stephen W., 80
Keating, Edward, 28
Kelsay, Sgt., 111
Kennedy, John F., 198, 216
Kettle Hill, 114
Keyes, Daniel M. 93, 94
Khomeini, Ayatollah, 237
Kimball, George, 77
Kincheloe, 85
King George's War, 29, 30
King George II, 25
King George III, 26
King George VI, 172
King Philip's War, 16-18, 25
King, William, 75
Knight, 88
Knowlton's Rangers, 57, 58
Knowlton, Thomas, 57, 58
Knox, Frank, 113
Korean War, 11, 129, 130, 137, 138, 142, 195, 196, 198, 201, 204-207, 212, 214, 231, 234
Krait, 156
Krueger, Walter, 151, 189, 192

L
Laclede Rangers, 80
Larned, Bill, 113
Larteguy, 9
Lee, Fitzhugh, 101
Lee, Henry, 63
Lee, Jeremiah, 50
Lee, Robert E., 99, 101, 105
Lehmann, T.R., 173

Lewis, Anthony, 21
Li, Tai, 164
Lincoln, Abraham, 81, 91, 101, 103, 105
Lincoln, Benjamin, 59
Little Big Horn, 109
Little Fork Rangers, 84
Liversedge, Harry, 126
Long Range Reconnaissance Patrol(LRRP), 107, 198, 232-234
Longstreet, 92
Loudoun Rangers, 91-94
Lyon, Ivan, 155

M
MacArthur, Arthur, 107
MacArthur, Douglas, 127, 151, 154
MacKay's Rangers, 23, 24
Mackay, Patrick, 23
MacPherson, James, 24
Mahan, Alfred T., 106
Mahon, Dennis H., 83
Maine, 112, 114
Makin Island, 124, 125
Marblehead Mariners, 49-53
Marcinko, Richard, 237, 238
Marine Force Recon, 128-132
Marine Raiders, 118, 123-128
Marion, Francis, 47, 48, 58-64, 102, 146
Marshall, George, 157
Massachusetts Rangers, 14
Massacre Bay, 122
McCaffrey, Joseph P., 128
McClellan, 92, 101
McClure, Robert A. 137, 213
McCullock, Ben, 79
McGee, John H., 201, 212
McGirt, 74
McGowen, John R. C., 191
McKinley, William, 116
McNeill, Jesse, 98, 100
McNeill, John H. 98-101
McNeill's Rangers, 86, 98-101
Means, Samuel C., 86, 91-93
Merrill, Frank D., 145, 182-185

ORDER FORM

Pathfinder Publishing of California
458 Dorothy Ave.
Ventura, CA 93003
Telephone (805) 642-9278   FAX (805) 650-3656

Please send me the following books from Pathfinder Publishing:

_____Copies of **Elite Warriors** Hard Cover, @ $22.95 $____
_____Copies of **Silent Warriors** Hard Cover, @ $22.95 $____
_____Copies of **Surviving a Japanese P.O.W. Camp**
          @ $9.95 $____
_____Copies of **Agony & Death on a Gold Rush Steamer**
          @ $8.95 $____
_____Copies of **Shipwrecks, Smugglers & Maritime**
          Mysteries @ $9.95 $____
_____Copies of **Living Creatively**
          With Chronic Illness @ $11.95 $____
_____Copies of **No Time For Goodbyes** @ $11.95 $____
_____Copies of **Surviving an Auto Accident** @ $9.95 $____
_____Copies of **Violence in our Schools, Hospitals and**
          Public Places   @ $22.95 Hard Cover $____
                    @ $14.95 Soft Cover $____
_____Copies of **Violence in the Workplace** @ $22.95 Hard $____
                    @ $14.95 Soft $____
                              Sub-Total $____
          Californians: Please add 7.25% tax. $____
          Shipping* $____
                              Grand Total $____

I understand that I may return the book for a full refund if not satisfied.
Name:_____

Address:_____
_____ZIP:_____
MASTERCARD and VISA orders accepted.
Card_____No._____Exp.Date_____
*SHIPPING CHARGES U.S.
Books: Enclose $3.25 for the first book and .50c for each additional book
(Foreign surface $4.50). UPS: Truck; $4.50 for first item, .50c for each
additional. UPS 2nd Day Air: $10.75 for first item, $1.00 for each
additional item.

THE AUTHORS

Lance Q. Zedric

Lance Quintin Zedric, born in Havana, Illinois, is a 1983 graduate of Monmouth College (Illinois), and holds a Master's Degree in History from Western Illinois University. During his four years in the U.S. Army, the author served as an intelligence analyst in Korea; at Fort Bragg, North Carolina; and in support of CENTCOM forces during the Gulf War. Mr. Zedric is the former Director of Public Information for Monmouth College and has published numerous magazine and newspaper articles on military history. He currently resides in Illinois, where he is a freelance writer and researcher. His first book, *Silent Warriors of World War II: The Alamo Scouts Behind Japanese Lines,* was published in 1995 by Pathfinder Publishing.

Michael F. Dilley

Michael Frederic Dilley is a former paratrooper, serving in XVIII Airborne Corps and the 82d Airborne Division. He retired from the U.S. Army in 1984 after duty as a counterintelligence agent, intelligence analyst, case officer, and interrogator. He served in Viet Nam for two years. During his last 18 months in the 82d Airborne, he helped to develop SERE training for high risk personnel. He has a B.A. in History from Columbia College in Missouri. Mr. Dilley is a staff writer for *Behind The Lines* magazine, specializing in military history articles about World War II special operations. He also reviews books with special operations themes for *Infantry* and *Behind The Lines.* His first book, *GALAHAD - A History of the 5307th Composite Unit (Provisional),* was published in 1996 by Merriam Press. He lives with his wife, Sue, in Davidsonville, Maryland.